Mind Power

Mind Power

William Walker Atkinson

SANAGE
PUBLISHING HOUSE

Paperback: 978-939-0896-48-6

Printed by: Manipal Technologies Limited, Manipal

Designed by:
allpublishingsolution.com

CONTENTS

THE HISTORY OF THIS BOOK

In 1907 appeared a little book entitled: "The Secret of Mental Magic," by William Walker Atkinson. In 1908, the material of said book was edited, revised, and elaborated by the author; portions of its sequel, "Mental Fascination," combined with it; and a large amount of entirely new material added thereto; the whole being published in new form under the title: "Mind Power, or The Law of Dynamic Mentation." In the present edition, the sub title has been changed to "The Secret of Mental Magic"—thus restoring the original title by which the book is best known to thousands of friendly readers.

Chicago, March 15, 1912.

CHAPTER 1

THE MENTAL DYNAMO

I wish to invite you to the consideration of a great principle of Nature—a great natural force that manifests its activities in the phenomena of Dynamic Mentation—a great Something the energies of which I have called "Mind Power."

My thought on the subject is based upon the fundamental conception that:

There exists in Nature a Dynamic Mental Principle—a Mind Power—pervading all space—immanent in all things—manifesting in an infinite variety of forms, degrees, and phases.

I hold that this energy, or force, or dynamic principle, is no respecter of persons. Its service, like that of the sun and rain, and all natural forces, is open to all—just and unjust; good and bad; high and low; rich and poor. It responds to the proper efforts, no matter by whom exerted, or for what purpose called into effect. But the proper effort must be exerted, consciously or unconsciously, else there will be no operation of the force. I believe that the activities of this dynamic mental principle are intimately correlated to manifestations of the mental operations known to us as desire, will, and imagination. We shall learn something of the laws and principles and modes of operation of its energies and activities, as we proceed with our consideration of it, in this work. It may be difficult for you to grasp this conception of Mind Power at the start—but it will grow upon your understanding as its activities are presented to you, one by one, like a great panorama.

My terms will be explained and illustrated by examples, as we proceed—so you need not analyze them at this point. It may be as well, however, to state that I have used the term "Dynamic" in its original Greek sense, *i. e.*, "powerful"; "possessing power," etc.

I have postulated of my conception of Mind Power that it

pervades all space—is immanent in all things—and manifests in an infinite variety of forms, degrees, and phases.

But, it may be urged, this is nothing more than science claims for the principle of physical energy—then is Mind Power identical with the physical energy of science?—is it nothing more than a high form of mechanical or material energy? No, Mind Power is very far from being a blind, mechanical energy—it is a living, mental force, which I hold is behind the manifestations of physical energy and mechanical force. It is not the physical energy of science, but is something of the nature of a living will, which is rather the cause of physical energy, than identical with it. Let us take a familiar example. You desire to move your hand—and it moves. Why? Because of the manifestation of the wonderful and mysterious force called "will" which is stored up within you, and which you have released to move the hand. You send a current of nerve force which is really a manifestation of Mind Power or will force from your brain, along the nerves of the arm, which contracts the muscles of the arm and hand, and your desire is gratified. Your desire, or wish, set into motion the Mind Power which acted upon the material substance of your body and caused it to act. What was it that flowed along the nerve wires? Was it electricity, or magnetism? No! it was that subtle and mysterious thing that I am calling Mind Power, and which is bound up with the will principle of mind.

Mind Power is an actual living force. It is the force that makes plants grow—and animal bodies grow—and which enables all living things to move and act. It is the force which enables the growing mushroom to raise up the slabs of paving stone—or causes the roots of a tree to split open the great boulders, into the crevices of which they have crept. Mind Power is not an abstraction or speculative nothing—it is an existent, living, mental, acting force, manifesting sometimes with an appalling power, and sometimes with a delicate, subtle touch that is almost imperceptible, but which accomplishes its purpose.

In order to reach a clear conception of the universality of Mind Power, let us consider its manifestations as we see them, unquestioned, in the universe—on the many planes of life and activity. Beginning with the more familiar instances of its operation and manifestation, let us then proceed to delve still deeper until we reach instances not so easily perceived; and then still further back until we find it in places and in things that are generally regarded as lacking in Mind Power and life.

And, here let me say that I hold that life and Mind Power are always found in company with each other—there is some close relationship between the two—they are probably twin phases of the same thing, or else twin manifestations of the same underlying reality. There is no life without mind and Mind Power—and no Mind Power, or mind, without life. And, further, I claim that there is nothing without life in the universe—nothing lifeless there, or anywhere. The universe is alive, and has mind and Mind Power in every part and particle of itself. This is not an original idea of my own, of course,—the leading scientific thinkers admit it today, and the Hindu philosophers have known it for fifty centuries. Do you doubt this? Then listen to these authorities who ably express the thought of their scientific schools.

Luther Burbank, that most wonderful man who has revolutionized our conceptions of plant life, and who has practically held Plant Life in the palm of his hand, says: "All my investigations have led me away from the idea of a dead material universe tossed about by various forces, to that of a universe which is absolutely all force, life, soul, thought, or whatever name we choose to call it. Every atom, molecule, plant, animal or planet, is only an aggregation of organized unit forces held in place by stronger forces, thus holding them for a time latent, though teeming with inconceivable power. All life on our planet is, so to speak, just on the outer fringe of this infinite ocean of force. The universe is not half dead, but all alive."

Dr. Saleeby, in his important scientific work, "*Evolution: the Master Key*," goes even still further in his claim of a living universe; and life accompanied by mind. He says, among other things: "Life is potential in matter; life energy is not a thing unique and created at a particular time in the past. If evolution be true, living matter has been evolved by natural processes from matter which is, apparently, not alive. But if life is a potential in matter, it is a thousand times more evident that mind is potential in life. The evolutionist is impelled to believe that mind is potential in matter. (I adopt that form of words for the moment, but not without future criticism.) The microscopic cell, a minute speck of matter that is to become man, has in it the promise and germ of mind. May we not then draw the inference that the elements of mind are present in those chemical elements—carbon, oxygen, hydrogen, nitrogen, sulphur, phosphorus, sodium, potassium, chlorine—that are found in the cell. Not only must we do so, but we must go further, since we know that each of these elements, and every other, is built up out of one invariable unit, the electron, and we must therefore assert that mind is potential in the unit of matter—the electron itself."

Flammarion, the eminent French scientist, says: "*The universe is a dynamism*. Life itself, from the most rudimentary cell up to the most complicated organism, is a special kind of movement, a movement determined and organized by a directing force. Visible matter, which stands to us at the present moment for the universe, and which certain classic doctrines consider as the origin of all things—movement, life, thought—is only a word void of meaning. The universe is a great organism, controlled by a dynamism of the psychical order. Mind gleams through its every atom. There is mind in everything, not only in human and animal life, but in plants, in minerals, in space." Prof. J. A. Fleming, in his work on "Waves, Air and Aether," says: "In its ultimate essence energy may be incomprehensible by us except as an exhibition of the direct operation of that which we call mind and will."

Let us then follow the hint given by the scientists—let us proceed to examine the evidences of the immanence of life and Mind Power in all of the things of the universe—things organic; things inorganic; and things beyond organism, shape and form—back into the very ether of space itself. And in the search we shall find these evidences everywhere—in all things. Nowhere does life and Mind Power escape us. Immanent in all things—manifesting in an infinite variety of forms, degrees, and phases, we find these twin principles. I invite you to join in one of the most interesting and fascinating explorations known to modern science.

We do not need any proof to demonstrate the existence of life, mind and Mind Power in man, or in the lower animals. The activities resulting from its presence are in constant evidence. And if we examine the plant kingdom we will see manifestations of life, mind, and Mind Power there also. Plants not only manifest "appetency," or "the instinctive tendency on the part of low forms of organic life, to perform certain acts necessary for their well being, particularly in the selection and absorption of the material substances necessary for their support and nutriments";—not only "instinct" or "involuntary and unreasoning prompting or impulse, and the response thereto";—but also, in certain cases, there appears mental action closely akin to conscious choice and will. I refer you to the many recent works on mind in plant life for illustrations and proofs of this statement. And biology shows us that there is life, mind, and Mind Power inherent in the cells of which our bodies, blood and the material of animal and plant life, is composed. These cells are "little lives," and manifest mental power and faculty. They perform their particular functions, and live, grow, reproduce themselves, and act just as do the tiny forms of animal life at the bottom of sea—the latter being but little more than single cells, or cell groups. The possession of memory on the part of the cells of organic matter, is an accepted scientific fact.

At this point the orthodox and conservative scientist usually stops, drawing a line between "organic" and "inorganic" matter. But the daring minds of advanced scientists of today have brushed aside the dividing line, and have moved to a position where they meet the Hindu philosophers and the occultists, and now admit and teach that life, mind and Mind Power invade the "inorganic" world to its utmost limits, and that universe is indeed alive and possesses Mind.

Some of the lower forms of "organic" life, so called, possess no organs, and are but masses of jelly like matter without signs of even rudimentary organs—and yet these life forms show evidences of desire, choice, and will. And Science has admitted the existence of life and mind in the crystals! the latter "growing" in a manner showing vital and selective energy, and even rudimentary sex. More than this, the metals and minerals, under scientific tests, have shown "responses" that are similar to the same action in organic life—showing life and rudimentary sensation, the latter of course being a manifestation of mind. Some of the cold, careful scientific records read like fairy tales to those not familiar with the wonderful achievements of recent science. I wish that I had the time and space to recount these tests—but I must hasten on. Enough to say that in mineral and metallic forms there has been found "response" indicating the existence of "sensation" in varying degrees; and that in the crystallization of minerals and metals there has been evidenced the action of the same instinctive mental life energy which as "appetency or instinct" builds up the bodies of living organic forms. If you wonder at this—think of the miracle which is performed every second by plants absorbing the minerals of the earth, which are then converted into living plant cells; then we eat the plants and convert the plant cells into animal cells which serve as the basis of our blood, muscles, organs, and even our brains. In fact, every particle of organic substance was evolved in this way. Think over this and you will see that Nature is One in her essence, and that she is alive and possesses Mind Power.

But we do not stop even at this advanced point. Minerals, and all forms of matter are composed of infinitesimal atoms, or particles. The particles combine by reason of some inherent "attraction" existing between certain of them, known as "chemical affinity," etc. Chemical affinity is a peculiar thing—it manifests in likes and dislikes, loves and hates; it is impossible to study these manifestations without recognizing an elementary manifestation of "like and dislike"—"love and hate." You think that this is far fetched, do you? Well, listen to these words from some of the leading scientists about this power to receive sensations, and power to respond to the same, and maybe you will change your mind. Haeckel, the great German scientist, holds that the atoms of which matter is composed may "receive sensations," and "respond to sensations." He dwells upon this fact in his latest works "*The Riddle of the Universe*," and "*The Wonders of Life*," and writes as follows regarding "sensation in the inorganic world": "I cannot imagine," Haeckel says, "the simplest chemical and physical process, without attributing the movements of the material particles to unconscious sensation." He also says, in another place: "The idea of chemical affinity consists in the fact that the various chemical elements perceive the qualitative differences in other elements—experience 'pleasure' or 'revulsion' atcontactwith them, and execute specific movements on this ground." He adds, later, that the "sensations" and "responses" in plant and animal life are "connected by a long series of evolutionary stages with the simpler forms of sensation that we find in the inorganic elements and that reveal themselves in chemical affinity." Nageli, another scientist, says: "If the molecules possess something that is related, however distantly, to sensation, it must be comfortable to be able to follow their attractions and repulsions; uncomfortable when they are forced to do otherwise." And so you see that Science now is preparing to admit elementary life and Mind Power in the atoms and particles of matter.

But we have not as yet reached the utmost limit of scientific investigation regarding the presence of mind in the universe. "Further than the atoms?" you may ask. Yes, further than the atoms! What is true regarding the atoms, is true of the *ions* or electrons of which they are composed—these tinier particles are attracted and repelled; form groups and combinations which regulate the kind of atom produced; and manifest the same kind of "affinity" that is noticeable in the atoms. And more than this—these particles, as well as all forms of physical energy, are believed to emerge from the ether, that subtle, tenuous, universal substance, which, although unseen, and intangible, is held to exist in order to account for the phenomena of the universe. If there is Mind in the particles that emerge from the Ether, is it too much to claim that there must be Mind in the Ether itself? Is this preposterous? Not so! Listen to the words of the following scientific authorities on the subject:

Flammarion says: "Mind gleams in every atom. There is mind in everything, not only in human and animal life, but in plants, in minerals in space!" Cope says: "The basis of life and mind lies back of the atoms, and may be found in the universal ether." Hemstreet says: "Mind in the ether is no more unnatural than mind in flesh and blood." Stockwell says: "The ether is coming to be apprehended as an immaterial, super physical substance, filling all space, carrying in its infinite, throbbing bosom the specks of aggregated dynamic force called worlds. It embodies the ultimate spiritual principle and represents the unity of those forces and energies from which spring, as their source, all phenomena, physical, mental and spiritual, as they are known to man." Dolhear says: "Possibly the ether may be the medium through which mind and matter react Out of the ether could emerge, under proper circumstances, other phenomena, such as life, or mind, or whatever may be in the substratum." And, so, we have the best of authority to support the inevitable conclusion that there must be Mind Power even in the ether.

For my own part, I go still further, and for several years back have been claiming that the Ether and the Universal Mind Power Principle are one and the same thing—that is, that that theoretical something that science has called "the Ether," is in reality the Universal Mind Power Principle from which all manifestations of activities emerge—the Universal Mental Dynamo! I cannot prove this, of course—but it is logical. But my argument does not depend even upon this—for admit that there is Mind Power in the ether, and my case is won. And in the ether it must be, even if the ether is not but another name for it. For if Mind Power is not in the ether, from whence does it come into the particles of matter, and in matter itself, organic and inorganic?

Resting the consideration for a moment, let me say that with mind as reason, intellect, etc., I have nothing to do in this book, for this is a consideration of the dynamic phase of mind—the Power phase—Mind Power, or Dynamic Mentation. I am trying to show you that Mind Power exists everywhere, and is manifest in every activity of the universe. "In every activity of the universe?" you say; "surely you do not include physical activity and energy such as natural forces etc.!" Yes, I do mean just that! "How can that be?" you ask, "what has Mind Power to do with electricity, light, heat, magnetism, gravitation, etc.?" It has everything to do with them, in my opinion. I will explain it to you in a few words, for I cannot go into this subject at length in this book, but must hasten on to the other parts of my subject.

Here it is in a nut shell: All the forms of natural physical energy, or forces, known as light, heat, electricity, magnetism, etc., are held by science to be forms of energy arising from the *vibration of the particles of matter*. Now what causes the vibration? Motion of the particles, of course! And what causes the particles to move? Just this, the attraction and repulsion existing between them! And what causes the particles to exhibit this attraction and repulsion toward each other? Now here is where we get to the heart of the matter; listen well! We have seen that the particles are attracted to, or repelled by, each other—in the matter of "likes and dislikes"; "love and hates"; or "pleasure or revulsion"; or "comfortable and uncomfortable experiences related, however distant, to sensation," etc. And these attractions and repulsions are held to result from "capacity to experience sensations" and the power to "respond to sensations." And both the power to receive and experience "sensations," and to respond thereto, *are manifestations of mentality*, which Haeckel has compared to "desire" and "will." And if mentality is the cause of the sensations and of the response there; and the latter are the causes of the attractions and repulsions; and the latter are the causes of the motion, to and fro, of the particles of matter; and the latter, in turn is the cause of the vibrations; and the vibrations are the causes of the manifestations of light, heat, electricity, magnetism, etc.,—then am I not justified in claiming *that mind and Mind Power are the motive force of all physical energy*?

And, am I not justified in postulating the existence of an universal mental dynamic principle? I tell you, friends, that the future will show that this dynamic mental principle is the source of energy—not energy the source of mind! I know that this is revolutionary, but I believe that it will meet the requirements of the future. I have been preaching this thing for several years now—and many have been the smiles; the jeers; and the sneers. But, from the beginning, I have felt a keen appreciation of the words of Galvini, when he said, bitterly: "I am attacked by two very opposite sects—the Scientists and the Know Nothings; both laugh at me, calling me the 'Frog's Dancing Master,' but I know that I have discovered one of the greatest forces in nature."

And, now, in conclusion, I must ask you to form a mental picture of this great universal dynamic mental principle; pervading all space; immanent in all things; and manifesting in an infinite variety of forms, degrees and phases. We can think of it only by means of symbols. Let us then consider it as a great living, throbbing, pulsating, mentating Ocean of Dynamic Mind Power. In the depths of that Ocean of Mind Power there is quiet, and calm and peace—the embodiment of latent power, and potential energy. On its surface are ripples, waves, great movements of energy, currents, whirlpools, eddies—phases of fierce tempest alternating with phases of calm and quiet. And from the depths of that Ocean of Mind Power, all mental and physical Power emerges—and to its bosom all must return. And in that ocean there is an infinite store of energy, from which may be drawn that which the human centers of consciousness and power require, when they learn the secret. This Ocean of Mind Power is our only source of dynamic energy—but we have at our disposal as much of its force as we can carry off over our channels of supply. It is the use of this power that we call Dynamic Mentation.

Now, do you understand what I mean by the Universal Principle of Dynamic Mind Power—this Universal Mental Dynamo?

Several years ago I told a friend of this conception, and after he had listened to me attentively and with interest, he reflected a few moments, and then suddenly asked: "But where do I come in?" And that is the question that many of you are asking now, no doubt. Well, while here I cannot dip into metaphysics or philosophical speculation, or even into my favorite occult sources, I will say that each of you is a Centre of Power in that Ocean of Dynamic Mind Power and each "I" is a master of the power. You have the Whole Thing back of you—and you are free to draw upon it for all that your channel will carry to you. And you are allowed to enlarge your channel. That is enough for this time—more will follow as we proceed.

CHAPTER 2

THE NATURE OF MIND POWER

At this point I am confronted with the question that naturally arises when one begins to consider an unfamiliar object, subject, or principle—the question of: "What is it?" "What *is* Mind Power" is a difficult question to answer, for it implies a knowledge of the thing "in itself," apart from its activities and manifestations. And this "thing it selfness" is something that the candid, scientific thinker admits is beyond the range of his thought and knowledge. Any attempt to answer such a question must involve one in a maze of metaphysical and philosophical speculation regarding something which is by nature unknowable. And so I may as well frankly state here that I do not purpose "guessing" at the "thing in itselfness" of Mind Power. For, at the best, any attempt at an answer would be merely a guess—for I do not *know*, neither do I know anyone else who *knows!*

I am acquainted with the numerous speculations of the ancient and modern philosophers and metaphysicians on the subject—I have read and studied them, and have rejected them as mere theories unsupported by facts. And I have made and rejected a dozen or more theories of my own on the subject—all vague, foolish speculations. I have studied the best of what has been written and thought regarding this "thing in itselfness" of mind and Mind Power, so you see my ignorance is not the ignorance that comes from lack of thought, or lack of acquaintance with the thoughts of others—but is rather the ignorance that comes as the result of much thought, and much study of the thoughts of others—the ignorance that is only realized through knowledge. Regarding these ultimate questions, the best thinkers freely confess their ignorance knowing that, as Nordau has said, they "have plucked that supremest fruit of the Tree of Knowledge—the consciousness of our ignorance." Like Pyrrhon, some twenty five centuries ago, they say "*Uden horizo*"—"I do not decide."

We do not know "things in themselves"—we *cannot* know them. If we knew the ultimate truths regarding the tiniest and most insignificant thing in the universe, we would know *everything that is*—for that tiniest thing is connected with, and related to everything in the universe, and that which underlies the universe—and to know the "thing in itself" of *anything* would be to know the great "Thing in Itself" of The All. All that we can do is to know and consider things by what they do; and how they act; and through their manifestations and activities; and the results and effects of the same—rather than by what they are in the abstract, or apart from their activities, manifestations, and the phenomena proceeding from them. Apart from their activities, manifestations and phenomena, things are but abstract no things so far as our understanding is concerned—airy "words" coined by the metaphysicians and philosophers in order to provide food for speculation, argument, and dispute without end. And we may as well admit the fact that all consideration of ultimate things—things in themselves—inevitably leads us to the conclusion that the only real Thing in Itself is a Something, underlying all things and yet a No Thing, and which transcends all of our experience, knowledge, reason, thought, *and even imagination*. And therein lies the folly of attempting to tell "just what" anything is.

In view of the facts mentioned, and which are held to be correct by the world's best thinkers, how much saner is it to devote our attention to the consideration of things as known through their activities, manifestations, and phenomena—knowing them by what they do, and and how they act; by the laws and principles of the activities and operations; rather than by speculations concerning their nature as abstract thing in themselves. This is the method of modern Science, as compared with those of speculative philosophy and metaphysics. But, "a little learning is a dangerous thing"; and "fools rush in where angels fear to tread." And so we shall never be at a loss for ingenious theories and "solutions" of ultimate problems. We have among us some who glibly inform us that they know "just what Mind is!" Such add to the gaiety of the nations, and therefore are useful and interesting. Did you ever hear of the youth at college, who when asked by his professor: "What is electricity?" answered "Well, sir, I *did* know, but I have forgotten!" The professor answered, dryly: "Now, isn't that too bad! Here is the only person in the world who ever knew just what electricity is—and he has forgotten! What a loss to the race!" Why do we not have courage enough to leave off this making of the speculative soap bubbles with which we have been amusing ourselves, and learn to answer honestly, "I do not *know*!" or, at least like modern Science, learn to frankly state: Here our knowledge of the subject ends; to morrow we *may* know more, but sufficient for the day is the knowledge thereof—and an inch of knowledge of facts is worth a mile of unsupported speculation and theory. As Thomas L. Harris has said:

"The theorist who dreams a rainbow dream,
And calls hypothesis 'philosophy,'
At best is but a paper financier
Who palms his specious promises for gold
Facts are the basis of philosophy;
Philosophy, the harmony of facts.
Seen in their right relation."

And, now, having confessed your ignorance and mine, let us proceed to a consideration of Mind Power as known by its activities.

In the first place, let me say that I do not hold that Mind Power is identical with mind. Rather does it seem to me to be correlated to mind, particularly in the operation of mind known as desire, will, and imagination. If you like, we may consider it to be the acting aspect of mind. Mind has three aspects—the aspect of being, or substance; the aspect of thought, with the sub divisions of reason, feeling, emotion, desire, will, etc., on both conscious and subconscious planes; and third, the aspect of ACTING. And it is in this aspect of action that mind is known as Mind Power.

While it is extremely likely that there is a certain employment and manifestation of Mind Power in the ordinary processes of reasoning, intellectual effort, etc., still Mind Power seems to be more closely connected with the more elementary phase of mentation, such as feeling, emotion, and particularly desire and will. We know that it is possessed by the lower forms of animal and plant life; even the inorganic forms; all of which existed and employed the force before intellect and reason manifested itself in man. And so I would impress upon you that while Mind Power may be called into operation by, and still more certainly may be directed by the intellect—still you must not make the mistake of identifying it with that phase of mind or attributing it solely to creatures possessing the same. It is a far more elementary and basic force, as you have seen in the preceding chapter.

Indeed, in order that you may understand the operations of Mind Power you may as well get into the habit of considering it as correlated to that which we call will, (as distinguished from intellect and reason).

By "will" I do not mean that phase or faculty of the mind which decides, determines, or chooses—although this customary use of the term is quite correct as applied to one phase of will. This deciding, choosing, determining faculty is one of the attributes of intellect and Self consciousness superimposed upon the elemental will in the direction of guiding, directing, turning and restraining—it is the Ego at the wheel, directing the Ship of Life by the Chart of Reason, the motive power being will, or Mind Power. Choice in the lower forms of life and activity, simply means yielding to the strongest desire, or aggregate of strongest desires, or average of strongest desires.

No, I did not mean will in the above sense, but in the more elementary sense of the term—the original sense, for the word is derived from the root meaning "to wish; to desire strongly." And, in this elementary sense, the word "will" is used to designate that primitive, original, universal mental principle in life, which manifests in desire for action, and in the response to that desire. In this sense will may be considered as Desire Will, both being held to be phases of the same thing—or rather the two poles of the same thing. The desire pole of this Desire Will is connected with that which we call emotion, feeling, etc., which arouses it into action.

The will pole of this Desire Will is connected with that principle of mental activity which we are considering under the name of Mind Power—the dynamic aspect of mind. I ask that you re read this paragraph, that you may fix this idea firmly in your mind, for upon it depends the correct understanding of much that I shall have to say in this work.

In Desire we find the first step toward Dynamic Mentation. Desire precedes action of will which releases the dynamic force of the mind—the Mind Power. Desire is the coiling up the steel spring of Will—there is always a state of "tension" about desire—a state of "coiled up energy" caused by "feeling," "emotion" or similar state which has been aroused by the sight of, or memory of, or thought of, some attractive object. The feeling" inspired by the attractive object coils up the spring of desire, and this "coiled up" energy supplies the "motive power" of the will. But, remember this, some desires are acted upon, while others are rejected—*neither men nor things act upon every desire*. There is the other pole of the Desire Will which must be called into action—and this leads us to a consideration of the matter of choice, determination, or decision, which is so often expressed by the term" "Will, " as I said a little further back.

This choosing or determining phase of will, is little more than an empty name or term, so far as is concerned the relation between desire and will action in the cases of things and creatures lower in the scale than man. For in these cases this choice, determination, or decision is based entirely upon the degree of "feeling," or the degree of attractiveness of the objects presenting themselves to the attention—the strongest feeling, attraction, or motive interest winning the day. (Fear is one of the strongest feelings influencing desire, and acts usually as a neutralizer of other feelings and desires, and is most potent as a motive influencing choice or decision—in fact, one is justified in regarding fear as the negative form of desire, being really a "desire not to.") With the advent of reason, and intellect, particularly when the self conscious ego appears, new elements are introduced, by reason of which man is enabled to deliberate and weigh motives, desires, feelings, emotions, etc., and thus the will of man is held to contain elements lacking in the general principle of will.

But the aspect of will with which we are much concerned is the aspect of action—the will pole of Desire Will. Just where desire passes into will is impossible to decide—the chances are that they blend into each other. But this we *do* know, that "something happens" at a certain stage of the mental operation, whereby the attention of the thing, or ego, passes from the pole of desire to the pole of will—and then, one of two things happens, *i. e.*, (1) either the "coiled up" spring of desire is released by the will, and the energy of desire is transmuted into the energy of will, which thus releases the Mind Power or dynamic quality of mind into action; or else: (2) the will refuses to be aroused, and desire slowly uncoils her spring, and the tension is relieved, gradually or at once. The will may be cultivated and developed so as to refuse to release the spring of desire into action—and in this inhibiting quality lies much of that which is called "strength of will"—it often requires more will not to do, than to do.

The aspect of "action" is the true dynamic quality of will. And with action all will is intimately and inseparably connected. As Prof. Halleck says: "Will concerns itself with action. The student must keep that fact before him, no matter how complex the matter seems." Action is the. "inner meaning" and reason of the will. And it is with this phase that we are concerned in the present work. Action is the essential aspect of Mind Power—the latter exists for the purpose of Acting. It is the essence of activity.

And so you will see that this "universal dynamic mental principle"—which I have called "Mind Power," is not that phase of mind which manifests as intellectual, reasoning processes; but is that phase of mind which is aroused by desire will—and which acts. It is manifest in the universe among forms of life below the plane of reason, as well as among those on that plane, and therefore precedes Reason in evolution. It also manifests along unconscious and automatic lines, and precedes the self conscious stage of man. It represents an elementary, primitive, fundamental, dynamic, mental force; and may be thought of as a raw, crude, undeveloped force, manifesting along the lines of instinctive action or appetency, rather than along the lines of intellect, reason, or the higher cognitive faculties. It is something far more elemental and basic than intellect. It is more nearly akin to the elemental life forces which we personify under the name of "Nature."

Whether or not that which we know as reason or intellect were evolved from an elemental Mind Stuff; or whether these higher forms of mentality are something of an entirely higher and distinct nature; or whether, as the occultists hold, intelligence is the result of the influence of a Spiritual Ego (something distinct from mind) upon an elementary Mind Stuff—these are questions belonging to other phases of the general subject of Being, with which we have nothing to do in the consideration of the subject before us. I have my own opinions and beliefs on these points, and so have each of you—we may differ regarding the same, but may still be able to examine the subject before us as co workers, in spite of our lack of agreement regarding questions of philosophy, metaphysics, or religion. We are dealing with a natural force—a universal energy—now and here, and should examine and study its principles just as we would were it electricity, magnetism, heat or light that we were studying. I am inviting you to a scientific study, not a metaphysical or philosophical speculation, doctrine or theory. These latter things have their own good places—but they have no place here at this time.

CHAPTER 3

MENTATIVE INDUCTION

As wonderful as is the manifestation of Mind Power within the limits of the form of the thing, cell, plant, animal, or person, and which produces the effects known as local action, movement, etc., there is still a greater wonder to be witnessed in the manifestation of the same power beyond the limits of the personality or form in which it originates. And it is to this manifestation of Mind Power that I am about to apply the term "Telementation."

I may as well explain my terms at this place and time. In the first place I use the term "Mentation," in the sense of "Mental activity"; the term being derived from the Latin word *mentis*, meaning "the mind"; and the suffix "ation"; meaning "action." So "Mentation" means "mental activity." From Mentation we derive Mentative, or "relating to mental activity"; Mentate, or "to manifest mental activity"; etc., etc.

From Mentation, also, I derive the term, "Telementation," which so far as I know, was originally coined by me several years ago. The word is derived from the Greek word, *tele*, meaning "far off"; andtheword"mentation," aboveexplained."Telementation" means "mental activity at a distance," or mentation exerted over space," or "long range mental influence," etc. I have been led to the coining of this new term designed to take the place of "telepathy," for the reason that the latter term is improper and misleading. "Telepathy," according to its root words, really means "to suffer at a distance," or the "feeling of the pain of another," the suffix "pathy," being derived from the Greek word meaning "to suffer." It may be used properly in connection with the sympathetic transference of pain, or disease, or similar mental state, but its use otherwise is improper. It is being discarded by the best scientific authorities, who prefer the term "Thought Transference," etc. I have thought it advisable to use the term "telementation" in this connection, believing that it meets the requirements of the case better than any other term of which I have any knowledge. I expect it to come into general use before long.

And now about the transference of mental states from one thing or person to another. I shall not attempt to go into a discussion of the phenomena of Thought Transference in this work, for the reason that it is too well established, and too generally known to require an argument in its favor from me. To thousands of careful investigators it is an established fact, and anyone who will take the time and trouble to conduct the experiments may reproduce the phenomena to his own satisfaction. Moreover there are instances of telementation arising in the everyday life of nearly every person, such instances being of the spontaneous order, that is, not having been expected or sought after. Those who are desirous of obtaining "proofs" of telementation, beyond their own personal experiences, are referred to the records of the English Society for Psychical Research, which contain the carefully noted reports of many very interesting cases which have been conducted by the society under the most careful supervision and scientific requirements. The circulation of Mind Power is as real a natural phenomenon as the circulation of air, water, or the blood.

There have been many theories advanced to account for telementation, and there has been much talk of "two minds," "dual mentality," etc., in this connection. In this work I shall have very little, if anything, to say regarding man's "two minds." I, of course, am fully conversant with the subject of the sub conscious and super conscious regions of the Mind, but I find this principle of telementation to have its roots still further back in the scale of evolution—back before "consciousness" as we know it, existed in the created forms of matter or life—back to the plane of "mind in inorganic matter"—and therefore, I shall not attempt to urge any "two mind" theories to account for it. In fact, I believe that the mind of man is a far more complex thing than a "dual mind" combination—there are many more planes and regions of mind than the "objective" and "subjective" minds of the "dual mind" authorities.

I find the basis for the theory of telementation far back in the scale—in fact at the lowest extreme of the scale of things. I find it in the atoms, or in the particles of which the atoms are composed. In the first chapter of this work I called your attention to the manifestation of Mind Power among the atoms and particles of matter, which was evidenced by action, motion, and movements resulting from "attraction and repulsion" of these atoms and particles. In other words I showed that physical forces were produced by the motions of the particles, or vibrations of the atoms, which arose from states of like and dislike; love and hate; attraction and repulsion; pleasure and pain; among these tiny particles of matter. And it is here that the elementary principle of telementation is noticeable—here is where it may be seen in full primitive force and operation. If you will think for a moment, you will see that the motions of the atoms are two fold, *viz.* (1) the voluntary motion of the atom toward the other atom to which it is attracted by chemical affinity; and (2) the movement of the atom occasioned by the "attractive force" exerted by the other atom, in the same manner that a magnet" draws" the needle to it.

Haeckel has told us that there is the voluntary movement of the atom itself, in response to the "desire" awakened in it by the attraction—how does it become aware of the presence of the other atom unless something passes between them? And that something must be in the nature of a mentative current, for there is nothing else to pass, because all other forms of energy being produced by vibrations of the atoms arising from mental states, the Mind Power must precede the physical energies, and must be the "something that passes between" the two atoms. Feeling the presence of the other atom, the first atom moves towards its affinity, voluntarily, and just as you move your arm or walk—the atom probably exerting a push upon the ether which must be to the atom or particle what the air is to the wing of the bird, or the water to the fin of the fish. But there is another cause of motion, as we have seen—the mutual pull of the attracting atoms.

And what manner or kind of energy is it that thus "draws" or "pulls" the other atom? It cannot be electricity, or magnetism, for those forces, as we have seen, are produced by a rate of vibration occasioned by the Mind Power in the atoms themselves—therefore we must go back to the antecedent force, which is Mind Power, and attribute to it the drawing or pulling force which moves the atoms toward each other.

That this attracting or pulling force is in operation between the particles of matter, there can be no doubt. No two atoms of matter are in absolute touch with each other—there is always a distance between them—a space which thus separates them—which never can be traversed or overcome. There seems to be an individuality in these tiny particles which, although allowing them to form combinations, nevertheless prevents absolute blending or amalgamation. There is always a "keep your distance," or "thus far and no further" principle in Nature which holds every particle of matter individual and alone. Every *ion*, electron, atom, and molecule of matter is alone, and separated even from its closest affinity by a "touch me not" circle of influence, which is also mentative in its nature, in my opinion. Even the hardest diamond, or piece of steel, is composed of molecules close together but yet separated by this circle of influence; and every molecule is composed of several atoms between which the same law operates; and every atom is composed of many *ions* or electrons, which have distances between them. So true is Nature in her proportions and laws, that scientists assert that in the hundreds of *ions* of which the tiniest atom is composed (and which atom is invisible to the sight by reason of its smallness) there is a "distance between" observed and maintained by these particles, which bears the same proportion to their sizes that the distance between the planets of our solar system bears to their particular sizes—in other words, that the *ions* composing an atom are akin to a minute solar system, each *ion* being attracted to the other, and yet "kept at its distance," the combined pull and push of the desire and the "keep off," respectively, tending to cause them to circle round and round each other.

And what is the force that traverses the space across which the particles themselves cannot travel? It is not electricity, or magnetism, for those forces are but the results of these circling and vibrations, and not their cause—and moreover science has not discovered electricity or magnetism between the atoms. And what holds the atoms and molecules of matter together, or rather in proximity—what causes their propinquity? Science answers: chemical affinity, and cohesion! But these terms are merely names, and science does not explain the nature of the force employed,—but it knows that it is not electricity or magnetism, or any other known physical force. I answer: It is Mind Power exerted over the intervening spaces by Telementation that attracts and holds these atoms and molecules in their places, and yet keeps them "at their distance." Mind Power, the existence of which in the atoms was postulated by Haeckel, and which always has been taught by the occultists.

And, so finding that telementation exists in the elementary forms of substance and physical things, I am justified in looking for its presence and manifestation from that point of the scale upward. And I believe that the vibrations of mental states, feelings, desires, etc., are transmitted from one mind to another by telementation, arousing similar states, feelings, desires, etc., in the receiving mind along the lines of what we call "induction" in physical science. But before considering induction, I would ask you to consider the following quotation from Flammarion, the eminent French scientist, who says:

> "We sum up, therefore, our preceding observations by the conclusion that one mind can act at a distance upon another, without the habitual medium of words, or any other visible means of communication. It appears to us altogether unreasonable to reject this conclusion if we accept the facts. This conclusion will be abundantly demonstrated. There is nothing unscientific, nothing romantic in admitting that an idea can influence a brain from a distance. The action of one human being upon another, from a distance, is a scientific fact; it is as certain as the existence of Paris, of Napoleon, of Oxygen, or of Sirius." He further states: "There can be no doubt that our psychical force creates a movement in the ether,

> which transmits itself afar like all movements of ether, and becomes perceptible to brains in harmony with our own. The transformation of a psychic action into an ethereal movement, and the reverse, may be analogous to what takes place on a telephone, where the receptive plate, which is identical with the plate at the other end, reconstructs the sonorous movement transmitted, not by means of sound, but by electricity."

As I have said, I account for the transference of mental states, etc., by the theory of "Mentative Induction," which I believe to be the theory more fully meeting the requirements of the case than any of the "dual mind" or similar hypotheses. The term "Mentative Induction" will be readily understood by those familiar with the phenomena of electricity. The word "induction" comes from the word "induce," which means "to influence." In electrical science the word induction is used in the sense of "the process whereby one body possessing magnetic or electrical properties reproduces that property in another body without direct contact."

In text books on physics a simple experiment is often given students to illustrate magnetic induction, as follows: A magnet is so placed that its poles project over the edge of a table upon which it rests. An iron nail, or steel needle, is held a little distance below the magnet so that it will not actually touch the latter but will be near enough to be magnetized by "induction," that is, without direct contact. The nail, or needle, will have an induced property of magnetism produced by the current from the magnet, and will support another nail, or needle, by direct contact. This induced magnetism renders the nail, or needle, a magnet, possessing all the properties of the original magnet, so long as the current flows.

And, just as a magnet may communicate its properties by induction so may an electrified body communicate electrical states in another body without actual contact. The text books are full of examples to illustrate this law. The theory accepted by Science is that the induction is the action of the electrical current through the ether, by waves of vibration. And I hold that just as the vibratory waves of magnetism and electricity pass through the ether and produce similar properties in other bodies by means of induction, so do the vibratory waves of Mind Power, from one mind, pass through the ether, and by induction set up similar mental states in the minds of other persons within the "field of induction."

I hold that just as the "excitement" of the particles of matter ("excitement" being merely "aroused activity") may manifest an energy that may be transmitted to another object, removed in space from the first, and then may arouse by induction a similar state of "excitement" in the particles of the second object—so may the "excitement" of the mind among the brain cells of the animal or person be transmitted by telementation to another animal or person in whom, by mentative induction, a similar state of excitement is generated or induced. I hold that there is the closest possible relationship between motive energy and emotive energy—in fact, that both are forms of the same thing. I shall not attempt to go into details regarding telementation or mentative induction at this place, for the reason that I shall bring out the principle in detail, from time to time, by pointing out the manifestations and activities of these principles. But I wish you to fix in your mind the elementary principles of Mind Power in its phases of telementation or "long distance effect," and of mentative induction, or the process by which "like begets like" on the mental plane as on the physical. The machinery of the mentative processes and activities being hidden from physical sight, we may understand these processes and activities better by using the illustration of corresponding physical processes and activities—particularly when the correspondences are more than mere resemblances, being operations of the same underlying natural laws. For this reason, the illustration or symbol of wireless telegraphy will help us to understand telementation; and electrical or magnetic induction will help us to understand the phenomena of mentative induction.

And, now let us pass on to a consideration of the activities and manifestations of Mind Power, in its phases of telementation and mentative induction, in living creatures, beginning with the lower animals.

CHAPTER 4

MENTAL MAGIC IN ANIMAL LIFE

I have spoken of the manifestation of Mind Power among the atoms and particles of matter, whereby the tiny corpuscles become aware of each other's proximity, and whereby they move voluntarily in response to the desire aroused by the attraction or affinity of the other atoms; and whereby they also exert a pull or drawing power on the other atoms, and respond to the same attracting force of the other particle. Ascending the scale, we find the crystals building up their forms by drawing material from the fluids in which they are immersed, and then building upon a set pattern and style, as truly as does the builder among the animals or among men.

Passing on to the low forms of animal life, we find tiny life forms in the slime of the ocean bed, which are apparently no more than tiny drops of glue—cells without a nucleus—which nevertheless perform the functions of all organic forms, being born, taking nutrition, assimilating, eliminating, growing old, and finally dying, after reproducing their kind by growth and division. But, the point that most concerns us is that although these creatures have no senses, or even rudimentary sense organs, they are aware of the approach of other creatures, and of their food. In some way they become "aware" of these things—how, man does not know. Moreover they are possessed of the power of motion, and exert their will in the direction of moving from place to place. Some of these forms of life, when viewed under even a strong microscope are seen to move by gliding from place to place, apparently at will, and with no perceptible employment of organs of motion such as false feet, fins, etc. They seem simply to *move by pure will*. How do they do this? How do they become aware of the approach of other creatures, without sense organs, or the rudiments of the same? It seems that mentation and telementation are manifested here.

Rising higher in the scale, we find many insects seemingly endowed with the faculty of becoming aware of the presence of other insects at distances so great as to render the ordinary senses of no avail. Students of ant life relate many remarkable instances of this kind. Ants at a distance seem to be able to communicate with their fellows, summoning assistance, and directing the movements of ant armies. A professor in an American university has related that upon one occasion he met with an instance of telementation on the part of a colony of ants. He stated that he had placed a breeding cage of ants inside of a stone house, the latter having walls sixteen inches thick, with no windows and but one door, the latter being so sealed and protected that it was impossible for even a tiny ant to enter its crevices. When approaching this house for the purpose of studying the progress of his ant colony, he would notice that other ants had collected on the outside of the walls, and were running about trying to get through the stone blocks. Then he tried the experiment of moving his ant cage from one part of the house to another—first placing it beside one wall, and then another, and so on, trying all positions and places. In each case, after each change, when he would emerge from the house he would find the outside ants grouped on the stone wall as near to the inside ants as possible, changing their position from side to side according to the position of the ant cage inside of the house. Many other instances of the possession of the power of telementation on the part of ants have been noted.

Another authority relates that a pair of foreign moths were brought to England. There were no other moths of that kind in the country. One of them, the male, escaped in a part of England many miles distant from the place to which the remaining moth, the female, was taken. The female moth was placed in a tiny cage for security, and then set out of doors during the night. In the morning, much to the entomologist's surprise, he found the male moth clinging to the tiny cage which contained the female. It was the same male, undoubtedly, for in size, coloring, appearance, etc., it corresponded exactly; besides which there was not another moth of that particular species known to be in England. Similar experiments have been conducted with insects, and there is held to be ample grounds for believing that insects attract their mates by means of some mental power beyond the range of the ordinary senses.

Schools of fish seem to have some method of instantaneous communication between the individual fishes composing them, for the entire school moves from side to side, turning sharply, etc., as if it were possessed of but a single mind. Some scientists have held that many of the lower animals who live in groups, schools, etc., have mental relations similar to those of the colonies of cells which seem to have a common mind. There is undoubtedly communication over distance of the cells of the blood in animals, and the phenomenon of the school of fish, just noted, may be analogous—at any rate, there is some sort of distant mental communication between the individual fishes. The same phenomenon is noted among flocks of birds, as many know who have witnessed the flights of large numbers of birds of different kinds. Wild animals undoubtedly have some subtle sense whereby they find each other when separated by long distances. The return of cats and dogs who have been carried miles from home—and the return of birds to their original places, after their migrations, may have a similar explanation—there may be subtle vibrations from places, people, and objects, which the animals sense at a distance.

That animals exert a mental control over their fellows by some form of manifestation of Mind Power, there seems to be but little doubt among those familiar with the ways of animals, particularly of wild animals. There is a manifestation of something besides physical strength and prowess on the part of the animal—*there is a mental something displayed!* A. E. McFarlane, in a recent magazine article on the subject of "Bad Animals," says: "Put two male baboons into the same cage, and they will open their mouths, show all their teeth, and 'blow' at each other. But one of them, even though he may possess the uglier dentition, will blow with a difference, with an inward shakiness that marks him for the under dog at once. No test of battle is needed at all. It is the same with the big cats. Put two, or four, or a dozen lions in together, and they also, probably without a single contest, will soon discover which one of them possesses the mettle of the master. Thereafter, he takes the choice of the meat; if he chooses, the rest shall not even begin to eat until he has finished; he goes first to the fresh pan of water. In short, he is 'king of the cage.'"

Among the animals we find many instances of the power of "charming" or "fascinating," both of which I hold to be but varying forms of manifestation of Mind Power in the direction of powerfully influencing the imagination, desire, or will of another by mentative induction. This mental fascination, among the animals, manifests along two lines, *viz.*, (1) along the lines of desire operating in the direction of sex manifestation, such as the winning of mates, etc.; and (2) along the lines of will operating in the direction of overcoming the prey of the animal, such as the "charming" of birds by serpents, or of smaller animals by tigers, etc. These cases are capable of liberal illustration and proof, and natural history affords us full authority for accepting the same.

I recently read an account of a naturalist, who related that one day in a tropical country he noticed a winged insect circling around and around a scorpion. After a bit, the insect made a series of desperate plunges at the scorpion, as if in a frantic desire to terminate the charm; the scorpion soon striking down the insect, and afterwards devouring it. It is related by travelers that when one comes suddenly in the presence of a lion, tiger, or leopard, his legs seem paralyzed, and the eyes of the beast seem to exert a peculiar fascination and power over him. I have seen a mouse manifest the same emotion in the presence of a cat; and the same is true of a rat in the presence of a ferret, or similar enemy. On the other hand, every observer has noticed the wonderful "charming" power that animals exert over others of their kind, of the opposite sex. If you have ever witnessed the courting of a bird, during the mating season, you will have a keen sense of the reality of the power employed. One of the birds, and it may be either a male or female, will be seen to actually "fascinate" or "charm" the one of the opposite sex, the latter lying still with quivering wings, and a helpless expression in its eyes. When compared with the attitude of the same bird, when charmed by a serpent, the resemblance will be striking.

I have before me a book written in 1847, which relates quite a number of instances of the operation of mental fascination among the lower animals. I will give you a few of them, condensed, and abbreviated. Prof. Silliman is quoted as stating that one day, while crossing the Hudson River, at Catskill, he passed along a narrow road with the river on one side, and a steep bank, covered by bushes, on the other side. His attention was attracted by the sight of a number of birds, of a variety of species, who were flying forward and backward across the road, turning and wheeling in strange gyrations, and with noisy chirpings, seemingly centering over a particular point of the road. Upon examination the professor found an enormous blacksnake, partly coiled, and partly erect, showing an appearance of great animation, with his eyes flashing like a brilliant diamond, and his tongue darting in and out. The snake was the center of the motion of the birds. The professor adds that although the snake disappeared in the bushes, frightened at the approach of the men, still the birds seemed too dazed to escape, and perched on the nearby bushes, evidently awaiting the reappearance of their "charmer."

The same book relates an incident of a man in Pennsylvania, who saw a large blacksnake charming a bird. The bird described gradually decreasing circles around the snake, at the same time uttering piteous cries. It seemed almost ready to drop into the jaws of the snake, when the man drove off the latter, when the bird arose with a song of joy.

Another case is related of a ground squirrel, which was observed running to and fro between a creek and a large tree a few yards distant. The squirrel's fur was badly ruffled, and he exhibited fright and distress. Investigation disclosed the head and neck of a rattlesnake, protruding from the hole of the tree, and pointing directly at the squirrel. The poor squirrel at last gave up the fight, and yielding to the fascination, laid himself down with his head very close to the snake's mouth. The snake then proceeded to swallow the squirrel, when his meal was interrupted with a cut of a carriage whip in the hands of the observer, and the squirrel, released from the spell, ran briskly away.

Dr. Good is quoted as having made quite a study of the curious fascinating power that rattlesnakes manifest over small animals, such as birds, squirrels, young hares, etc. He relates that these animals seem incapable of drawing their eyes away from those of the snake, and, although seemingly struggling to get away, they still gradually approach the snake, as though urged toward him, or attracted by a power superior to their natural instincts. He goes on to state that the animal creeps nearer and nearer, until at last it is drawn into the serpent's mouth, which has been open all the while to receive it. Dr. Barrow is quoted as relating many instances of this kind, known to peasants in all parts of the world. Valliant, the African traveler, tells of an instance in which he witnessed a shrike in the very act of being fascinated by a large snake at a distance, the fiery eyes and open mouth of which were gradually approaching the bird, the latter manifesting convulsive trembling and uttering piercing shrieks of distress. The traveler shot the snake, but upon picking up the bird, he found it dead—killed either by fear or the power of the serpent, or perhaps by the violent breaking of the spell. He measured the distance between the snake and the bird and found it to be three and one half feet.

A case is related in one of the early reports of the Philosophical Society, in which a mouse was put in a cage with a viper, by way of an experiment. The mouse at first seemed greatly agitated, which state was followed by a condition of fascination, the mouse drawing nearer and nearer to the viper which remained motionless with distended jaws, and glistening eyes. The mouse, finally, actually entered the jaws of the viper, and was devoured.

Bruse, the African traveler, relates that the natives of an interior tribe seem to be protected by nature against the bite of scorpions and vipers. They are said to handle these creatures fearlessly, the latter seeming to be robbed of their power of resistance. He states that the creatures seem to sicken the moment they are touched by these natives, and are sometimes so exhausted by the invisible fascinating power that they perish shortly. He says, "I have constantly observed that however lively the viper was before, upon being seized by any of these barbarians, he seemed as if taken with sickness and feebleness, and frequently would shut his eyes, and would never turn his mouth toward the arm that held him."

Personally, I have seen a somewhat similar case. When I was a boy, in Maryland, I knew of a farmhand who was called a "snake charmer." How he did it, I never could find out, but he would exert some kind of influence over all kinds of snakes, poisonous ones included, and would cause them to remain fascinated until with a quick movement he would grab them

by the neck with his bare hands. This man generally carried a few pet snakes around with him for company. They seemed perfectly contented, and would poke their heads up from out of his pockets, in order to look at some one else with whom he might be talking. The negroes on the farm had a mortal terror of this man, and would walk a couple of miles rather than pass by his house.

The power of charming animals, dogs and wild beasts is undoubtedly possessed by some men, in varying degrees. And nearly everyone has known of men who could "charm" the wildest horses, as if by magic. I have read of some burglars who seemed able to quiet the most ferocious watch dogs. The Swedish writer, Lindecrantz, tells of certain natives of Lapland who are possessed of some process of charming dogs, to such an extent that they have been known to cow the most savage great hound, causing him to fly from them with all the signs of abject fear. Many of my readers have seen, or heard of, the horse "whisperers" found in various parts of the country, who will shut themselves in a stable with a fierce horse, and by "whispering" to him will manage to tame him completely, and make him passive to their will.

There are cases recorded in which men who have been "charmed" by a snake, have afterwards given in their experience. One of these cases relates that the man was walking in his garden when he suddenly came into the presence of a snake whose eyes gleamed in a peculiar manner. He found himself fascinated, as if by a spell, and unable to withdraw his eyes from those of the creature. The snake, he stated afterward, seemed to begin to increase immensely in size, and assumed, in rapid succession, a mixture of brilliant colors. He grew dizzy and would have fallen in the direction of the snake, had not his wife approached, throwing her arms about him, and breaking the spell. Another similar case is related, in which a man found his companion standing still on the road, with his eyes fixed intently upon those of a huge rattlesnake which was regarding him fixedly with gleaming eyes, scintillating in its raised head. The man was leaning toward the snake, and would have fallen toward it in a few moments. He was crying, feebly, but piteously, "He will bite me! He will kill me!" "Sure, he will," replied his friend, "why don't you run away? Why are you staying here?" But the man seemed perfectly dazed, and distracted, and could not answer. The companion finally picked up a stick and struck at the snake, which glided away savagely. The fascinated man was sick for several hours afterward.

When I was a boy, I had a somewhat similar personal experience, although not nearly so serious. Walking one day among a grove of trees belonging to my grandfather, I found myself standing staring intently at a snake about two feet long whose eyes glistened like large diamonds. In a moment I ceased to see anything but those awful eyes which glistened and displayed all the prismatic colors to my frightened glance. It lasted but a moment, however, for the snake glided away, seemingly as anxious to get away from me as I was to part company with him. I cannot say whether the spell would have been broken by me, if the snake had not moved away—perhaps it might, or perhaps not. All that I remember now, after the passage of thirty five years or more, is that I did not seem to feel fear after the first shock, my feeling and emotion seemingly being that of great wonder, and amazement arising from what I saw in those eyes.

But I have said enough regarding the manifestation of mentative induction among the lower animals. There are many interesting instances of this sort, scattered through the pages of books on animal life, and nearly everyone who has lived in the woods, or among wild life knows of many cases illustrating this fact which have come under his own observation. I have mentioned these features of the subject merely for the purpose of showing you that we have to deal with a general natural principle which manifests throughout all life. This book has to deal with the manifestation of this force among men. But in closing this chapter, I would ask you to notice the resemblance between the manifestation of the force among the animals, on the one hand, and among mankind on the other.

The animals employ the force for two purposes, *i. e.*, the captivating of mates, and the capture of prey. And how do men and women use it? Along similar lines! Yes, I mean this, as startling as it may appear. For is not the use of fascination, in the direction of attracting the other sex akin to the sex charming noticed among the birds and animals? And is not the use of fascination in the direction of influencing men and women along the lines of business, or personal interest, akin to the "charming" of prey by wild animals, serpents, etc.? You may see that evolution simply changes the form of use in this and other natural qualities, and power—the force or power remaining the same, under all of the changes. And, does it not become important for us to understand, study, and guard ourselves against the employment of such an elemental force as this, which manifests along all planes of life, from lowest to highest?

CHAPTER 5

MENTAL MAGIC IN HUMAN LIFE

Passing on from the lower animal life to the plane of human life, we find on all sides many manifestations of Mind Power along the lines of telementation and mentative induction. Now, as never before, is this mighty force being employed for worthy or unworthy purposes in everyday human life. On the one hand we hear and see it being used for the curing of the ills to which the flesh is heir, many of which ills, by the way, having been brought on by improper methods of thinking; by the adverse suggestions of advertisements describing diseases, urging patent medicines, etc.; as well as by the ignorance of the masses of people regarding the effect of negative thoughts and depressing auto suggestions. We also see Mind Power employed through the channel of suggestion, being exerted to bring about better and more positive mental states among those who have been manifesting negative mental conditions. We also witness the exploitation of Mind Power, under various names by numerous cults, sects, and organizations, through many schools, teachers, and publications—under many different names, and backed up by various "authorities." We also see the same force being improperly used in hypnotic exhibitions, and in other forms calculated to weaken the wills and positive mentality of other persons. But it is all the same power—no matter how used. Like any other natural force, it may either be used for the service of mankind, or for its hurt.

I would caution the student of this work from being misled by the many names and terms used by teachers and writers describing some form of Mind Power, and which the said persons claim to be "something new," or "something different"—it is always the same old thing—as old as creation, and just as universal as is electricity or light. When you have become acquainted with the fundamental principles underlying this great natural force, you will be able to recognize it, always, beneath its many disguises, garbs, titles and formulas. The same old Mind Power, you will find it.

Whether in the form of personal magnetism, or the subtle fascinating charm of one mind over another—that form of mental force that influences as if by an irresistible charm; that bewitches, allures, charms, enchants, attracts; or in what has been called fascination, in which one person is able to influence another by exercising a powerful influence upon his or her affections, emotions, passions or thoughts; or in some of the other similar forms of the exercise of an unseen, inexplicable influence upon others; or in the phenomena known as "psychologism," etc., with which all are more or less familiar; or in the phenomena attendant upon the revival of the ancient occultism in the last twenty years, under various names and forms, the fundamental principle of which consists in forms of mental "treatments" of one kind or another, present or "absent"; or in the phenomena of what has been called "suggestion," of which we hear so much in scientific circles; or in the various forms of mind or faith cures, of which so much has been heard of late years, and upon which a number of religions and cults have been built; or in the repulsive forms of mental influence, known as Black Magic, etc., etc.—we have the same fundamental principle, and manifestation of some phase of the general phenomena of Mind Power. The same cause is under all its manifestations—"good" or "bad," "black" or "white." It is all the operation of the one great law, or principle of Nature.

We see on all sides men who seem to exert a wonderful and mysterious mental influence upon others—upon those associated with them, or upon the public mind. Leaders spring into prominence, apparently owing their power to some mysterious influence over the minds and wills of others. Some attain power and position—others attain wealth and social state, by reason of some inner force. When we meet certain people, we become at once impressed by a something about them that makes its power and influence felt by us. They seem to radiate a peculiar force that bends our wills captive, and causes us to fall in with their desires, to a greater or lesser extent.

We know that when some people enter a room, they bring with them an indefinable influence that becomes apparent to all. Certain houses and stores have atmospheres of their own, which are perceptible to those entering them. Some places are depressing to all who live or do business in them. Some salesmen impart a sense of confidence and trust at once, while others cause the reverse. Some persons attract—others repel.

Some people seem to have a way of influencing the minds of others with whom they come in contact, so that these others will rally around the self constituted leader, and thus cults, religion, and "isms" are formed. We all know how far a strong "magnetic" leader may carry his followers. We have seen many instances of it during the past twenty years. People have followed some of these leaders like a flock of sheep. And they will always do so, until the underlying principle is understood and people protect themselves.

And all of these things go to form part of the phenomena of Mind Power. Surely the subject is worth investigating.

Now, as never before, the subject of the mystic forces of Mind Power is attracting the attention of the majority of thinking people. In ages past, the knowledge of the subject was possessed by but the few, who jealously guarded it from the minds of the masses, the latter obtaining but scraps of the hidden knowledge, and that adulterated with the grossest superstition and attributed to the particular form of primitive religion prevailing in the particular place, at that particular time. And even now, notwithstanding the popular interest in the subject, but very few have arrived at a scientific understanding of the matter, and the majority take their knowledge of the New Psychology in the capsule of dogma and theory advanced by some particular cult or sect.

Mind Power has been known to the race, in one form or another, from time before history was written. In the earliest records we find many traces of it among all peoples. And, even today, it is known and practiced, in a more or less ignorant manner, by all races, from the people of the highest civilization known to us, down to the ignorant African Bushmen.

Many have been turned away from a serious consideration of the subject by the fact that many of its forms have been accompanied by the grossest superstition, and the most absurd repulsive ceremonies. They have failed to see that underlying all the extravagant ideas and methods of application, there was to be found a fundamental law of Nature, as real and as constant as any other natural law or force. And, inasmuch as this law is in constant operation, and all are subject to its influence and effect, does it not become the duty of intelligent people to acquaint themselves with this mighty force or law, in order that they may understand its workings; take advantage of its benefits; and protect themselves against its misuse? Believing that there is but one answer to this question, this book has been written in order to throw light on a subject commonly left in the dark, or at least in the twilight of the human understanding.

I am fully aware of the fact that many ingenious theories have been advanced by modern writers attempting to account for the phenomena of Mind Power. But all students of the subject are aware that these theories, cleverly as they have been designed, are more or less self contradictory, and many a reader has thrown aside the subject in disgust after a vain attempt at reconciling the opposing views. And to make the matter worse, various cults and sects and "isms" have sprung into existence, the promulgators and leaders of which have used the accepted phenomena of Mind Power as a foundation upon which to build airy structures of religion, philosophy, and metaphysics.

Many of these cults have practically claimed a monopoly of the great natural force, and have assumed the right to be the sole custodians of the secrets thereof, alleging that they have the "only real article—all others are base imitators," notwithstanding that all of them show that they have arrived at at least a working knowledge of the force, and are obtaining results—each obtaining about the same percentage of successes, notwithstanding the fact that each denies the other the fact of possessing the information and right to use it. Is it not apparent to any intelligent observer that they are all using the same great natural force, in spite of their conflicting theories—and that their results are obtained in spite of their theories, rather than because of them?

In a former work, which has served as a basis for the present one, I grouped the phenomena of the manifestations of Mind Power under the general term of "Mental Magic," the use of the term being justified by the following facts: The word "Magic" was derived from the Persian word "*mag*," meaning "a priest." The Persian priests were "wonder workers," or "magicians," the latter word being derived from the word "Magi," the name of the hereditary caste of priests of ancient Persia and Medea. This Magian order, or esoteric cult of the Zoroastrian priesthood, represented the center of ancient occultism at that period of the world's history, and its influence was felt in all parts of the world, and continues down to this time. So highly were its members respected and considered, that the term "Wise Men," and "Magi" were synonymous. The "Three Wise Men" mentioned as appearing at the birth of Christ (Matt. II) were known as the Magi, or "wise men from the East."

From the word "Magi" came the term "Magic," which Webster has defined as follows: "The hidden wisdom supposed to be possessed by the Magi; relating to the occult powers of nature; mastery of secret forces in nature; having extraordinary properties; seemingly requiring more than human power, etc." So we may consider the word "magic" to mean: "mastery of the occult forces of nature," the term indicating the existence of such forces, and the possibility of the mastery or control of them. And in ancient times, "magic" was always believed to be connected in some way with the use of the mind, particularly in its aspects of will, desire, and imagination. Effects were believed to result because some magician either "willed it"; "desired it to be"; or else "imagined it would occur";—in each case the result happening as a materialization of the mental conception or wish. "Wishing" was always believed to be a magical operation, and if we examine a "wish" we see it is composed of the use of the imagination, coupled with desire, and backed up with will. And so, I felt that I was justified in using the term "Mental Magic" in considering the various phenomena resulting from the manifestation of Mind Power.

But by the use of the term "Mental Magic," I meant more than the mere mental control of the "occult forces of nature." I meant that these "occult forces of nature" are themselves mental in character and nature, and that their control or mastery means simply the conscious use, control, mastery, and application of certain mental forces, called "occult," that are possessed by the race, and are used by all, either consciously or unconsciously. The mastery or control of these forces, means that one may learn to "knowingly" apply that which all have been using blindly and unknowingly. And as knowledge and intelligent use always means Power, the knowledge of the principles of these forces, and the consequent intelligent application of them brings power to those acquiring it.

While it is true that that which is known as "magic" has always been mixed up with a mass of credulity, superstition, and meaningless forms and ceremonies, the close student will see that these excrescences and appendages necessarily arose from the superstitions of the mass of the people, and to the various forms of primitive religions that the race has fostered during the procession of the centuries and ages. The magicians were nearly always priests in the old days, that being the only career open to them, and one that enabled them to erect the barrier of primitive religious rites between their wisdom and the ignorance of the race.

The careful student will be able to trace the possession of something real and true always manifesting among the various forms and ceremonies of the various ancient cults. There was always to be found an esoteric or inner cult, within the mass of the exoteric or ignorant priesthood and followers of the temples. There was always the light of Truth burning in the holy of holies of the temples, for those who were sufficiently advanced to worship at its shrine.

And, among the dim records of the ancient mysteries that have come down to us from ancient India, Egypt, Persia, Chaldea, Babylon, Greece, and Rome, and the other old centers of civilization and culture, we may always find the underlying principle of the existence of some mighty force connected with the human mind—or more particularly, the will—that was at the bottom of the mysteries, and magic, and miracles. Back of all the ceremonies, rites, and incantations was the esoteric idea that the will was the real force employed under the mask of incantation and rites assumed to impress the imaginations and minds of the populace. Back of the amulet and charm was the working of the will of the person wearing them, which was called into effect by the faith or imagination (a real power and not a fancy as many believe) of the man ignorant of the real force.

As the writer on this subject in the Encyclopædia Britannica has truly said (although he was ignorant of the truth underlying the silly forms): "There being an evident relation between an objectand the thoughtof it, it becomes one of the chief practices of the sorcerer to try to make things happen by thinking about them." And the same writer in another place speaks of: "The element in Magic, not depending upon 'spirits,' depends upon imagined powers and correspondences in nature, of which the adepts avail themselves in order to discover hidden knowledge, and to act upon the world around them by means beyond the ordinary capabilities of men. Thus by mere effort of will," etc., etc.

And the student who will look under the surface, and read between the lines, will be able to see the evidence of "Mental Magic" underlying all the forms of magic, mystery, and wonder working miracles of all times and ages, and people—of all kinds, character or name. Behind all the masks he will see the features of this use of the Mind Power of man—always the same, in spite of the fantastic and grotesque masks and trappings.

I could fill pages with recitals of the many disguises under which Mind Power masquerades, but I must hurry on the telling "how," and I can do no more than to hastily call your attention to the many evidences of the use of this power in all parts of the world, and in all times. The ancient mysteries of Egypt, Greece, etc.; were systems of forms and ceremonies, wherein were hidden the use of Mind Power. The sick were brought to the temples and healed. The minds of the populace were filled with the thoughts of victory impressed upon them by the will and subtle suggestions of the priests. What we know in these days as "Mental Suggestions," including that which we now call "affirmations" or "auto suggestions," were understood and skillfully used by the priests, or magicians, in order to control the people.

And it must not be for a moment supposed that these forces were used for evil purposes. On the contrary, the priests were the real governing classes—the powers behind the throne—and they felt the responsibility of power, and endeavored by their knowledge of the occult forces of the mind to lead the people in the right path. Of course, selfish men there have always been, and we hear of cases away back in the early days of history where this power was prostituted for evil and selfish purposes, just as power is always capable of wrong application. In all ages we learn of the healing of the sick by mental power, for Mental Healing presents an unbroken line from the earliest days down to the present, concealed often under fancy trappings, but the same in principle always. And what we call "Mental Suggestion" has always been in force in the hands of the leaders of the race to influence, for good or evil, those under them. The great leaders of men have always been adept in the use of Mind Power, although many of them have never suspected the sources of their power.

To many it may seem almost sacrilegious to state that the highest uses of Mind Power, such as leading the race up to higher ideas, aims and accomplishments—to success, happiness and health—are merely higher forms of the same force that is used by the ignorant and repulsive savage in his rites, and dark practice. But it is true. Mind Power is like any other great natural force—it is above good or evil. It is neither good nor evil, but may be used for either. This is true of electricity, steam, explosives and every other natural force. And we might as well look this fact squarely in the face, and govern ourselves accordingly.

The same force that is used by the modern "healer," when he or she "treats" a patient for health, success, or some other desirable quality, is the same used by the black Voodoo; the Congo sorcerer; the Salem witch; the Hawaiian "Kahuna," who prays people into sickness and death; the medicine man of the American Indian, with his charms and incantations; the wizards and enchanters of the Middle Ages; the practitioner of "adverse treatments," or "malicious mental magnetism," of the modern cults. The same force pervades all, just as the same life force flows through the saint and sinner; the angel and demon; the dove and the serpent; the lamb and the tiger—Nature's one force through all.

And just as Mind Power is brought into operation through the prayers of the faithful of all religions, before their shrines, images and holy objects, so may the force be brought into operation through the fetiches, conjurations, enchantments, charms, spells and devil worships of the ignorant and depraved minds. The secret is this: The power does not come from the supposed source, but from within the mind of the man employing it. And, still more startling, to the uninitiated, is this statement, which is equally true: The power of the mind of the person affected is the real cause of the effect, rather than the power of the mind of the supposed causer, the latter merely calling into operation the power of the mind of the person affected.

Passing from the past to the present age, we see in greater use than ever this wonderful Mind Power. No longer the property of the few, the information has filtered out among the masses, through various sources, and we see the force in use on all sides. Often, the persons using it have not the true knowledge of its real nature, and such persons often involve themselves in a terrible whirlpool of effects by reason of a selfish and base employment of this power. Many are playing with this force like children playing with dynamite.

It is one of the purposes of this book to call the attention of such people to the nature of the force they are employing, and the possible, nay, probable, results of a misuse of it. Not that they are punished for such misuse, but rather by reason of it. Black magicians are invariably caught in the meshes of their own nets—are entangled in the psychic machinery of their own manufacture—and are blown up by their own psychic high explosives.

In concluding this little consideration of the subject, I would call the attention of the student to the fact that now, for the first time in the history of the world, Mind Power is being employed for furthering commercial aims and ends. Mental treatments for wealth and success are commonly known and advertised; instructions in the use of suggestion for commercial purposes are furnished both personally, and in correspondence courses; the laws and principles are explained, partially, at least, in books written for the instruction of those selling or advertising goods, and otherwise soliciting the patronage of the public.

It is true that the few strong men in business life have always made use of this force, consciously or unconsciously, but never before has it been taught generally as a part of a business education. It has been reserved for America to recognize the force, and to boldly apply it in this way, *i. e.*, to the making of dollars. And other countries are fast falling in line. And in view of this fact, is it not time that those who know of the real nature, principles, and laws of this force should give to the world their knowledge, that the race may know with what they are dealing—and may he enabled to extract the good from it by proper use, and, seeing the evil possibilities of improper use, may avoid such prostitution of one of nature's greatest forces.

Many students of the occult have sought to keep from the general public a knowledge of the fundamental principles of the great law of nature underlying the phenomena of Mind Power. They have claimed that it was "dangerous" for people generally to know that such a force existed and could be used. They have held that such knowledge should be carefully guarded by the few, and that its very existence should be denied to the many.

This may have been good reasoning in the earlier days of the world, when the masses were grossly ignorant, and when the only knowledge was locked up in the minds of the caste of priests and other leaders of the race. But the argument no longer applies, for the general intelligence of the race has refused to allow any locked doors in the Temple of Knowledge, and has insisted that all doors be thrown open to them. The result has been that a considerable body of occult knowledge has been opened to the gaze of the public, and they are clamoring for more. Much of the knowledge possessed by the public regarding Mind Power is but quasi knowledge—half truths—and the time has come when the whole truth should be taught. The time has arrived when the public should be made acquainted with the great force underlying the phenomena of Mind Power. People should be instructed regarding this force; its laws and operation; its intelligent and proper use, with directions designed to protect people against its improper use against them, on the partof others—this latter a mostimportant matter in these days of occult and psychic investigation on the part of the public, and the attempted base and selfish uses to which some are putting the occult mental forces of Nature.

It is too late to deny or ignore the existence of the mighty mental force in Nature that underlies the various forms of phenomena that go to form the outward phase of Mind Power, good and bad. Too much has been witnessed by the public concerning these matters for them to be hushed by the old cry, "There's nothing in it but imagination." On the one hand they have witnessed the various "treatments" of the healers, tending toward the cure of disease, the attainment of success, etc. And on the other, they have heard whispers of "adverse treatments," etc., and have heard of, or read, the various courses of instruction in hypnotism, mesmerism, etc., etc., and have seen evidences of the good and bad effects of what has been called "suggestion," in all of its forms. And they are beginning to realize that all of these things, differing as they may seem, have a common root in some one natural force. And they are demanding, like the man from Missouri, to "be shown." And they have a right to demand this.

The race has always recognized the existence of a mighty force of Nature which man has employed, consciously or unconsciously, in the direction of influencing his fellow men; other forms of life, and even the so called lifeless things around him. In the earlier days this use of the force was called "magic" (black and white); mystical art; divine power; miracle; fascination; charming; enchantment; wonder working; necromancy, etc., and in its more base and evil uses, black art; witchcraft; sorcery; voodooism, etc. For it must be remembered that this great force of nature is capable of base as well as of noble use.

Like any other great natural force—like electricity; the power of explosives; steam; the X rays; radium, etc.—this great force is capable of the highest and most beneficial uses by man when properly applied and is also capable of being applied to the most harmful purposes. Different as are the results arising from the varying applications, the force is the same in each case. The forces of Nature are not possessed of a sense of good and evil—their function and purpose is to act in obedience to the laws of their nature without regard to the question of good and evil to those by whom, or against whom, they are employed. This may seem like a terrible thing, but a moment's thought will satisfy you that it is true of all natural forces, and the question of good and evil, and its reward or punishment, belongs to another plane of life.

But, it may be asked, why do I wish to inform the public about a force, unknown to many, which is capable of evil as well as of good use and results. The answer is simple. Ignorance is no protection against anything, for the knowledge is always possessed of the few who may use it on the ignorant many without suspicion; the greater publicity is given to a thing, and the better it is understood, the better may its good effects be obtained and the less the danger of its improper use—forewarned is forearmed. If a thing is good, the greater publicity given it the greater the good—if it is evil, the brighter the searchlight turned upon it, the less danger is there attendant upon it.

The danger of all evils lies in the darkness of concealment, not in the daylight of publicity. "Turn on the Light" has always been the watchword of progress and civilization. And more particularly is this so at this, the first decade of the Twentieth Century, when the interest in occultism and kindred subjects has made a number of people acquainted with Mind Power, and has acquainted them with its uses, under various names and theories. And in many cases it is being practiced upon people who are unfamiliar with the subject, and therefore it is time that some one should "turn on the light," that it may be seen by all men and known for what it is—capable of the highest and the lowest uses, but a great force of Nature.

And with this exposition of it, goes the remedy and protection against improper use, as well as the knowledge of its wonderful proper uses. If it be a bane—here is the antidote. But it is not necessarily a bane, any more than steam, electricity, and explosives are a bane to mankind. What would be thought of people who would suppress knowledge of all natural laws, because of the possibility of improper use? Ignorance is no protection. Truth and fact must be followed to the end, and it will be discovered that, in Nature, every force that may be possible of hurtful use, may be guarded against by natural means.

So much for the unpleasant side. But there is a very pleasant side to this subject of Mind Power. This force has come to man just when he most needs it. He has used the so called mechanical forces to clear away the obstacles that Nature put into his way in order to develop him into a Man, and now he turns to higher forms of energy and work—he is crying for new worlds to conquer. And these new worlds will be conquered by the mind, rather than by the muscle. Great things are before the race, and one of the greatest forces in Nature in the work of the building up of the Super Man, will be this force called Mind Power. By it man will be enabled to fight off the forces of ignorance and materialism, and to draw to himself knowledge from the Universal Mind that will enable him to accomplish the heretofore Impossible.

In this book I shall treat Mind Power as I would any other great force or energy of Nature, *i. e.*, in a scientific manner, stating the principles plainly and without concealment, and also giving in full what I and other experimenters along the lines of this subject have learned of the methods beneficial, and the reverse, concerning the applications of these principles. In the case of the beneficial application, full directions will be given that the student may avail himself of the force to the fullest extent. In the cases where the subject of the harmful use of the force is alluded to, the student will be instructed how the same may he prevented, obviated, and neutralized, so that full protection is assured. This is what I should do in lessons upon electricity, steam, or explosives—and that is the course I purpose following in this work.

It is possible that this course may bring upon me the adverse criticism of those who believe "that the public is not ready for such knowledge," and that "such things should be reserved for the few." To such people, and all others, I would say that I have no sympathy with such an attitude, and I believe that the race is ready for *all the Truth*, and that that which is proper for the few is proper for the many. I believe that the greater the degree of knowledge the greater the degree of power and advancement. I believe that ignorance is not happiness; and that to keep a man ignorant of a natural fact, in order that he may escape its effect, is like allowing him to smoke when seated on a keg of powder rather than to acquaint him with a knowledge of explosives—or, to use another figure, to advise him to bury his head in the sand like an ostrich, rather than to look upon the approach of a possible danger. I do not believe in such sophistry! I do not believe in Ignorance! I do not believe in Darkness! Therefore, I purpose to "turn on the light!"

CHAPTER 6

THE MENTATIVE POLES

Whatever Mind Power may be, in its ultimate nature, it is true that in its "working nature" or phase of operation it seems to work along similar lines to those followed by electricity. Like electricity, Mind Power undoubtedly has two poles, or phases. Like electricity, it travels in currents. Like electricity, it operates by induction. Like electricity, it is vibratory in its manifestation. And, like the higher forms of energy—super electrical in nature—it possesses radio activity, or radiant energy—that is, like many other forms of radiant energy, it is constantly throwing off streams of active energy, in the shape of "rays"; "vibrations," or "waves." Recent scientific discoveries have proven this, and in the next few years the world will be startled by additional discoveries along these lines. Already we are receiving hints of "Mental Photographs," or "Radiographs," and before long we shall have "Tele Mentometers," that will register the telemental waves.

The brain I regard as in the nature of a "transformer" of the Universal Mind Power, or possibly as a "converter" of the force into mentation. The brain cannot *create* Mind Power; its office is merely to "transform" or "convert" the existent energy into usable forms and phases. Science agrees in the belief that in all brain processes there is an employment of some kind of energy, and a "burning up" of brain substance. Just as there is a constant "burning up" of the elements of an electrical battery in the production of electricity, so is there a "burning up" of brain matter in the production of Mentation. And yet Science teaches us that no electricity is ever "created"—simply a portion of the universal electricity is "converted" or "transformed." And I believe that the same holds good in mental action in the brain.

And now it is time for us to begin our consideration of the two Mentative Poles.

In this book I shall hold to the fact there is evident in the manifestation of Mind Power, in any and all forms, two distinct poles, or phases. I find myself compelled to coin two more terms for these poles or phases, for there are none now in common use. I shall call these two Mentative Poles respectively "The Emotive Pole" and "The Motive Pole." The word "Motive" means: "That which acts; wills; moves; chooses; controls." The word "Emotive" means: "That which manifests feeling; emotion; agitation; passion; sensation; etc.:" These definitions apply to my use of the terms in these lessons. You will be able to fix these two ideas connected with the Mentative Poles by thinking of the Motive Pole as "Will"; and of the Emotive Pole as "Feeling."

The Emotive Pole manifests actively as Desire Force. The Motive Pole manifests actively as Will Power.

These two poles play a most important part along the lines of telementation. Not only does desire cause the response of one's own will, but both desire and will are active forces in themselves, and act and react upon the desire and will poles of mentality of others. We shall see many evidences of this as these lessons progress. In fact, the entire theory and practice of Mind Power depends upon this underlying principle.

Your strong Desire Force is able to rouse the will of another mind in response thereto. It may likewise set up vibrations in that other mind, awakening there similar desires. Your Will Power may arouse desire in the mind of another, and cause action in accordance therewith. It may also overpower the will of another, and lead it captive. Your combined will and desire pouring out in the mentative current may produce a combined effect upon the minds of others by telemental induction. These two poles of the mind are both active and powerful in their effect. Both may be roused into intense activity, according to well known laws, as we shall see. Let us take a few moments' time and consider the subject of Desire Force and Will Power, before we proceed further.

Those who have studied the phenomena of Mind Power have generally accepted the theory that the effect upon other people was produced by the "thought" of the sender, and all the teachings upon the subject have been along this line. I, too, fell into this error, and for many years taught of the power of "thought," etc. But I have come to modify my views on the subject.

Of course, everyone who has paid any attention to the subject knows that thought transference is a fact, telementation being an established reality. But there is a very great difference between the fact that "thoughts" may be sent and received like telegraphic messages, on the one hand, and that persons may be influenced and affected, and bent to the desire or will of another on the other hand. It is like the difference between thinking and doing in ordinary life. One may send his thoughts so that another may receive them—but what of this? What has this to do with the doing and compelling? It is evident that the real force must be looked for in some far more elementary and vital operation of the mind, than logical and reasoning thought. What is thought? Webster defines it as "An exercise of the mind in any of its higher forms; reflection, cogitation." Nothing very dynamic about this, surely. We must look for something in the mind having more elementary force and power.

Let us think a moment. What part of the mind seems to produce the greatest moving power and strength? Is it not chiefly that region of the mind that produces what we call emotions—feelings—desires—cravings—passions? Does not this part of the mind really cause the greatest incentive action on our part? Is not the whole moving force largely summed up in the two words desire and will? Think of this a moment.

Why did you do this thing, and that thing? Is it because you thought about it by cold, logical reasoning, and acted upon the impulse given thereby? Or, was it not because you *wanted* to do it—*desired* to do it—felt like doing it? Is not always the feeling or desire precedent to and the originator of the action? And, as for thought, is it not used merely as an instrument to think up the best ways of manifesting the feeling or desire? Think of this—is it not so? Did you ever do a thing (except under compulsion) that you did not desire to do? And was not the desire the preceding cause of your every action?

Desire is the great inciting power of the mind. Desire is "that which incites to action." And you always act upon the strongest desire—subject always to the restraining influence of the reason, and the restricting or impelling influence of the will. I will tell you more about this wonderful thing, the will, in a moment or two, but let us now think of desire, for that is the real emotive power.

Desire originates in the sub conscious regions of the mind, and often we can feel her there, before she emerges into consciousness, stirring us up with feelings of vague discontent and unrest. After a bit, gathering enough force, she emerges into the conscious field, and then begins to demand expression. Now remember, that when I say desire, I mean all kinds of desire, high and low. Many people think of desire as only the craving of a low nature, but desire really means a feeling that wants something—and that something may be the very highest aspiration of the human mind.

Now, this desire in all of its manifestations has a mighty power of attraction and influence. It manifests as the Law of Mentative Attraction which is constantly drawing toward us the things we desire, and also drawing us toward them. Not only is this true on the conscious plane, but even on the subconscious. Our desires constitute our nature, and our nature is always operating the mighty power of Mentative Attraction.

The trouble with the most of us is that we allow our Desire Force to be scattered, and diffused, thereby lessening its attractive power. It is only when we learn the secret of concentration and focusing the Desire Force by the will that we are able to get results above the average. The will is the director and controller of the Desire Force, and upon its training and management depends the powerful use of the latter.

Desire Force not only has its effect upon the person, and others near him, but it may be, and often is, sent for thousands of miles where it affects and influences others, in ways. Desire Force is the mighty force which makes many of the phases of Mind Power possible. It spreads out from the mind of the person affecting and influencing others even at other parts of the world, if concentrated and directed by the will. It is a force beside which the X ray and electricity fade into insignificance. It moves not merely blind, lifeless things, but the living minds, thoughts, emotions, passions and actions of men. It is the force that rules the world, and its destinies. Like any other great natural force it is capable of being used for good or evil. It is neither good nor evil—it is either or both, according to the mind in which it originates.

What phase of mental effort is more apt to be a motive force—the cold, lifeless thought about an abstract metaphysical proposition, or a mathematical problem, on the one hand; and a warm vital wave of "feeling," emotion or passion, such as love, hate, ambition, aspiration, courage and desire on the other? And remember that these last mentioned all belong to the "feeling" side of the mind, and all are manifestations of elementary desire.

Desire is at the bottom of all feeling. Before we can love or hate, there must be desire. Before we can have ambition or aspiration there must be desire. Before we can manifest courage and energy there must be desire. Desire for something must underlie all life action—desire conscious or subconscious. Abstract thought is a cold, bare thing, lacking vitality and warmth—desire is filled with life, throbbing, longing, wanting, craving, insisting, and ever pressing outward toward action. Desire indeed is the phase of our mental action that is a motive force.

And not only does desire incite us to action—move us to accomplish its ends, but it also, when sufficiently strong, surges out from our minds in great waves and clouds of invisible and subtle energy or force, and travels here and there toward the object of its inner urge—affecting, attracting, drawing, forcing the desired thing into submission to its cravings and demand. In the presence of some strong man or woman—that is, in the presence of one whose desire burns fiercely and strongly, and whose will has learned to concentrate the Desire Force—one may actually feel the impact of the elementary principle of mind as it vibrates in great waves from the brain and nervous system of such a one. Who has not met people who actually seemed to be living desire and will?

The source of Desire Force exists in every person, and it may be developed to a wonderful degree. The desires of many of you—of the majority of the race, in fact—never get further than the faint, "want to" stage. These people "wish" for things in a faint, pink tea way. They never want a thing hard enough to stir their Desire Force into action and make the thing come to them, or else make it take them to the thing. The majority of people do not know how to desire. They do not know what it is to be filled with that intense, eager, longing, craving, ravenous desire that fills them with a new and mighty force, and makes them *demand* things instead of merely asking for them. They are like sheep, pigeons, or rabbits, and sit meekly around while the strong ones of the race—the ones filled with masterful desire—walk around and pick up every good thing in sight. And it serves them right, too, for they are not exercising the force which Nature has given them for the purpose of self protection and use. They have had the elementary vigor and virility bleached out of them by the "refinements" of one phase of civilization, and have nearly lost all that goes to make up manly men, and natural women. They have become beggars—mendicants of nature, instead of masters of her.

The forces of Nature are at the disposal of the man of vigor and determination and desire. Such a one has but to knock at the door of attainment and have it opened to him. Instead of doing this, the majority of us sit around the doorsteps whining that the door shall be opened to us. In the name of Human Power, friends, get up, and fill yourself with powerful desire, then march up to the door and smite it fiercely with your mailed fist, demanding masterfully, "Open for me, the Master!" And, lo! it will fly open at your call.

I have shown you that Desire Force is the great force underlying the phenomena of Mental Magic. But Desire Force without the aid of the will is like steam unconfined and undirected, and gunpowder fired in the open air—both wasted energy. The will is the lever and director of the great power of desire and without its aid the latter is almost inoperative and ineffectual. Let us examine into the operation of the will.

The will has two offices in connection with desire. These two offices may be spoken of as (1) the directing office; and (2) the protecting office.

The will acts as the arouser, director, restrainer, concentrator, and manager of the great occult force of desire. What is generally known as Will Power is often in reality merely Desire Force strongly concentrated and directed to a focus by the power of the will. Remember this, please, for it will enable you to form a better idea of the subject of Will Power. Often when you hear Will Power spoken of, whatever is attributed to it is really said of and attributed to Desire Force controlled, directed, and focused by will. The effort of the will is operated in the direction of this directing, focusing, concentrating, etc., and in the degree that the will is trained to do this so is the degree of "Will Power" of the individual. Not only is the will able to do this, but it is able also to direct the Desire Force into the mind of other persons, awakening similar vibrations there, and then by its own power the will is able to direct the Desire Force of the other persons into action, taking away that office from the will of the other persons, if their will be not strong enough in its protective office to resist the attack.

The idea of Will Power is more familiar to the minds of people than is that of Desire Force. All recognize the wonderful power of the will, and know of many instances of great accomplishment by reason of its power. And, yet, how few have stopped to consider that unless there was a preceding desire, there could be no manifestation of will. Unless a person desires, that is, *wants* to do a thing, he will manifest no Will Power. But, on the other hand, one may desire to do a thing, and unless the will is aroused and applied, no action will occur. Desire arouses will; and will may stimulate desire. The two act and react upon each other. The two should work in unison, and the trained individual has both under control and pulling well together, like a well trained team.

Will Power is more than a mere determination to act, although that mental attitude and action is manifested in Will Power. It is a living force. Desire is the sister, and will the brother twin. And both, together, manifest that which we know as Dynamic Mentation.

Will Power is more than a mere mental faculty—it is a mighty attribute, the influence of which may extend far beyond the mind of the person manifesting it. The greatest feats of the occult magicians depend upon telementation operated by trained Will Power. And the so called "great" men of history, ancient and modern, had their source of strength in this Will Power, which they trained and developed to an extraordinary degree.

The exercise of will shows itself in two ways, (1) the mastery of one's own mind; and (2) the mastery of the minds of others. The second is well nigh impossible unless the first be accomplished. One must first train his mind so that he will hold it firmly in the grasp of the will, and prevent it from jumping this way and that way, instead of moving ahead to its purpose. When one has so trained his mind to be obedient to his will, that it can be held steady and "one pointed," as the Hindus say, then is he in a position to direct his mentative currents upon others to the best advantage. But so long as his mind is in a stage of disorganization, one faculty pulling this way, and another that way, and so on, he cannot hope to concentrate upon others the force that is being wasted in keeping order at home. When the mind is mastered by the will, then may new territory be conquered.

The term, Will Power, is commonly used in connection with the manifestation of firmness, or determination. The determined will is known as a mighty factor toward attainment and accomplishment. And I think it well to consider this fact at this point, for back of all outward manifestations of mentative influence along active lines, lies this determined will of the individual. The more determined and firm the will of the individual, the stronger the mentative influence emitted and emanated by him. This statement should not require proof, for its truth is apparent to all who have made a study of man and his powers. It has been recognized by writers in all times. Here are a few quotations that will tend to fix the matter firmly in your mind, and create in you a desire to manifest the determined will—the lever that directs and concentrates Mind Power.

Buxton said: "The longer I live, the more certain I am that the great difference between men, between the feeble and the powerful, the great and the insignificant, is energy—invincible determination or a purpose once fixed, and then victory or death. That quality will do anything that can be done in this world—and no talents, no circumstances, no opportunities will make a two legged creature a man without it."

Donald G. Mitchell said: "Resolve is what makes a man manifest; not puny resolve, not crude determination, not errant purpose—but that strong and indefatigable will which treads down difficulties and danger, as a boy treads down the heaving frostlands of winter; which kindles his eye and brain with a proud pulse beat toward the unattainable. Will makes men giants."

Disraeli said: "I have brought myself by long meditation to the conviction that a human being with a settled purpose must accomplish it, and that nothing can resist a will which will stake even existence upon its fulfillment."

Sir John Simpson said: "A passionate desire and an unwearied will can perform impossibilities, or what may seem to be such to the cold and feeble."

John Foster said: "It is wonderful how even the casualties of life seem to bow to a spirit that will not bow to them, and yield to subserve a design which they may, in their first apparent tendency, threaten to frustrate. When a firm, decisive spirit is recognized, it is curious to see how the space clears around a man and leaves him room and freedom."

As we have seen, the use of the will as the projector of mentative currents is the real base of all mentative induction, under whatever name it may manifest. And the phase of will known as telementation is the form the results of which strike the observer with the greatest force. The will currents of a strong man reach out far beyond the limits of his brain, and influence people and things, causing them to be inclined toward his wishes. Many men have worked their will upon others far removed, and much that is known as thought transference, telepathy, mental influence, etc., is really this working of the will currents over space. What occultists have called "thought forms," etc., are really manifestations of the energy of the will. Will is a living force, that can be projected and operated at a distance. It has a property of reacting upon others, and permeating them with a mental essence not their own, unless they repel the invasion or fortify themselves against the aggression.

Desire and will are more elementary forms of mentation than thought. They underlie thought. Without desire and will there can he no thought. They ever precede thought; and are closely allied to the essence of what we call "feeling." Many people live almost altogether on the feeling plane, and exercise but little thought. The infant feels, desires and wills before it can think. Desire and will are really the medium from which thought is evolved.

A modern writer on mysticism has said: "There is no force in the universe except will force," meaning, of course, the great natural force of energy called will, of which desire and will in man are expressions. Desire is a natural force, and can be used, managed, controlled and directed just as can be any other natural force. And what we know as Will Power is the positive phase of directed desire. The Orientals have trained and cultivated this Will Power to degrees that seem miraculous to the Western mind, and by this trained Will Power they perform the so called "miracles" that confound the Western scientist. But even the 'West has its men of "Iron Will," whose influence is felt on all sides, and whose power is openly acknowledged by the public. In the East these men are generally hermits and sages, while in the West they are generally "men of action," leaders, "captains of industry," etc.

Mind Power is the essence of all mentative induction. It includes the positive, forcing, impelling, compelling, driving phase called will as its motive pole, and as its emotive pole it has that attracting, drawing, pulling, luring, charming, fascinating, something that we call desire. Mind Power manifests in the phases of both desire and will, as we generally use these terms, for it is composed of the elements of both. Will may be said to represent the masculine side of Mind Power, and desire the feminine side. It may help you to fix in your mind the attributes, characteristics and nature of these two phases of mentative energy by associating them with the idea of masculine and feminine.

I wish that you would learn to think of the Desire Force as the warm, ardent, fiery, forceful energy, underlying the manifestations of Mind Power; and of the Will Power as the cold, keen, strong, directing, controlling projector of the energy. By fixing these mental images in your mind, you will be better able to manifest the two phases as occasion arises.

Besides its office as the director of the energy, the will serves a very important office as the restrainer of Desire Force. When under the control of the "I" of the person, and taking the suggestion of reason and judgment, it is able to prevent one from expressing undesirable or hurtful desires.

It refuses to project the Desire Force, or to allow the desire to take effect in action. It also turns back the desire upon itself, and refuses to allow it to manifest. It is the utmost importance that the individual acquire a mastery of his will, for by doing so he will be able not only to express his desires with the greatest force and effect, but will also be enabled to restrain hurtful desires, and to prevent their manifestation upon the plane of action.

And the will has still another important office. It acts as a protector. The will repels the influence or vibrations of another mind, and renders its possessor immune to undesirable thought waves. It creates a protective aura around the individual, which will turn aside the thought waves or vibrations which may reach him, whether such be sent directly to him or whether they are the vibrations emanating from minds of others and unconsciously sent forth. The will when properly used acts as an insulator for attacks upon the desire pole of one's mind, and prevents the vibrations from reaching their mark. And if it be well trained and strengthened it will be able also to resist the most powerful attacks upon it by the wills of others, and will beat back the vibrations which would force their way into its stronghold to take it captive.

CHAPTER 7

DESIRE AND WILL IN FABLE

I herewith reproduce "The Fable of the Mentative Couple," a bit of writing in the lighter vein perpetrated by myself about a year ago. My excuse for writing this tale, and for reproducing it now, is that it carries with it a decided moral, and teaches an important truth. It brings out the distinction existing between the Motive and the Emotive phases of the mind, and beneath its flippancy is concealed some good, sound psychological truth.

I ask that you read it, in connection with what I have just told you regarding the offices of the will, desire, imagination, etc. It will show you, in figurative style, the operation of the two poles of the Desire Will. And it will show you how the emotive pole or phase, if left unguarded by the protective faculties, will be led into all sorts of trouble. It will also show you how the protective faculty may be disarmed and overcome by a diversion of its attention from its task. There are several important psychological facts brought out in this little fable, and a number of important "morals" to be deduced therefrom. I trust that you will seek for the truth and principles underlying the trifling words of the fable. Just as important truths may be conveyed in the fairy tales of the child, so may just as important facts be taught by the fairy tale fable of the Mentative Couple intended for the "grown ups."

Each of us, man or woman, has a Mentative Castle, in which dwells a Mentative Couple—Volos and Emotione. And Volos often strays away, leaving Emotione unprotected. And the fascinating stranger often puts in an appearance. And Emotione often is beguiled by his wiles. And Volos often is fooled by having his attention and interest distracted by clever schemes, leaving Emotione unprotected again.

So, while recognizing the value of Emotione, learn to keep Volos at home at the gate of the castle, and do not allow him to be "side tracked." Heed the advice of the wise man of the fable. There is an important lesson for *you* in this fable if you will take the trouble to find it.

THE FABLE OF THE MENTATIVE COUPLE.

Once upon a time there lived in the land of Mentalvania, in a wonderful building called The Mentative Castle, a man and a woman, called "The Mentative Couple." They were happy though married. They lived in harmony, because they were useful to one another, and neither was complete without the presence of the other—and neither did his nor her best work, unless the other was present and assisting.

Well, now, the man was called "Volos" (which is the same as the English name "Will"), and the woman was called "Emotione," which in the language of that country meant something like a combination of emotion, desire and imagination.

Now, the chronicle informs us that these two people had natures entirely different from each other, as has been said. We are told that Volos was of a stern, inflexible, strong, positive nature; apt to stick to a thing once begun; full of the "will to live" and "vitality"; full of determination and spirit with a strong dash of the "let me alone" and "get out of my way" in his make up; with a taste for meeting difficulties and overcoming obstacles; with a goodly habit of reaching out and taking hold of what Emotione wanted and needed; and a powerful lot of self respect and self reliance in him. He was apt to be firm although his firmness was not the stubbornness of the mule. His general keynote was strength. He was a good warrior and defender of his castle. But Emotione was of an entirely different type, temperament, and character. She was most impressionable, imaginative, emotional, credulous, fanciful, full of desire, curious, sympathetic and easily persuaded. While Volos was all willing and thinking, Emotione was all feeling.

Volos was a strong character, but lacked certain qualities that make for success—but these qualities Emotione possessed, and she supplied the deficiency in Volos. Volos had to "figure out" everything, while Emotione had intuition, and jumped at a conclusion in a way remarkable to Volos, who couldn't understand the process at all. When he would ask Emotione for an explanation, she would say, lightly, "Oh, just *because!*" which answer would often provoke profane and irreverent discourse on the part of Volos. But, nevertheless, he learned to respect these "becauses" of Emotione, and found that they helped him in his business. Emotione would dream out things, and see things a long way ahead, and then Volos would proceed to put these plans into operation. Volos couldn't see very far ahead of his nose, while Emotione could see miles beyond, and years ahead. And besides this faculty of Mental imagery that came in so useful in Volos' business, Emotione also possessed a burning and ardent desire for things, which she managed to communicate to Volos, thereby causing him to get out and do things that otherwise he would never have dreamed of doing. Emotione was like fire, and Volos like water. The water would hold the fire in check, but at the same time the Fire would heat up the Water and the result would be the Steam of Action. And, so, you see these two—this Mentative Couple—formed a fine co partnership, and prospered mightily.

But, alas! the tempter entered Eden—and the attractive stranger meandered in the direction of the Mentative Castle, and when he reached there trouble occurred. And this is what happened:

One day Volos was absent from the castle, being engaged in some arduous enterprise. And consequently the castle was unguarded. Volos had provided against this by instructing Emotione that she was to keep the castle gate closed tight, when he was away from home, and never to gaze without in his absence, for there was some mysterious danger lurking without when he was away. Emotione had faithfully followed the directions of her liege lord, although her womanly curiosity was piqued thereat. Many the time she had heard strange knockings at the castle gate, but she heeded them not, and even refrained from looking out of the little peep hole in the gate—though this last was much against her inclination, for she could see no harm in "just looking."

But, to return to our tale. This particular day when Volos was absent from home, her curiosity was too much for Emotione when she heard the strange knockings at the gate. And, breaking her rule, she ventured to peep without. Looking down she saw a most attractive stranger, with a fascinating smile on his lips. He looked almost as strong as Volos, but he seemed to have a dash of the woman in him, besides. He had the strength, but also the charm that Emotione recognized as being a part of her own nature. "Ah" sighed Emotione, "here is a man who can understand me." The fascinating stranger smiled sweetly, and looking her in the eyes, masterfully asked to be admitted. "No, no," replied Emotione, "I cannot let you in, for Volos told me not to." "Ah, fair lady," said the Stranger softly. "Volos means all right, but he is rather old fogyish, and behind the times. He does not 'understand,' as do you and I. Pray, let me in." And, like Mother Eve, Emotione took the bait.

Well, to make a long story short, when Volos came home he found that Emotione had subscribed to a set of "Villeveaux Modern Art," a beautiful work published by the De Luxe Bros. of Fifth Avenue, to be issued in 824 weekly parts, at the nominal price of $5 a part—739 parts of which were already out, and would be delivered shortly. She had also given a number of side orders for manifold wares, which had dazzled her untrained and unguarded fancy. Volos cried aloud to the gods of his land—but it was too late, the contracts had been signed.

But this was but the beginning. Volos did not understand just what was the matter, and contented himself with scolding Emotione, whereat she wept bitterly. But the poison went on with its deadly work. And when Volos again was absent from home, the habit reasserted itself, and when the fascinating stranger again called at the castle, he was admitted. And when Volos returned, he found the castle furnished from dungeon to watch tower with costly rugs, and furniture, and various other articles, bought from "Morganstern's Popular Installment House," at $1,000 down and $100 per week. He also found that the castle had been lightning rodded from ground to turret, on each wing, tower, and annex; and that sundry promissory notes, containing a law proof, judgment confessed clause, had been given in exchange therefor. And then Volos swore by the Beard of Mars, the war god, that he would have no more of this—he would remain at home thereafter. And he did.

But the subtle stranger was onto the game, in all of its details. And this is how he played it on Volos, even though the latter remained at home.

A few days after Volos had determined to remain at home, there came a band of mountebanks, singing, dancing, and performing juggling tricks. Volos sat on the great stone beside the open castle gate, and his attention was attracted by the sounds and sights. Faster the dancers whirled—louder beat the drums—sweeter grew the singing—more bewildering grew the feats of jugglery—until poor Volos forgot all about the open castle gate, so rapt was he at the strange sights, sounds, dances, and feats of jugglery. Then one of the mountebank gang (who was really the attractive stranger disguised in motley array) slipped, unseen, past Volos, and in a moment was engaged in eager conversation with the impressionable Emotione.

Volos watched the crowd until it moved away, and then entering the castle, and closing the gate behind him, was confronted by Emotione, in tears, for she dreaded the coming storm. "Alack a day, woe is me," she cried, "I am again in trouble, O, Volos, my liege lord! I have just ordered from the fascinating stranger, who slipped past you at the gate, a baby grand, self playing, automatic, liquid air valved, radium carburetter, piano playing, Organette, upon which I may play for you all classes of music, ranging from Vogner's *Gotterdammerung* to the popular "Merry Widow Waltz" with feeling, depth of expression, and soulful understanding, according to the words of the fascinating stranger who took my order."

"Gadzooks!" ejaculated Volos, "Fain would I cry aloud the name of that production of Vogner's just mentioned by thee. And by my halidom, e'en shalt thou soon be performing the waltz just mentioned by thy false red lips! Zounds! Of a truth I have been stung again by that fascinating stranger. I must gaze no more upon these fleeting scenes of merriment and amazement, lest I be again decorated with the asses' ears. Aha! Volos is himself again, and the next time the fascinating stranger appears upon the scene, he shall be smitten hip and thigh with my trusty battle axe, and my snickersee shall pierce his foul carcass!"

But, alas! even once more was poor Volos deceived and trifled with—once more poor Emotione fascinated by the stranger. And it came about in this way.

On the day of his last undoing, Volos sat on the open step, in front of the narrowly opened castle door. "No man shall pass me now," cried he. But fate willed otherwise. For as he sat there, there approached many people who took seat upon the steps before the gate, and engaged Volos in long heated, and wearisome discourses regarding the outlook for the crops; the presidential campaign; the Japanese question; race suicide; the new theology; how old was Ann; the problem of the final outcome of the collision between the irresistible force and the immovable body; the canals on Mars; what Roosevelt will do with his big stick when his term expires; and many other weighty, interesting, and fascinating topics of general interest. Most agreeable were these visitors, and most considerate of Volos' feelings were they. And although they seemed to differ from him at the beginning of each argument, still they courteously allowed him to convince them inch by inch, until they finally acknowledged that he was invincible in argument, and invulnerable in logic. "'Tis passing strange," quoth Volos, "but nevertheless 'tis true—that *I always find myself on the right side of every question*. And the wonder grows when they all admit it in the end. Verily, am I developing into a wise guy!"

And, pondering thus, he fell sweetly asleep from the rigor of the disputes; the flattering attentions shown him; the joy of the victory; and the exceeding amount of attention and interest he had expended, for human nature has its limitations, even in the case of one so strong as Volos. And while he slumbered, the fascinating stranger (who was really the leader of the argumentative visiting committee), crept into the house and unloaded upon Emotione a choice collection of gilt edged mining stock (pure *gilt*, all the way through in fact); a bunch of flying machine bonds, and a 5,000 monkey power, vestibuled drawing room, observation car Automobile called the "Yellow Peril." And when Volos discovered what had happened he wept aloud, crying bitterly, "Odds bones; s'death—of a cert am I the Baron E. Z. Mark." And thereupon he sent for the wise man who dwelt in the next barony.

The wise man came, and after hearing the story said: "My children, yours is a sad case, butmatters may be adjusted without a visit to Sioux Falls, and without the raising of the question of alimony. The trouble is as follows: "Volos, without Emotione, has no desire or incentive to do things. He has no wants to satisfy, and therefore does nothing. He needs Emotione to supply the desire. And without her he has no feeling—he is nothing but a hard shell clam. Therefore he needs her to supply the feeling, for verily, and of a truth, feeling is the spice of life. And without her he has no imagination, and cannot see beyond the end of his nose—and what is life without imagination? Gadzooks, one might as well be a mummy!

"And on the other hand, Emotione without Volos, is a consuming fire of desire; an unrestrained imagination; an intuitive faculty degenerated into the basest superstition, most deplorable credulity, and the idlest fancy. Volos has no desire, emotion, or imagination of his own—and Emotione has no will of her own. "Verily, cannot it be seen by all that this couple needs one another the worst way? Each, alone, is but an incomplete half. United they stand—divided they fall. In union alone is there strength for them.

"And more than this, each, without the other, falls a prey to the wiles of some fascinating stranger. We have seen how Emotione was fascinated and controlled by the stranger who gained access to the castle. But I have also seen (by my magic art) that when Volos was away from home on important business, and not having Emotione along to keep him straight, he fell a victim to the wiles of the Desire and Imagination of a fair stranger across the river, and did her bidding, and used his will to perform her tasks, instead of those desired by his own Emotione. Verily, art these people quits with one another and should now begin over again. True it is that harmony will be theirs only when they are together.

"And this is the secret of the undoing of Emotione. Without the will of Volos to protect her, direct her, and advise her, Emotione allowed her desire imagination, and emotion to run wild and unrestrained. And so she became so impressionable as to allow herself to be mastered by the will of the stranger, who took advantage of the same and gathered to himself many choice orders for things. And even when Volos sat by the door watching the players, dancers, and jugglers, his *attention* was so centered on what he saw, that the fascinating stranger slipped through the gate—it was even as if Volos had been absent from home. And, again, when Volos allowed himself to become engaged in weighty discourse with the visiting committee, and used up his energy and force in argument and dispute with them—and when he permitted himself to be 'jollied' into a false security by these United Brethren of the Blarney Stone—he relaxed his vigilance, and allowed himself to become tired, drowsy and sleepy, and so fell into a doze at his post, and the stranger again entered and took Emotione's orders for goods.

"And this then is the Remedy (as my successor, Lawson of Boston, will say in the centuries to follow)—this is the Remedy. Each person of this Mentative Couple must stick close to the other. Volos must have no 'important business' across the river, which will allow Emotione to be without a protector and adviser. And Emotione must stick close to Volos, and satisfy her curiosity, imagination, emotion and desire, by setting him to work out things for her—to do things dreamed of by her—to get her things she desires—to express the things felt by her. This is the secret of success, dear Mentative Couple—mutual work by desire and will, working in unison and harmony—each faithful to the other—each guarding the other from the fascinating strangers that beset each when separated. Now, then children, stick close to each other!"

And saying this, the Wise Man vanished from sight.

And the moral of this fable of the Mentative Couple is this: That the mind of every man and woman is a Mentative Castle, wherein dwells a Volos and an Emotione. And what happened to the couple in the fable, may happen, and does happen, to many in everyday life. The will, straying from home, and paying attention to other attractions leaves the castle unguarded, and the fascinating stranger enters. And, again, the will has its attention distracted by passing objects of interest, and forgets the castle door. And again, the will allows itself to be fatigued, tired, and jollied by useless argument, and talk, and cogitation, at the instigation of the designing fascinating stranger, and the latter slips past the gate.

And in each case, inside the gate is Emotione unprotected and innocent, true to her own nature, credulous, imaginative, fanciful, desireful, and emotional—is it any wonder that she "orders goods" that are not wanted by the family? And the remedy of the wise man as given to the Mentative Couple may be, and should be, applied by every man and woman in his or her Mental Castle. And this then is the moral of the fable.

And thus endeth the fable of the Mentative Couple, who dwell in the Mentative Castle, in Mentalvania, in the days of old when brave knights held their sway and fair ladies had their way.

The End of the Fable of the Mentative Couple.

CHAPTER 8

MIND POWER IN ACTION

And now let us consider the subject of the operation of Mind Power, in the phase of its employment, consciously or unconsciously, to affect the minds of others. It is true that this subject will be considered in detail in the chapter on Personal Magnetism and Telementation, but it will be well for us to take a glance at the general workings at this point. I shall cover the points briefly, the elaboration being made at the proper points in the lessons.

In the first place, let us consider the matter of mentative induction. As you have seen, the currents of Mind Power flow in vibratory waves from the mind of the individual, and act upon the minds of others according to the laws of mentative induction. They thus set up corresponding vibrations, and therefore corresponding mental states of feelings, in the minds of such people. In other words, these vibrations "induce" or set up by induction in the minds of others, mental states similar to those existing in the mind of the mentator.

These induced mental states are similar in quality and nature to those in the original mind. But, of course, they are less in degree; for a part of the original energy has been dissipated in many directions, and then again, a certain amount of force is lost according to the degree of resistance in the receiving mind. If the receiving mind sets up, consciously or unconsciously, a considerable resistance to the vibrations, it will either entirely neutralize or repel them, or else rob them of much of their power. If, on the contrary, the receiving mind be in its nature more or less in accord with the vibrations, it will set up little or no resistance, and the induced condition will be very nearly as strong as the original impulse.

The ether, or fine substance filling space, is constantly filled with these mentative currents, of all kinds and degrees, streaming out from the minds of all kinds of people. These currents, of course, come in contact with each other, and often either combine or else act to neutralize each other. For instance, currents of a certain degree or kind of vibration (that is, of a certain mental state) when they come in contact with other currents of similar vibration, will tend to coalesce and combine, there being a harmony and attraction existing between them. But if they are opposing vibrations they will antagonize each other and act in the direction of neutralizing each other's force. If they are of equal strength, both will lose power, but if one is much stronger than the other it will lose only in the inverse ratio of its strength, and the weaker will suffer likewise. That is, the weaker will lose twice as much power as the stronger, and the stronger will lose only half as much as the weaker—supposing that the stronger is of twice the strength of the weaker.

In this way is accounted for the well known fact that places, towns, cities, etc., have their own "personal atmospheres," which affect persons living in them or visiting them. These "personal atmospheres" of towns arise from a combining, neutralizing, etc., of the various vibrations arising from mentative currents from the minds of the people living in the town. An average vibration is struck, which is strongly felt by all within the "field of induction" of that town. A little thought will make it clear to you that this is a correct statement of the mental conditions manifest in various towns, cities, etc., all over the world.

Each place has its own individuality, which soon makes its impression on those taking up their abode in it. It is more than geographical and atmospheric conditions, although, of course, these play their parts, as we all know. The average mental state of the people living in the town strikes the key note. The stronger vibrations affect the average, and give a mental tone to the place. The best proof of this effect being caused by mental vibrations is found in the fact that two towns only a few miles from each other, each having the same atmospheric and geographical conditions, will manifest entirely different mental atmospheres.

People often ask: "If it be true that the ether is filled with mentative currents, why are we not affected more than we are?"

The answer is that they are affected more than they imagine, but they are still affected much less than one would suppose at first thought, for the reason that the currents conflict with each other and rob each other of their force. And then again, Nature instinctively affords a safeguard and sets up additional powers of resistance. Just as Nature protects the hearing sense of those who are surrounded with many and constant noises, until they fail to hear anything but an unaccustomed noise—just as she operates upon the smelling sense of the chemist until he fails to notice the odors which are most apparent to the stranger entering his shop—so does she give additional unconscious resisting power to people situated within an active field of mentative induction.

Bring a person from a quiet place into a bustling, active city, and he is apt to be swept off his feet at first with the "spirit of the place"—he will either be swept into its prevailing life with an almost irresistible impulse, or else he will be repelled by reason of the inharmonious mentative currents. In either case, however, he will be intensely aware of the vibrations. But, the same man, after a time, will fail to be so affected—he will be better able to resist the vibrations and will manage to live with a greater peace and poise than at first, although he will, of course, alter his nature more or less in harmony with the prevailing tone of the place. He will "feel" the vibrations less as time goes on. Some people have so developed this resisting power that they are almost immune, while others have so little power of resistance that they are swept here and there by each strong wave of mentative energy that reaches them—they are always in some field of induction and being swayed by its vibrations.

This phase of mentative induction explains the phenomena of those great waves of feeling that sweep over a country, such as the emotion that followed the sinking of the Maine in the harbor of Havana. You will remember the first shock that came to you when you read the account in the morning papers. Then there came upon you a growing sense of some impending event of great moment, mingled with a feeling of horror and indignation, followed by an almost irresistible desire to join in a movement to avenge the outrage. This latter feeling grew perceptibly as wave after wave of feeling passed over the country in mentative currents, setting up increased mental feeling by induction. Older people will remember many similar waves that swept over the land in past days.

These things are common, and give you a clue to the apparent mystery of the action of mobs composed of a number of individuals who combine in numbers and then commit acts that no one man of the lot would think of perpetrating singly or individually. The conscience of the mob is apparently a thing apart from the individual consciences of the units composing it. After the excitement—the morning after—many, if not all, of the persons concerned, felt a sickening horror and wonder at their work. A mob is a cyclonic center of mentative currents, resembling a whirlpool or whirlwind, with an active center and a less active circumference.

Great waves of religious fervor noticeable in communities during the progress of "revivals" are accounted for in the same way. A few active revivalists start a whirlwind of fervid feeling and emotion, and it spreads out in constantly widening circles, increasing until a climax is reached, and then a diminishing strength is apparent, which gradually settles down into the accustomed mental state of the community.

These whirlwinds or whirlpools of emotional excitement, of whatever kind, are, of course, strengthened by the constantly repeated suggestions of those participating in it, which with the constantly growing volume of mentative energy being thrown forth serves to add fuel to the fire. This force would go on forever, steadily gaining in strength and volume, were it not for a provision of nature which causes the law of rise and fall; increase and decrease; that universal law of rhythm, to manifest in this as in all else in her domain. Everything has its rise, its climax, and its decline.

So much for these general waves of mentative energy, or mentative currents. But there is another phase to be considered—many phases, in fact. Let us examine them.

First there are mentative currents, arising from the strong centered desire of some person, who forming a strong mental image, by means of visualization, creates for himself a center of desire force, which guided by his will power attracts to himself all that will fit into his plans. He constitutes himself a mentative center, around his visualized idea, and constantly sends out strong mentative currents charged with the strongest, most ardent desire force, guided, directed, and projected by his developed Will Power. He thus sets into operation the great mental Law of Attraction, of which the early writers on Mental Science talked so much. These mentative currents, charged with desire, spread out, and soon begin a rotary movement like a whirlpool, sweeping around and around, always drawing in toward its center persons and things tending to fit in with the plans of the center.

The original desire in the man's mind is reproduced in kind in the minds of thousands of people by the law of mentative induction, and they all fall in with the plan, the degree, of course, depending upon the degree of positivity or negativity of the receptive mind, multiplied by the degree of positivity of the mentator. The great plans of the so called "Captains of Industry" are carried out by reason of this law.

Many of these great centers of Desire Force—these successful men, who attract to them that which they want, and those whom they need—do not realize the nature of the force that they are using, but there are a constantly increasing number who do know it, and they are "working it for all it is worth." Many of these steady, cool business leaders are really deeply versed in occult laws. If the true facts of the case were to creep out, there would be the greatest sensation that the country has ever known.

Then there is still another phase of the matter. I allude to the cases of men who (generally consciously, but sometimes unconsciously) are focusing their mentative currents directly upon some person or persons who are necessary to their plans and desires. They are filled with desire to have these persons do thus and so, or not do thus and so, as the case may be. These men, according to their degree of concentration and will power direct to the other person or persons strong mentative currents of Desire Force, and by mentative induction set up vibrations of a corresponding rate in the minds of these others, the degree of effect produced, of course, depending upon the degree of negativity of the recipient. This effect is produced in two ways, both according to the law of mentative induction.

The first way is to set up corresponding desire vibrations in the mind of the other, so that it will in turn cause his will to carry out the desire. A variation of this is to direct the desire force toward the will of the other, and thus "entice" or "charm" the other's will into compliance with the desire of the sender. This will be understood if you will remember what I have said about the resemblance of the desire pole to the feminine, and the will pole to the masculine. You will see an illustration of this in every phase of mentative influence.

The second way is for the will of the sender to force its way past the will of the other and boldly "make love" to the desire of the other, and endeavor to "seduce" it by mere strength and persistency until it accedes to his wishes. The variation of this is seen in the case where the attacking will boldly grapples with the will of the other, and by sheer superiority of power overcomes it and makes it captive and obedient. This latter is very rare, except in cases of personal interviews between the two persons, aided by telementation between interviews.

You will notice that the phase in which the desire pole of the mentator does the work is along the lines of feminine action, the force being of a charming, fascinating, drawing, coaxing nature; and where the will is employed, the action is decidedly masculine, the attack being made boldly, and with a show of strength, the subtlety of the desire attraction being absent. The giants in the art of mentative attraction combine poles in their attacks and work, and thus in the words of "Uncle Remus": "Dey cotch 'em comin', and dey cotch 'em goin'," like "Brer Fox."

Then again, there is the use of mentative induction, in what is known as "Personal Magnetism," which we will see in other chapters of this book. In this phase the mentator pours forth his mentative currents, either in a general way, or else in a concentrated, directed manner, toward the other, in a personal interview. This is the secretof whatis called "personalmagnetism," and also of that unaccountable (to the uninformed) manner which some people have of overpowering others by sheer "strength of will." The "personal magnetism" phase of personal influence is the phase of feminine activity; and the "force of will" phase is the phase of masculine activity.

Then there is that form of mentative induction called "mental suggestion," which I take up in later chapters. Although suggestion has to do with words, etc., rather than with mentative currents, still the principle is the same—the mental state is "induced" by words or physical things which are the result of feeling and mental states, just as is the phonographic record the result of the original speech which it is able to reproduce when the diaphragm is brought in contact with it by means of the needle. And then there is very little mental suggestion that is not accomplished with mentative currents—very little, indeed.

In closing this lesson I wish to caution my readers to refrain from manifesting or feeling anything like fear at what I have said about the use of mentative energy by other people. Remember, that fear in itself is the most negative influence and most weakening mental state known. It renders negative the most positive man if freely indulged in. No matter how potent may be these mentative currents, there are none that may not be rendered impotent, and ineffectual by your own will power set in motion by your own desire force. Each and every one of you have within you, and under your own control, a force that will render you perfectly and absolutely immune from undesirable mentative influence, no matter who may use it against you.

Nature has blessed all of us in this respect—it makes no bane without its antidote, and does not depart from its rule in this phase any more than in any other. It supplies the means of self protection to everyone, and always furnishes the defensive weapon to match the offensive one. As a matter of fact, you are defending yourself constantly, although you may not know it.

Much of this defensive work is done along subconscious lines, but you are doing much of it consciously by the use of your will and spirit of individuality. You are using the mental "No!" all the time—that is, unless you are some poor creature who is afraid to say "No!" even mentally, and if you are that, then this book is doubly needed by you.

I shall instruct every student of this book, in many different ways, as we proceed with the lessons in this art of self protection. No one who studies this book need ever again fear any undue influence on the part of others. I purpose to make mental masters of you, and to teach you to throw off the bonds and shackles of mental slavery. I intend to make you strong, positive individuals, instead of weak, negative personalities.

There is nothing to be afraid of except fear—so the sooner you cast off fear the better you will be, and the more advanced on the road to mastery. While this is not the place for exercises, still I want each and every one of you to start right in now and form a mental attitude of fearlessness and strength, that you may begin at once to send forth mentative currents of that rate of vibration. If you do so—and you will, I know—then you will begin to notice an improvement at once. You will begin to realize your increasing power, and you will also see that others are beginning to feel it. Begin today—this moment—to radiate mentative currents of strength and power in all directions. Stimulate the currents by arousing a strong, intense, burning desire to be strong and to radiate strength vibrations—then back this up by the application of a strong, steady, masterful and dominant will—and then "the trick will be done."

But right here, remember, first, last, and all the time, that it is nota mere matter of thinking—buta matter of feeling. Thoughts are cold, but feelings are warm, alive and vital. Therefore you must not merely think "I Am Strong," or say it like a parrot—but you must stir up your nature to its depth, until you can really feel that you are indeed strong and possessed of the radiant energy of mentative force. Feeling is living thought. Everything that is worth while was produced by this feeling thought. Feeling—Desire—Emotion—Passion—Wanting—Willing—Demanding—these are the things that have creative power. So do not deceive yourself with this "holding the thought," or any such nonsense of which you have heard so much until you get sick at the mention of the words. It is not simply "holding the thought," it is "holding the desire," and backing it up with the will, that does the work. To create a thing you must want it with a burning, eager want that brooks no denial—backed up by a will that knows no such word as "can't" or "no."

CHAPTER 9

PERSONAL MAGNETISM

Perhaps the most interesting manifestation of Mind Power along the lines of telementation and mentative induction, at least to the beginner in the study of the subject, is the phase known as "Personal Magnetism." We may as well begin by considering the use of the word "magnetism" in connection with mental influence, etc. We often hear of "personal magnetism"; "mental magnetism"; "magnetic personality"; "magnetic attraction"; "magnetic influence," etc., etc., used in the sense of mental attraction; personal influence; fascination; charming; psychological influence, etc. Let us see just why the term is used. The explanation involves an interesting bit of little known occult history.

The word "magnetism," of course, arises from the word "magnet." Now here is an interesting bit of history. You will see in the dictionaries that the term "magnet" was given the lodestone, or natural magnet, because it was first discovered near Magnesia, a town in Asia Minor. This explanation is most amusing to those familiar with the records of the old occult brotherhoods, for the latter know that instead of the magnet being named after the town, the town was named after the magnet, the latter being known centuries before the town of Magnesia was built.

The natural magnet was known in China, India, and Persia thousands of years ago. Its name "magnet," arose from the same Persian word as "magic," namely, "*mag*," signifying the esoteric priesthood or Magians. The name was given because the power of the natural magnet resembled the mental power exerted by the Magians, and the stone was called literally "the Magian Stone," or the "Magic Stone," hence the words "magnet" and "magnetism." So you see we come by our use of the word in a perfectly natural way.

An interesting fact (and one that goes to prove that minds work in accustomed channels) is to be noted in the circumstance that the mysterious phenomena of Mesmerism, etc., noticed in Europe and America during the past century or so, came to be naturally called "Animal Magnetism"; "Personal Magnetism," etc., the mind of the public intuitively connecting the phenomena with that of the magnet, which it very much resembles. And, in our day, we speak of people being "very magnetic," "lacking magnetism," having a "magnetic presence," etc., etc. And so history repeats itself. The magnet which was originally called the "Magian or Magic Stone." because its force resembled the mentative attraction manifested by the Magi or Magians, serves to give a name to similar manifestation of mental force centuries after. The "magnet" gives back to the Twentieth Century Magians the name it borrowed from the Magians of Ancient Persia. It has repaid the debt.

While the phase of Mind Power which has to do with the operation of the force upon distant minds and objects is perhaps the most startling, still that phase which is called "Personal Magnetism" is one of the most important and remarkable. Its very frequent occurrence often causes us to overlook it, but it is the phase which is effectively used by those who understand it, and the one against which it behooves us to guard ourselves.

All have noticed that some individuals seem to have a "winning way" about them, and are able to induce others to fall into their way of thinking, and to do what they wish done. The so called "magnetic" man is able to sway audiences or individuals by his mystic power, and one often fails to realize just how it was done when he recalls the words spoken, or reads them in cold type the morning after. The secret lies not alone in what is said, or even in how it is said, but rather in how great a degree personal magnetism was emanated by the speaker.

Many persons who have dealings with the public in the direction of selling goods; securing subscriptions; selling life insurance, etc., etc., have acquired a degree of the art of using personal magnetism, often being unconscious of the force they are employing. And many large employers of agents have schools wherein the agents are taught the psychology of suggestion, personal influence, etc., and more or less of personal magnetism although under some other name. And, more than this, every person who is in earnest, when talking to another person manifests more or less personal magnetism, unconsciously, or consciously.

While the statement may bring down upon my head the wrath of those who believe that the phenomena of the "old fashioned revival" are due to the "workings of the Spirit," I do not hesitate to affirm that all students of psychology know that the greater part of the fervor is due to emotional excitement produced by personal magnetism, manifesting along both the lines of mentative currents and suggestion. Anyone who has ever attended a negro revival or camp meeting has carried away with him a memory of the effects of a certain kind of personal magnetism upon a certain type of emotional minds.

And not alone in the field of "emotional religion" does this force manifest itself so strongly—it is just as plainly demonstrated in the case of "emotional politics." Let any man sit down and sanely consider the performances of the average man of the rank and file of either of the political parties during a campaign. See how men are swayed by emotional appeals to their prejudices and party spirit. See how they allow themselves to be blinded by glittering promises and statements, without a shred of reasonable argument, until they become fanatics.

Their emotions are skillfully played upon by the leaders and speakers, and the currentof personal magnetism, and suggestion, spreads over the body of the party until they become a mob possessed of certain fixed ideas that have taken possession of them. Families are split by factional differences, and hatred reigns when love formerly had its abode. The excitement grows fiercer and fiercer, until at last the day of the election is at hand, and the country goes into a paroxysm of emotional excitement. Then the result is announced. The next day every one suffers from a relapse, and the country begins to laugh over what has happened.

After the sting of defeat has worn off, and the elation of victory has melted away, it is found that the country is moving along about as usual—not going to the dogs because some man is defeated, nor taking great leaps forward because some other man has been elected Town Supervisor, or President, as the case may be. The people play their parts year after year—that is the majority of them—being swayed by emotional excitement rather than by reason, thought, or intelligence. And the men who pull the mental strings grin to themselves as they think over "what fools these mortals be," and prepare themselves to pull the same strings again upon the next occasion, and to make their sheep like followers again dance to the tune of "My party, right or wrong, my party."

And in both revival and political campaign the moving spirit is the same. Our old friend, personal magnetism, operates through the force of a few "feelings" conveyed from the minds of the few to the minds of the many, aided and abetted in its subtle influence by its mate, mental suggestion. Gaining force under the force of the desire and will of each person who adds his force to the original impulse it swells in volume until, like the rolling snowballs, it grows to mammoth proportions and sweeps all before it.

You have often heard that "enthusiasm is infectious." Did you ever wonder why? Have you ever wondered why you enjoyed a theatrical performance more when the house was filled than when only half its seating capacity was used? Have you ever understood the cause of the wave of enthusiasm that has swept over the large audience, including yourself, until you felt all in a mental glow? Have you ever realized that what is known as "the psychology of the crowd," by which term is meant the influence that can be gained over a crowd, whereas the separate individuals composing the crowd could not be so affected, is due to personal magnetism and mental suggestion which is started into operation and then spread from mind to mind by the added desire and will manifested in mental states and their associated physical actions?

And there is another fact to be remembered while we are considering audiences and crowds. I allude to the fact that the speaker is affected by the personal magnetism of the audience, which flows back upon him, giving him increased power to send again to them his own ideas, awakening fresh emotional excitement in them. It is action and, reaction always.

It is of the greatest importance that one understands the causes of these "mental epidemics," for when the cause is once understood one is far less liable to be carried away by emotional excitement spread in this way. Many sober, sensible people have been swept off their feet by these waves of personal magnetism, and have done and said things that would otherwise have been impossible for them. They have allowed the personal magnetism to reach their minds through the emotive pole, arousing ideas and desires that otherwise would have been impossible.

We have seen, or heard, of respectable citizens, including the members of the so called learned professions, lawyers, doctors, teachers, preachers, joining in mobs and allowing themselves to be carried away by the personal magnetism and suggestion of the more excitable members thereof, and participating in acts that afterwards seemed like horrible nightmares to them. The emotional nature is always very near the surface, in the majority of men, and it should be ever guarded from outside arousing influences. The motive pole of the mind—the will power, should ever be on guard to resist this invasion of the emotive pole—desire force. And so should the will ever be on guard to neutralize the personal magnetism of others who in personal interviews seek to bend the minds of their hearers to their ideas, and by thus arousing desire mould them so as to work their wills upon them.

In all of these cases of personal magnetism, and mental suggestion whether along the lines of personal influencing, appeals, artful suggestion, etc., as well as in the cases of "mental epidemic," the effect is produced by the mentator, or suggestor, obtaining the voluntary attention of the other or others, and thus holding his will engaged, and his emotive pole of mind thus unguarded, while he pours in his mentative currents, or suggestions (usually both) into the emotive pole of his hearers. He thus induces in them the desires, emotions and feelings which act as motive forces, causing them to act according to his wishes and will.

The person affected is rendered unable to reason correctly, or intelligently, for his will is "on a vacation," and his reason is swayed by his desires, emotions and feelings thus induced, the necessary support of the will being lacking. The will of the man sending the mentative currents, or mental suggestions, is in control, instead of the wills of the hearers and persons influenced. In the cases of widespread "mental contagion" the influence spreads from mind to mind, along the same lines, and according to the same laws.

I trust that what I have said along these lines will appeal to the student in the direction of causing him to interpose a resistance to these currents and suggestions in cases such as I have mentioned. The remedy is in his own hands—simply the interposition of the will, in the manner of which I shall speak as we proceed. Surround yourself with an armor of will power which will act as a shield against influences of this sort, and which will beat them back upon their senders. If people but understood this law they would cause these selfish mentative currents to be reflected back upon the sender until he was swept away in the whirlwind of his own raising.

It is apparent to all students of human nature that there is a wonderful difference in the degrees of what is called "personal force" observable in different persons with whom we come in contact. Some are very "forceful," and others are quite "forceless," and others form varying degrees between these two extremes. This difference in "personal force" depends upon the degree of dynamic "positivity" or negativity" in the "magnetism" of each person.

The man who is able to manifest a strong degree of Mind Power along the lines of motive polarity, or Will power, becomes dynamically "positive." I use the word "positive" in this connection in the sense of Webster's definition: "having the power to direct action or influence." Passing down the scale, through varying and lessening degrees of "positivity," we reach the case of the man who is almost devoid of this power of manifesting Mind Power—and his condition we call that of dynamic "negativity." By "negative," as I use it here, I mean: "non positive; lacking the power of direct action or influence. "

Now, every person has his own degree of dynamic "positivity." Each one is dynamically positive to some others, and dynamically negative to others still—unless indeed one has reached the limit of positivity or negativity, which limit cannot be definitely fixed. Two persons meet each other. At once there ensues a silent, quiet struggle between their dynamic mentation, depending for its intensity upon the importance of the meeting. Still, in any and all events, the struggle ensues, usually unconsciously. It may be over in a moment, or it may last a long time, but from that struggle, sooner or later, one or the other must emerge a victor, unless, as is rarely the case, they are of equal degrees of positivity. And there is no mistake about the result—each one recognizes himself as the victor, or the defeated, and adjusts himself to his relative position.

I do not mean by this that the degree of dynamic positivity is fixed permanently in either person. For the contrary is the case. One of the persons who is really stronger, usually, may be weaker at that particular time owing to his will being fatigued, or by reason of his having relaxed his will power, as is often the case. And in such a case, the defeated one may be the victor at the next encounter, or may even rally his energies in a moment later and turn the tables. One may have a strong will, in moments of activity, and yet in moments of passivity he may relax it very much. And, a still more important fact: One may so increase his will power that he will be able to completely dominate those who formerly over mastered and even over awed him. All of us know of instances of this kind in our own personal experiences.

At the extreme dynamic positive pole are to be found those wonderfully forceful men who seem to dominate all with whom they come in contact. These people fairly paralyze the wills of those around them, and induce emotive states almost at will. When in deep, earnest, mentative effort, they seem to actually "plunge" their will into the mind of the other persons, and set themselves up as the dominant force therein, taking the others' wills captive and holding them obedient to the master will of the positive man. Such men are of course rare, and whenever they exist they make a strong mark on the history of their times, local or general. I do not like to Quote Napoleon Bonaparte as an example, for he has been used to illustrate almost everything. But still, the mind intuitively flies to him in thinking of the dominant will. Napoleon had a marvelous will—an almost superhuman will. It was manifested not only on the world at large, but also upon those closest to him in the way of personal contact. This man worked his will on those around him, and forced his desires upon them, also. He dominated everything and everybody, and his contemporaries, even his enemies, testify to this marvelous personal power. He is a very good example of this extreme positive type.

Passing down the scale, we see men of strong personal force in all walks of life. These men formerly played the part of warriors or rulers of kingdoms, but the increasing importance of commercial life in the world's affairs has developed and brought forth a new type of these positive men, who now show themselves as "captains of industry," prominent figures in "frenzied finance," makers and rulers of the great "trusts" of this country, and others. A little lower in the scale of personal force we find men of marked power, but still a little less strong than those above them. And so we pass down, through the varying degrees of the scale, meeting the average man and woman, and then on to the "weaklings" of the race. At the extreme negative end of the scale we find those impressionable creatures, known to students of experimental psychology as "somnambules," or "impressionables," who have merely to be told to do a thing, in an authoritative manner, in order to have them attempt to do it, or at least to feel impelled to do so.

There are many people upon whom the phenomena of extreme mental suggestion may be produced while they are wide awake. They will feel the "burn" on their hands, caused by your finger, if you but suggest it to them in the right way. They will be unable to draw apart their hands, which have been fastened together by your strong suggestion. They will be drawn backward, or forward, by your suggestion. There are many people of this kind, some more impressionable than others, but all quite impressionable, who will be driven this way or that way by those who understand the subject. Fortunately, this fact is not generally recognized, or else we should hear of still more cases of "strange influence," etc., in the newspapers. But the subject is becoming more widely discussed and known now, and it is only a question of time when the law will be compelled to take cognizance of it.

Fortunately, however, the extreme negative condition may be overcome by one, by developing his will and learning the principles underlying the subject. Knowledge of the nature of the subject robs the force of much of its effect, the latter depending largely upon the passive ignorance of the subject. Give him the proper instruction, and he will be able to interpose a resistance. Every man has his present place on the scale, but he may improve his position!

Personal magnetism bears a close resemblance to that which in olden times was frequently caned "Mental Fascination." "Fascination" means "the act of fascinating, or state of being fascinated." The word "fascinate" springs from the Latin word "*Fascinare*," meaning "to enchant; bewitch, charm by eyes or tongue; captivate, attract," etc. The definition of the English word, "fascinate," is as follows: "To act upon by some powerful or irresistible influence; to influence by an irresistible charm; to allure, or excite, irresistibly or powerfully; to charm, captivate, or attract powerfully; to influence the imagination, reason or will of another, in an uncontrollable manner; to enchant, captivate or allure, powerfully or irresistibly."

The above definition is condensed from a number of the best dictionaries, and gives the essence of the idea embodied in the word. In this work I use the term "Personal Magnetism" in the sense of: *The action of Mind Power in the direction of powerfully influencing the imagination, desire, or will of another*. This is my own broad definition which includes all the varied phenomena.

CHAPTER 10

EXAMPLES OF DYNAMIC MENTATION

The story of dynamic mentation runs along with the history of the human race, for it has always been known to man in some form. Coming to primitive man along with other inheritances from still lower forms, it was used from the beginning. Its earliest forms were similar to its employment by the lower animals, such as has been mentioned in a preceding chapter. The positive minds of the race influenced and dominated the more negative ones. Without understanding its laws, the positive barbarians discovered that they possessed a stronger power of inducing mental states among their negative companions, and were thus enabled to work their will upon them. Many of the leaders of barbarian races owe their positions of prominence and leadership to this law of mental induction.

But along with the rise of leaders there was manifested a similar rise in power and influence of the priests. All races have had their priests, and have today. A priest is a man whose office is that of a mediator between men and their divinities—one who claims to represent the supernatural entities in their dealings with men—a religious, or spiritual "middle man," as it were (I use this expression in all seriousness, and with no desire to speak lightly of the priestly offices, which have played an important part in the history of the race). The priests, not being occupied with warfare, or agriculture, and by reason of their support being contributed by the people, found plenty of time to "think," a somewhat rare privilege in the early days (and even in these times, for that matter). And, so, there gradually arose, among all peoples, a priestly caste that possessed the bulk of intelligence of the race. These priests soon began to recognize the importance of Mind Power, and they studied its underlying principles and laws of operation. This of course gave them an additional hold on the people, and a power over them. There seems to be no doubt but that even in the early days of the race, the priestly caste held a very wide knowledge of the laws and practice of dynamic mentation.

In the heart of Africa today, we find the Voodoo men, or conjurers, or medicine men, well versed in the application of Mind Power. It was also known among the early American Indians, although their degenerated descendants seem to have lost the knowledge, except in a few instances. The power of the priesthood among primitive races, is based almost entirely upon some form of dynamic mentation. And, as we see the race ascending in the scale, so do we see the priests displaying a broader and fuller knowledge of the subject in question. The history of the oriental races show that a full knowledge of the operation of Mind Power has been possessed by them for thousands of years. In the pictured stories of the Egyptians, the traces of which appear in their ruined temples and other buildings, we see that they understood the art perfectly. In ancient Persia and Chaldea, the art arose to great heights. In fact, among all of the advanced ancient races of men, we find an important place given to the subject before us.

Among the Ancient Mysteries, and the various ceremonies of the temples, of the early races, we see many instances of the use of this power. Back of the rites and ceremonies were always the underlying principle and application. In the early use of the force, its employment was largely along the lines of healing. But still we read in the pages of early history of many instances of mental fascination, pure and simple. That which was afterward called Mesmerism, hypnotism, etc., was well known to the ancients, and, in fact, some of the recorded results coming down to us from the past, have never been equalled by modern experimenters. Some of the feats of the modern Hindu magicians, or fakirs, have never been equalled by Western hypnotists.

Ancient history is full of instances of the operation of dynamic mentation among the people of the early days. It is related that Julius Caesar, while quite a young man, fell in with pirates near the Isle of Rhodes, who captured his ship, and took him prisoner. They held him for several weeks, while awaiting the ransom money being raised by his relatives. Plutarch writes that while the young Caesar was the captive of the pirates, he asserted his mastery over them to such an extent that he seemed a ruler rather than a prisoner. When he wished to rest or sleep, he forbade them to make any noise, and they obeyed him without question. He abused them and ordered them around like servants, and they did not seem able to disobey him. He did not hesitate to threaten them with death when he regained his liberty, and they did not resent it—and he afterward made good his threats.

It is related of Alcibiades, the Athenian, that he once made a bet with some of the young Athenian nobles, that he would publicly box the ears of Hipponikos, a venerable and greatly respected citizen. Not only did he bet that he would do this thing, but be also claimed that he would afterward compel the old man to give him his favorite daughter in marriage. The day following, when Hipponikos came out, Alcibiades walked up to him and gave him a resounding box on the ears. The old man seemed dazed and bewildered and retired to his home. A great public outcry arose, and the young man seemed likely to fall a victim to the indignation of the citizens. But the next day Alcibiades went to the home of Hipponikos and, after making a pretence of baring his back for punishment, he managed to induce in the old man a feeling of good humor and mirth, and obtained his pardon and goodwill, the latter increasing daily thereafter until finally he grew so devoted to the young man that he offered him the hand of his daughter in marriage, which was accepted. Anyone who is acquainted with the recorded character of the Athenians will realize what a wonderful occurrence this was. It was a striking exhibition of dynamic mentation, without a question.

All the great generals of history have possessed this quality. Caesar, Alexander the Great, Napoleon, Frederick the Great, and the modern mystic warrior, Gen. Gordon, all managed their men in a mysterious and wonderful manner, so that their troops worshiped them as almost gods, and went to their death willingly and joyfully. The single instance of Napoleon, when he returned from Elba, and confronted the Bourbon army drawn up to capture him, should satisfy anyone of the possession of the greatest dynamic power by this wonderful man. You remember that the troops were drawn up confronting Napoleon, their muskets leveled at his breast in obedience to the command "Aim!" Napoleon, who was on foot, marched deliberately toward the troops, with measured tread, gazing directly into their eyes. Then the officers shouted, "Fire!" A single shot would have killed Napoleon, and would have brought to the man who fired it a fortune from the Bourbon King. *But not a man obeyed the order*, so completely were they under the spell of Napoleon's fascination. Instead of firing, they threw down their guns and ran joyfully toward the Corsican, shouting. "*Vive l'Empereur!*" Their officers fled, and Napoleon, placing himself at the head of the troops, marched on to Paris. Other troops flocked to his standard at each point where he confronted them, although they had been sent out to capture or kill him. By the time the gates of Paris were reached, he was at the head of an immense army. The fascination manifested by this man was one of the most marked instances of its possession of which we have any record. And it seems to endure to this day—almost a century after his death. The very mention of his name makes one's blood tingle.

All great leaders of men, statesmen, orators and politicians have the power of dynamic mentation developed to a considerable degree. If you have ever come in contact with a man of this sort, you will always remember the impression he made upon you. Every man who knew James G. Blaine will remember his "personal magnetism," of which so much was said during his lifetime. Anyone who heard the famous speech of Wm. J. Bryan, at the Chicago Convention, in which he made use of the famous expression: "*Thou shalt not press upon the brow of Labor the crown of thorns; thou shalt not crucify Mankind upon a Cross of Gold*," needs no further proof of the reality of dynamic mentation.

Bryan was almost unknown to the majority of the delegates, and no thought of nominating him was entertained by them. But his "magnetism" was so great that it swept the convention like a mighty tidal wave, carrying all before it, and Bryan was carried around the hall on the shoulders of the delegates, who afterward made him their nominee for President. And although defeated twice, this man still possesses a wonderful fascination over hundreds of thousands of people in this country, who would rally around his standard at any time that he would sound the call. Henry Ward Beecher, at the great meeting in England, manifested the same power. The whole meeting was against him, and drowned his words by hoots, yells, and other noises. But Beecher looked them straight in the eye, and gradually *cowed* them into subjection, and then talked to them for two hours, and fairly carried the meeting by storm. He was but one man facing thousands of other men hostile to him, and determined to prevent him from speaking. But the single man won—by his dynamic will. It was not alone the words, in these cases—it was the Mind Power behind the words.

Fothergill relates the following remarkable incidents in the life of Hugo, Bishop of Lincoln, which is another illustration of one phase of dynamic mentation:

> "Perhaps no exhibition of heroism was ever more remarkable than when Hugo, Bishop of Lincoln, bearded Richard Crœur de Lion, in the church of Roche d' Andeli. In pursuit of war in Normandy, Richard demanded more supplies from his barons, and the bishop refused to supply any men; the see of Lincoln was bound to military service, he admitted, but only within the four seas of Britain. Richard was not a man to be lightly crossed, and Hugo was summoned to Normandy. So enraged was the king with the spiritual peer that when he presented himself in Normandy to answer the charge against him, two friendly barons met him to urge upon him the necessity for sending a conciliatory message to the king before entering his presence. The bishop declined the advice. The king was sitting at mass when the prelate walked up to him and, despite the monarch's frown, said, "Kiss me, my lord king." The king turned away his face. Hugo shook him and repeated his request. "Thou hast

not deserved it," growled the king fiercely. "I have," returned the prelate, and shook him all the harder. The king yielded, the kiss was given; and the bishop passed calmly on to take part in the service. Mere indifference to death could never have produced such a result. There was something more. As well as utterly fearless, Bishop Hugo possessed a will power of most unusual character, of which several instances are on record. Not only did he face the king and justify his refusal to supply men in the council chamber afterwards; but he went farther, and rebuked him for infidelity to his queen. The Lion was tamed for the moment. The king acknowledged nothing, but restrained his passion, observing afterwards, 'If all bishops were like my lord of Lincoln, not a prince among us could lift his head among them.' Such is the story as told by Froude. Yet Richard was the last man to permit a liberty to be taken with him, as his whole history showed.

"Hugo was such a remarkable illustration of what high will power can do, that another story may be related of him. King Henry Plantagenet had made Hugo Bishop of Lincoln; yet shortly afterwards, on preferring a request for a prebendal stall for a courtier, his request was refused. Hugo had already braved his wrath once, and the king, despite the episode of Thomas a Becket, was savagely angry. Henry was with his suite in Woodstock Park, and sat down on the ground pretending to be mending his glove when the bishop approached him. The king took no notice of his spiritual peer. After a brief pause Hugo, pushing aside an earl, sat down by the king's side. Watching the royal proceedings he remarked—'Your Highness reminds me of your cousins at

> Falaise.' Falaise was famous for its leather work, and it was at Falaise that Duke Robert met Arlotta the tanner's daughter, the mother of William the Conqueror. This reference to his ancestry was too much for the king, who was utterly worsted in the discussion which followed."

Can anyone doubt the existence of the subtle force of Mind Power in the instances just related? There was Mind Power behind the words, actions and courage of Hugo—without it he would have failed.

CHAPTER 11

DYNAMIC INDIVIDUALITY

For the purpose of illustrating the personal qualities of the dynamically positive man, along the lines of Personal Influence, I shall proceed to describe these qualities as existing in a person whom I will call the Dynamic Individual. Let us consider this man as an actually existent individual, in our treatment of him. You must endeavor to imagine him in this way, that you may understand his qualities. He is a very positive man, magnetically—one of the examples of a strong, forceful man of affairs, who is constantly meeting people, and having relations with them. How does such a man act, talk, look, move and conduct himself. Let us see!

In the first place, let us consider his appearance. He may be tall or short; dark or fair; stout or slender—these things do not count. But, notice this, that no matter which of the characteristics just mentioned he may possess or lack, he has a certain "air about him" that all may recognize, once they have seen it in any one. Let us notice this "air" carefully, for it may give us a clue.

The principal feature aboutthis "air" of the Dynamic Individual is its suggestion of self confidence and fearlessness. Our man seems to have a certainty of an inward power and force about him. Not the blustering, self important air manifested by the pinchbeck imitators of our man, but a calm, contained, poised consciousness of strength and self confidence. Our man seems to feel that there is "something in him" that gives him a strength and firmness unknown to the majority of people. Every such man has this inner consciousness, and I shall tell you what it is.

As I said in the first chapter, there exists in Nature a Universal Dynamic Mental Principle. In this principle each individual is a Center of Power. This Dynamic Principle in its outward manifestations of one pole of its energy, at least, resembles a universal will. That is, while its inner nature cannot be known, yet in the outer aspect of one of its poles of energy it resembles a universal will in operation everywhere. And, so, we are justified in thinking of it as Universal Will Power.

The more positive a man becomes, in dynamic mentation, the closer does he become in contact with this Universal Will. And the closer he is to this Universal Will, the more positive does he become. It is a case of action and re action. "To him that hath shall be given" applies in this case. The quality of dynamic positivity draws one to the Universal Will, and the nearness to this will renders one more and more positive.

But there is this to be noted in connection with this truth. When a man feels the sense of power that comes from a mental relation with the Universal Will, and allows the energy to flow through him, and to manifest in his acts, he has a reservoir of will power back of him which is inexhaustible and never failing. But if, in his conceit arising from some successful action, he begins to think that the power is due to some "personal strength," then he becomes "conceited" and "the pride of personality" grows upon him. This is where he makes his mistake. By this personal view of the matter he fences himself off from the Universal Will and limits his force to that portion which is locked up within his own mind, induced there by the will of the universe. Such a one separates himself from the source of power and puts up a barrier between himself and the universal supply. This is in accordance with the inner teachings of the great schools of occultism, and which teachings agree perfectly with the latest theories of modern Science. There is a great ocean of Universal Will, in which we are but centers of activity, and if we will but open ourselves to the power and will contained therein, we will have an unfailing store of power upon which to draw.

Let us pause for a moment and see what forces are combined in this active mentative center. In the first place we see that the dual aspect of the Mind Power manifests itself always. That which we have called the Desire Force, and that which we have called the Will Power, appear as the two mentative poles. You know this well, for you have studied the previous chapters wherein this point is brought out and illustrated. But here is an aspect of the matter that I did not bring out in those chapters. I allude to the resemblance of the two phases of Mind Power, *i. e.*, Desire Force and Will Power, to the physical phenomena of magnetism and electricity respectively.

Desire Force, like magnetism, manifests in a drawing, pulling, attracting power; while Will Power, like electricity, manifests in a pushing, compelling, driving power. Desire Force, like magnetism, tends to draw things inward and to itself; while Will Power, like electricity, tends to drive things outward and away from itself. This dual manifestation of energy is seen all through Nature in all of its manifold forms and conditions. There is ever the drawing in to a center—and there is ever the pushing outward from the center. And this law manifests upon the mental plane as well as upon the physical plane.

We have heard much of people being "magnetic," that is, having the power to attract persons to them—but that is merely one phase of the operation of dynamic mentation. We do not hear so much about people being "electric," and yet the term is just as proper and applicable as the term "magnetic." "Electric" people are the people in whom Will Power is strongly developed and manifest. These people "get after" others and make them do things. They are the active, energetic, forceful men and women who get behind things and push them along. All great leaders possess this phase of energy to a marked degree. The mere mention of the matter to you will cause you to think of instances of people who possess mentative "electricity." There are men who are able to make the crowd around them do their bidding—they are able to work their will upon the mass of people. These men are seen to possess a strange power, but very few understand it. It is entirely different from the fascinating, alluring, charming, attractive personality of the "magnetic" man, for it forces, and compels by sheer force of character and will, instead of drawing and attracting. You will see why I have spoken of these two phases as masculine and feminine respectively when you consider their different manner of manifestation.

But, while both of these forms of power, the "magnetic" and the "electric," have their strong points and advantages, I hold that the highly developed Individual must have both of these phases developed highly. In short, instead of being merely very "magnetic," on the one hand, or very "electric," on the other hand, the ideal man must be "electro magnetic." In other words, he must have both sides of his mentative energy highly developed and in full operation. In this way he is able to manifest a combined influence which will make him a very giant of dynamic mentation—a Dynamic Individual.

I would advise all who wish to become dynamic individuals to cultivate the mental image of the Universal Will—think of it as a great ocean of Will Power, in which you live, and move, and have your being. Feel yourself in touch with it. Think about your relation to it, constantly, and you will find that your mind will gradually open out to admit of the inflow of its power. And when you learn to know the real source of power, then you will no longer deceive yourself and attempt to shut off the flow of the Universal Will by erecting petty personal barriers of conceit.

This inner consciousness of the dynamic individual, especially if he understands its true nature, will react on a man's personal manner and appearance and cause to manifest in him that calm, serene, positive "air" of power, will and strength, that the great leaders of men always possess. And that "air" is in itself a mighty suggestion to others, for the world has learned to associate it with power and ability. Just as the feeling manifests itself in action, so will the outward action tend to induce the inward feeling, as I have told you. If you will endeavor to imitate and reproduce the outward carriage, manner, "air" and demeanor of this dynamic individual, you will have taken a step toward inducing a corresponding Mental State in yourself. But do not remain satisfied with this—go right to the fountainhead and receive your power direct from the Universal Will.

But there is something else about the dynamic individual which is different from Will Power. The will is a cold, keen, powerful force, devoid of color—it is like a great natural force devoid of feeling or emotion, although acting in response thereto. What other great force is manifesting strongly in our dynamic individual? Desire Force? Yes, that is the other great force within him—Desire Force.

No matter how strong a will a man may have, even though he gets in the closest touch with the Universal Will, he will accomplish nothing unless he be possessed of a developed desire. One must "want" to do things, before he wills to do them. Let us see what this Desire Force is.

The Universal Mind Power seems to be a strong something, containing within it all the force and energy there is in existence. It does not seem to have the attributes of personality about it, except when it becomes manifested in personal minds, or centers of power. When a personal center, or personal mind, is established in the Universal, then there seems to spring into manifestation a creative desire, which constantly urges toward outward expression.

This Desire Force is seen all through Nature, in all of her forms, and is inherent in all that we call Life Energy—that is, the energy which prompts the building up of form and shape. This Desire Force causes the seed to sprout and the plant to grow—the cell to multiply, and the higher forms to evolve from the lower. It is the essence of the great Creative Life Energy ever manifest in Nature. It is essentially a feminine principle, and is constantly desiring to "give birth," "bring forth," "create." It stirs the will into action, and never is satisfied unless it is performing creative work, mental or physical.

Now, there are persons who seem to possess but very little of this Desire Force, except on the physical plane. Their mental plane manifests very little of this force, and consequently they accomplish little or nothing of the world's work, and merely carry out the desires of others. But there are others who have this force manifested most strongly within them. They are possessed of a craving, longing, desiring force that impels them to "do things." That is, it fills them with ardent desires, along mentative lines of creation, which are ever crying out for satisfaction. The strong men and women of the world have this Desire Force highly developed, and its effort toward expression is what causes these people to accomplish things. Now do not mistake me. This desire is not always in the direction of "owning things," but rather in the direction of "doing things." It is true that when one's desires are along the line of accumulation, the force will be bent in that direction; but it may be less along these lines, and in that case the accumulation will be a mere incident of the "doing."

Our dynamic individual has a great deal of Desire Force within him. He "wants" to do certain things, and he wants to do them very much. He wishes to accomplish certain ends, and the desire becomes an ardent, glowing force that stirs up the desires in those around him, and at the same time incites his own will into action. His Desire Force combines with his will, and wonderful things are accomplished.

When you come into contact with a man of intense desire, you can fairly feel the force emanating from him. Our dynamic individual has learned to concentrate his Desire Force. When he wants some particular thing, he forgets about the minor things, and focuses his desire upon the particular thing craved by him, and thus draws it toward him with intense energy. The will drives, forces, impels and compels, with a "push"—the Desire Force draws, induces, pulls toward one, with an irresistible "pull." When our dynamic individual meets you, and wants you to do something, you can feel the pull of his Desire Force, drawing, coaxing, inducing, alluring, and attracting you toward him and his objects.

One who wishes to "do things" should keep the flame of his desire burning bright. He should continually pour upon it the oil of suggestion, and place before it the lantern slides of the mental images of the thing desired. If you will study the man of strong desire, you will see that he draws everything toward him that he wants. He has a "pull" upon things and leaves nothing undone in the direction of his want. He is hungry and thirsty with desire, and he seeks satisfaction wherever it may be found, his wits being sharpened by the intensity of the desire. And he draws people to him by the very strength of his Desire Force. You will find that people will instinctively fall in with the suggestions and urgings of the strong desire man. People, as a rule, are "drawn" rather than "pushed" or forced into a thing. The seductive, drawing, charming, fascinating force of men is that of Desire Force, not of Will Power. Yes, again I say to you that he who would succeed must, of necessity, keep his fire of desire burning bright and fierce, else it will not awaken into action his own will, nor stir the desire in others.

We talk much about Will Power, and its possession, but the majority of men fail because they do not desire things hard enough. They must want things "the worst way," and then they will bend everything toward getting them. This is true in the case of both good and evil desires—the law is the same in both cases, and operates along the same line. We are acquainted with the disastrous consequences attendant upon the possession of evil desires, and have seen many instances of the harm wrought upon others by reason thereof. But did you ever stop to think that the same degree and intensity of desire, turned in the right direction, would accomplish wonders of good works? If you will put into your plans of proper attainment and aspiration the same degree of energy that the evil man puts into his schemes of selfish gratification, you will be able to move mountains of difficulties.

This Desire Force in the dynamic individual is that which causes us to feel that "he wants this thing, and is going to have it." You know the feeling, if you have come into contact with strong men. And they draw their own to them by the exercise of this elementary force of Nature. They learn that by mentally drawing to themselves a supply of the Universal Energy they are enabled to transform it into Desire Force, as well as Will Power—the emotive pole is charged, as well as the motive pole. Both draw from the same source, and both have a constant source of supply. And both may manifest a wonderful degree of this transformed energy, in the shape of Will Power and Desire Force. In our dynamic individual, both poles are fully charged, and in active operation.

Now I have said enough about the theory of the dynamic individual. I shall ask you to read over what I have said above several times—in fact reread it until you thoroughly understand it. And then I shall take you on to the practical work and exercises calculated to develop in you the qualities of that individual. Taking it for granted that you have carefully considered what I have just said, I shall ask you to perform the following exercises, etc.:

Exercise I. In order to realize the reality of the statement that you are a centre of Mind Power, you must first enter into a realization of the existence of a Great Ocean of Mind Power itself. Do not pass over this lightly, for it is most important. You must begin to create a mental picture of the Universe as a Great Ocean of Living Mind Power, vibrating with life and force and power. Endeavor to make this mental picture so clear that you can "see it with your mind's eye," and until it becomes a reality to you. Picture yourself *as alone in the Universe* and surrounded on all sides with a vibrating, pulsating sea of energy, or power. See that power is locked up in that ocean, and that the ocean exists everywhere. Shut out from your mental field all other persons, things or conditions. *Imagine yourself as alone in the great Ocean of Power.* You must practice frequently upon this mental picture until you are able to visualize it distinctly. This does not mean that you have to actually *see* it, just as you do this printed page; but that you should be able to actually *feel* it. You will begin to understand just what I mean after you have practiced this a little. This Great Ocean of Mind Power must become real to you—and you must practice until it does so become.

The importance of the above exercise may be understood when I tell you that it will be impossible for you to manifest more than a moderate degree of power until you are able to realize yourself as a real centre. And it will be impossible for you to realize yourself as such a centre until you realize the existence of the Ocean of Power itself. For how can you think of yourself as a centre of power, in an Ocean of Power, until you realize the existence of the Ocean itself? The Universal Ocean of Mind Power contains within itself *all* the Mind Power, force and energy that there is. It is the source from which all forms of energy arise. It is filled with an infinite number of tiny centres of energy, of which you are one. And in the degree that you draw upon it for strength, so will you receive strength. By all means endeavor to clearly visualize this Great Mind Power Ocean, for it is the source of all the force with which you are filled and which you hope to acquire. Enter into this great realization, friends, for it is *the first step to power.*

Exercise II. The second exercise, which will tend to increase your vibration as a centre of Power, is as follows: Picture yourself clearly as a Centre of Power in the Mentative Ocean. While seeing the Ocean on all sides of you, you must see Yourself as *the Centre of it*. Do not be frightened at this idea, for it is based on the Truth. The highest occult teaching informs us that the Great Mentative Ocean *has its centre everywhere and its circumference nowhere*. That is, that being infinite in space, there is no finite spot that is *really* its centre and yet, on the other hand, every point of activity may be called its centre. Being extended in every direction infinitely, its circumference is nonexistent. Therefore you are most certainly justified in considering yourself as a centre of the Ocean of Mind Power. Each dynamic individual is such a centre, and each has his world circling and revolving around him. Some have a small world, and some have mighty ones. There are centres so mighty and exalted that the human mind cannot grasp their importance. But even the tiniest point of activity is a centre in itself. So hesitate not, but begin to form a mental picture of yourself as a centre of power.

Practice this exercise until you can clearly *feel* yourself as a centre of power. You must learn to think of yourself as a focal point of force in the great Ocean of Mind Power. Just as the great body of electricity manifests itself in tiny points of activity, so does Mind Power express itself in you who are a point of activity within itself. In urging you to perfect yourself in this realization I would impress upon you the fact, known to all advanced occultists, that in the measure of your realization of this mighty quality of the Ego will be the measure of the power possessed by you. All of the strong men of our times, and of all ages, have had this realization, intuitively or instinctively; that is, although they may not have known the philosophy or science of the matter, they have *felt* this sense of the power of the Ego in themselves, which gave them the confidence to do things and the Will Power and Desire Force to carry out their undertakings. It is this feeling of inherent strength that makes men strong and successful and positive. And this feeling and realization may be developed and unfolded within anyone, providing he *wants it "sufficiently."* By the exercise of your desire and will you may build up this realization of power, and in the building up there will come to you a constantly increasing stream of desire and will. In the measure of your expression will be the measure of your impression from the source of all positive impression.

Exercise III. The third exercise consists in the realization of the nature of the Power. This force, energy or power with which you are being filled, and which you are now attracting toward your centre, consists of the electrical manifestation of Will Power and the magnetic manifestation of Desire Force. These two constitute the dual phases of the one force—Mind Power. And, therefore, you must begin to realize that these qualities are within you in order that you may be able to express them, and thus gain the additional and increased power that comes to those who do express them. You must begin to realize that you have a will which is capable of impressing itself on the things, persons and circumstances of your world—and you must begin to realize that you have a desire which attracts to you the things, people and circumstances of your world, and which, in fact, draws to you the very material from which your world is made. When you realize this dual force within you, it will begin to express itself automatically. The act of realization causes the mental machinery to begin to work smoothly and effectively. Therefore picture to yourself this dual force within you. See yourself as influencing, and acting upon the world around you. See yourself as a power in the land. And also see yourself as an attracting force, drawing to you that which you need and want and require, consciously and unconsciously. Picture yourself as a *Dynamic Individual.* You are an individual because you are a centre of power. You are dynamic because you possess the Electric Will and the Magnetic Desire—the twin poles of Mind Power.

Carry with you this thought constantly and repeat it often to yourself and you will find it a source of Power—you will find the Power pouring into you when you say or think it. When you feel weak, or when you feel the need of additional Power, use this Statement of Power:

"I AM DYNAMIC!"

And when you say it, or think it, you must picture to yourself just what you mean by the statement, hence the importance of knowing *just what is meant.* Do not pass over this Statement of Power as unimportant, but try it in actual practice and you will realize what a Battery of Power you have become. Those around you will soon become aware of a new sense of power within you.

Keep this Statement of Power to yourself. Do not invite the ridicule of those around you by telling them the source of your Power. Do not bother about them—if they are individuals themselves they will understand without being told; and if they are not all the telling in the world would not make it clear to them. Hoe your own row and mind your own business—and let them do the same. No one can build up his individuality except from within. And each must work out his own salvation and climb the ladder of attainment for himself. And the sooner that people learn this the better will it be for all. Don't be a leaner, or a leaning post. Don't lean on anyone else—and don't let anyone lean on you.

There has been too much of this foolish business about living other people's lives for them, or letting other people live your life for you. Each man or woman must grow into an individual by his or her own work and life. There is no such thing as vicarious individuality. Don't be afraid to "assert the I"—to claim your rightful heritage and birthright to be an individual, and not a parasite. And don't be afraid to shake off and trim off the parasitic persons that have encumbered your own unfoldment toward individuality. Let the parasites take root in the earth, just as you have done; let them fasten their roots in the great body of strength and power instead of in the mental body of someone else; let them stop their second hand nourishment and learn to draw from the first source. This is the only way, and the lack of the knowledge of it is filling the world with weaklings instead of with individuals. Therefore think of these things; hold them well in mind when you make your Statement of Power:

"I AM DYNAMIC!"

In considering the qualities that go to make up the person in whom Dynamic Mentation is likely to be strongly developed, I may mention the following:

1. *Physical Well Being*; for there is a certain strength about a man or woman in strong, robust health, that must be taken into consideration. It is true that some persons not physically well, but unhealthy, have exercised strong powers, but this was *in spite of* their lack of physical health, and owing to a strong will which allowed them to master even this obstacle. But, all else being equal, there is a power about a strong, healthy, vigorous person that makes itself felt.
2. *Belief in One's Self*; for without this no one manifests positivity. Believe in your own power and ability, and you impress others with the same belief. Confidence is contagious. Cultivate the "I Can and I Will."
3. *Poise*; for the calm, well poised, imperturbable man has an enormous advantage over one lacking these qualities. The man who meets any emergency without "losing his head" has something about him that makes him looked up to as a natural leader—he has one of the qualities of positivity. Cultivate the calm masterful mood.
4. *Fearlessness*; for fear is the most negative emotion in the being of man. Fearlessness is a most positive quality, just as fear is the most negative. Cultivate the "I Dare—I Do!"
5. *Concentration*; for this "one pointedness" focuses the Will Power upon the object. Do one thing at a time, and do it with all the power that there is in you.
6. *Fixity of Purpose*; for you must learn to know what you want to do, and then "stick to it" until it is done. Cultivate the Bull dog quality—it is needed.

To those who recognize the need of the above mentioned qualities, but who lack them, I would recommend the careful study and determined application of the principles stated in the chapters of this book, entitled, "*Mental Architecture*," "*Making over oneself*" and "*Mind Building*", respectively.

CHAPTER 12

MENTAL ATMOSPHERE

Our dynamic individual places himself in a receptive attitude only toward the great Universal Will, and in a positive attitude toward all else. In this way he really becomes a most active center of Power, which becomes manifest to all with whom he comes in contact. He may not realize just what he is doing, and may know nothing of the truth herein stated, but, still he feels that he is "in touch with something" that aids and assists him and which gives him strength and dynamic force. He may talk about his "luck," or his "lucky star," or he may secretly believe himself specially favored by Providence (this is a secret belief of the majority of successful men)—but the fact remains that every positive and successful man feels, underneath it all, that he has something back of him. And this belief takes form in action and causes him to manifest that "air" of calm, positive power and self confidence noticeable in such men in every instance.

You will readily see, from what has been said, that the "Personal Atmospheres" of persons depend upon the character of their mental states, and are the result of the mental currents emanating from them. Every person has his or her own mentative aura, or body of radiant mentative energy, which flows from them in all directions. These mentative atmospheres affect the people with whom one comes in contact. You know people who seem to carry with them an atmosphere of "feeling" which affects a roomful of people, or even a building. This atmosphere may be positive or negative in its effect—that is, stimulating or depressing. All of these things arise in the way which I have mentioned. It is related of Rachel, the great French actress, that although she was not beautiful in form or face, still she had that indescribable charm of personality about her that caused everyone to consider her a beautiful woman, so great was her fascinating charm.

That which so many call "Personal Magnetism," as distinguished from Personal Force, consists of this mentative atmosphere, or radiant mentative energy, which induces in all within its field a feeling of similar emotion or vibration. The charm of the "fascinating person" is accounted for in the same way. It is all a matter of the mentative currents inducing feeling in others. The power called "Fascination," which has been known in all times and countries, arises from the same cause. It operates by the strong mentative currents pouring from one's mind, and inducing mental states in others.

The mentative force emanating from each individual creates a mental atmosphere around him which often extends a considerable distance from his body, especially in the case of strong individuals, whose mental atmosphere is felt when they enter a room or public place. Persons whose personality is weaker have a mental atmosphere extending only a few inches from their bodies, and which is scarcely perceptible to those coming in contact with them.

The man who feels himself to be a dynamic individual carries with him an aura of mental atmosphere of positive strength, which is plainly felt by those coming in contact with him. People say about such a man that he "has something about him" which impresses them, but which they fail to understand. It will be worth your while to study this mental atmosphere of some strong man with whom you come in contact, for now that you have the secret of the matter you may take some valuable lessons from him.

I cannot very well describe this "air" to you, for unless you have met a man of this kind you will not understand it. But it is a very different thing from the pompous, self sufficient, self important, fussy air and demeanor manifested by the cheap imitators of these great men. The dynamic individual does not tell you how great, or smart, or important he is—he leaves that for his cheap imitators; he makes you feel his strength by his very manner and atmosphere, without saying a word. He has that "something about him" that people notice and wonder at. And that "something" comes from his conscious or unconscious relation to the Universal Will.

The "little fellow" who thinks he is one of the "big ones" believes that his strength comes from his personality, and sooner or later he stumbles because of this error. But the real "big ones" of life know better; they may not understand it all, but some way they feel that there is a "something" back of them from which they are able to draw strength and power, and believing this, they are filled with courage and daring and radiate their power on all sides. They may talk of their "lucky star" or "special providence," or else believe themselves to be "specially favored of God" (as is the case with at least one of the "big men" of modern finance), but no matter what may be their special interpretations of this "something," they all recognize its existence and trust to it. And this conviction and realization gives to the strong individuals that, air of calm, positive power and self confidence that impresses those with whom they come in contact and which forms their mental atmosphere.

And in giving you instructions in the art of building for yourselves a positive mental atmosphere I can do no better than to refer you back to first principles and again bid you to realize that you are a dynamic focus—a centre of power—in the great Universal Will, having the dual attribute of Will Power and Desire Force. In short, that you are a living dynamo.

If you will but get this realization firmly fixed in your mind you will automatically create for yourself a most positive mental atmosphere that will be felt by all with whom you come in contact. So first, last and all the time build up this realization. Say to yourself, "I am Dynamic!"—then think it out; dream it out; act it out. And, of course, always realize what all this means. You are the channel through which is pouring the Universal Will Power and in the degree that you *allow the current to so flow through you*, so will be the power you are able to manifest.

When you wish to manifest a special degree of power just let this statement: "I am Dynamic!" flame out in vivid letters in your mind. When you feel that you are being approached by some other person of strong will, whom you do not wish to influence you, just bring this statement into effect, and you will actually see the effect of it upon the other person. He will feel your strong mental atmosphere and will cease trying to affect you. And even when there is no special need for making the statement of power it will be well for you to keep it burning bright within you, for by so doing you strengthen your realization, and your mental atmosphere reflects the inner

So much for the general mental atmosphere. As we proceed we shall see that the dynamic individual creates special mental atmosphere around him by his mental states, depending upon his will or desire at the time. Not only does his will and desire affect other persons directly by means of mental currents, but mentative induction is also set up by the mental atmosphere, without any special effort on his part.

In this place I wish to call your attention to the importance of always maintaining your positivity as a means of mental training. Do not allow yourself to become negative to others, even where there is nothing lost by so doing, for by this neglect you create a negative habit which will cause you trouble to overcome later. If a person comes into your presence and his personality seems likely to dominate or overpower yours, by all means interpose a mental resistance right then and there. It is not necessary for you to manifest the same in words, for that would make you ridiculous in many cases; nor is it necessary for you to give any special physical expression to your mental state. Simply look the person in the eye, carelessly and without any special effort, at the same time making the mental statement, "I am Dynamic!" and you will find that your positivity will rise until it is equal with his, and your feeling of negativity will disappear. In exceptional cases you may add mentally, "I am more dynamic than you!"

It will be well for you to practice the creation of special mental atmospheres in order to establish the habit and thus render it easier to avail yourself of the same on special occasions. Opportunities of all kinds will present themselves to you in everyday life. The gist of the matter is to surround yourself with a mental aura of such a nature that people will act toward you as you wish them to do. A few examples may help you to get a clearer idea of what I mean, so I herewith give you the same.

I know a lady, living in Chicago, who was constantly complaining that people were "always running over her" on State Street (the crowded retail street of the great Western metropolis). She said that they were always crowding her off the sidewalk and pushing, bumping and jostling her in a most annoying manner. She asked me for instructions as to what thought she should use to prevent individuals from so acting. I answered that I did not think it was necessary to consider the separate individuals in the case, but that she should "treat" *the crowd as a whole*, by means of a protective mental atmosphere. I then advised her to build up a mental atmosphere around this statement: "People respect my rights; they will not unduly impose on me in the street; I deny the power of the crowd to impose on me." And she followed this advice, and in a short time had built up a protective mental atmosphere which acted almost magically upon the crowd, who stepped aside and gave her a full right of way on the pavement. She would simply go on her way calmly, serenely and undisturbed, and *the crowd let her alone*. I must add that I think that the original trouble arose from a subconscious dislike of crowds and an extreme shrinking from people, the result being that this dislike acted almost as does fear, and really attracted to her the interference of people. The new mental atmosphere dispelled the old one and gave her an additional positivity besides.

In this connection I would call your attention to that remarkable psychological fact that *fear acts as an attracting force*, in a negative way. If you *want* a thing very much you attract it to you—and if you *fear* it very much you do likewise. This apparent contradiction has bothered many students of the subject, but it seems very plain to me. I think the explanation is that in both cases a vivid mental picture is held, and the attraction results along the line of visualization, which always tends to materialize the mental image.

Another case, from actual experience. Another lady, also a resident of Chicago, complained that the clerks in the great department stores would not treat her courteously, but would keep her waiting without paying her any attention, and in other wayswouldtreatherlikea"humandoor mat." Shesaidshewould not have minded this so much if other women were treated likewise, but that while she was ignored others would receive the greatest attention, the clerks "falling over themselves" to wait upon them. I told her that she had gradually built up around her a mental atmosphere of expectancy—that she had fallen into the habit of *expecting such treatment*, and consequently she got what she expected. I think that in the beginning she had manifested a timid, "humble," meek, "worm of the dust" state of mind when she entered the big stores, which somewhat overawed her. And then, after this drew upon her the neglect of the clerks, who seem very ready to wipe their feet on human door mats, she grew to regularly expect the shabby treatment. It was not a matter of dress, or anything of that kind, for she dressed well—and, for that matter, I know women who dress poorly who never get any such treatment, for they understand the underlying mental laws too well for that. It was simply a matter of a negative mental atmosphere.

I told her to "brace up" and create a new mental atmosphere, around this general statement: "The clerks like me; they like to wait on me; they give me every attention; they do this *because they like me*, and also because I insist upon it as my right!" The charm worked in a short time, and now the good lady reports that the clerks not only treat her well but even take the trouble to call her attention to desirable selections, special bargains, and all the rest of it. The cure was perfect.

I call your attention to the above statement—please note that the first part of it operated along the lines of Desire Force, and the latter part along the lines of Will Power. The statement of the first mentioned lady (the one who objected to street crowding) was altogether along the lines of Will Power. I ask the students to study and analyze each of these cases, because by so doing they will be able to apply the principles in cases coming under their own observation, and also in their own cases.

I once directed a lady who complained that she was unpopular, and that "nobody loved her," etc., etc., to apply a similar method. She created a new mental atmosphere around her along the lines of the general statement: "People *like me*; they find me *attractive*; they *love me*, and *like to be in my company*." After a time she reported that from a state of "wall flower dom" she had become quite a favorite, and in fact was at a loss to adjust herself to the changed conditions, finding somewhat of an embarrassment of "likings" and "lovings." This was a case of Desire Force pure and simple.

Now do not imagine for a moment that in the above cases, and hundreds of others known to me personally, the desired result was obtained merely from repeating, parrot like, or like a phonograph, the words of the statement. This talk of the power of mere words, and all the rest of such talk, has wearied me greatly. I have seen and heard so much of this nonsense since I have become acquainted with certain people who consider themselves "in the New Thought" that I dislike to use the words "statement" or "affirmation." These people have imagined that by the mere repetition of *words* they could work miracles. Pshaw! What nonsense! They remind me of the Chinese, and certain other people who write long prayers on slips of paper and allow them to flutter in the breeze, hoping that the gods will accept their prayers at face value while the prayer makers are amusing themselves elsewhere. Sometimes they attach little bells to the prayers in order to attract the attention of the gods. Others paste the prayers on water wheels, turned by the streams, thereby claiming credit for a prayer at each turn of the wheel. Cheap praying that! Oh, don't laugh—some of you are just as foolish. You have been making your statements and affirmations in the same spirit, and now feel disappointed because "nothing happened." Of course nothing happened; how could it be otherwise?

I have said over and over again—and now say it over again another time—that *the words of themselves are nothing*; the real virtue lies *in the feeling behind the words*. If there is no feeling there is no result. In order to get the results you must erect the framework of words, and then build around it the structure of feeling, and expectation, and visualization. That's the way to do it. The words are merely the skeleton—the flesh and blood are the feelings and materialized visualizations.

The ladies mentioned above, whom I have used as "typical cases" to illustrate the principle—did not rest content with words, *for I wouldn't allow them to do so*. I kept after them, insisting upon their using the proper mental exercises and methods—that's what did the work. And now I shall give you the same instruction and directions that I gave them—adapt them to your own cases and you will be likewise successful.

The kernel of the process of creating the mental atmosphere lies in what is called "visualization." Visualization is simply the creation of a strong mental image of the thing desired, the perfecting it each day until it becomes almost as clear as an existing material thing. Then the visualization tends to materialize itself—that is, it begins to build around itself actual material conditions corresponding with the mental framework. The statement of words is the pattern around which the visualized mental images form themselves. And the mental image is the framework around which the actual material conditions form themselves. The lady above mentioned made her mental image of the street conduct of the crowd—and the people unconsciously felt it and built themselves around it. So in the case of the lady in the department store, and the others mentioned. The mental image manifested itself as a mental atmosphere, and gradually materialized.

The thing to do in visualizing is to bring the positive imagination to see and feel the thing as actually existent. Then by constant practice and meditation the mental atmosphere becomes formed, and the rest is all a matter of time. *See yourself as you wish to be. See others as you wish them to be. See conditions as you wish them to be.* Think them out—dream them out—act them out. And materialization will follow upon visualization, even as visualization followed upon the statement.

In this connection, however, I must call your attention to the fact that the degrees of receptivity of other people to your mental atmospheres and mental pictures depend entirely upon their degree of positivity. They respond only in the degree that they respond to other mentative influences. The strong avoid influences to which the weak yield, in this as in every other phase of the phenomena. But do not let that cause fear on your part. You may make yourself positive—you have had the instructions given you, and it is now your own work to do the rest.

I might write a whole book on this subject of visualization in the phase of forming mental atmospheres—but I have herein given you the underlying principles, and have also given you a few illustrative examples—you must do the rest yourselves. If you have carefully read this book, and have studied *between the lines* as well as the lines themselves, you will have grasped the little details of the matter which will not be apparent to those who have not done so. Each will find in this book that for which he or she is ready—and not a bit more. I think the careful students among you will readily understand just what I mean by this. If you do not understand, then I cannot help you out, and you must wait until you unfold in understanding. But I would say that a re reading of this work is advisable—several re readings, in fact. *Each time that you re read it you will find something new that you had previously overlooked*, and each reading will discover *many hidden meanings now suddenly made plain*.

The man who wishes to be successful in his dealings with his fellow men must surround himself with a positive mental atmosphere. He must create an atmosphere of self reliance and positivity that will overcome the negativity of those with whom he comes in contact. This positive mental atmosphere is that subtle influence that emanates from the strong men of affairs, and which affects, influences and controls people to a greater degree than the flow of words which many affect, believing it to be the key of success. When you come in contact with one having a mental atmosphere of this kind you are affected by it, consciously and unconsciously. And if it has this effect on you in the case of other persons, why should you not reach out and possess this power yourself? Why should you not be a positive instead of a negative?

The directions and exercises given in this chapter, coupled with the instruction given in other chapters of the book, should enable you to develop around yourself a most positive mental atmosphere, that will make you a power. But it all depends upon yourself—you must exercise your will and desire, just as you would do were they muscles that you wished to develop. The rule operates in the mental as well as in the physical world. In addition to the exercises given in preceding chapters, I would suggest that the following may prove useful to some of you, in special cases, in forming the positive mental atmosphere. I shall merely give you the verbal framework, and you must build around it the mental picture, which in turn produces the mental atmosphere. But, remember, even in practising these exercises never lose sight of the main Statement of Power, "I am Dynamic!" for that statement will impart life, vitality and energy to the other mental images and statements.

Here are the statements referred to—the verbal framework around which you are to build your mental picture that you wish to materialize on the objective plane. You will find them useful in many cases:

MENTAL FRAMEWORK.

I. I surround myself with an atmosphere of success.

II. I am positive. I have a strong will. I make a positive impression on those coming into my mental atmosphere.

III. I am fearless—absolutely fearless—nothing can harm me.

IV. I kill out all worry and discouragement—I radiate hope, cheerfulness and good nature. I am bright, cheerful and happy, and make all around me *feel* the same way.

V. I am well poised, calm and self controlled.

VI. I have a perfect mastery over my temper, emotions and passions, and all recognize this to be a fact.

VII. I am at ease here, and all bashfulness and timidity has departed. I am calm, at ease and feel at home.

VIII. People like me—I am surrounded with a mental atmosphere that causes people to like me.

IX. I am master of my surroundings—nothing disturbs me—nothing affects me adversely—I am master.

X. I am surrounded with a mental atmosphere of protection. No one's adverse thoughts, currents or suggestions can penetrate this protective armor. I am safe from mental attacks. I am safe, strong and positive.

In using any of the above statements be sure to follow my advice and instructions regarding the mental images, etc., which *put flesh on these verbal skeletons and make a living force out of the dry bones of words*. Remember the importance of mental imaging and visualization in this matter of creating mental atmospheres.

CHAPTER 13

CHANNELS OF INFLUENCE

In the last chapter I spoke of the effect of mental atmospheres with which people surround themselves. You will notice that in my discussion of that part of the subject I spoke only of the *general influence* exerted upon others, and not of the direct personal influence exerted by one man upon another in personal intercourse. Let us now consider the channels of direct personal influence.

As I have told you elsewhere, every time two people meet there ensues a silent mental conflict, or struggle for supremacy, from which one or the other emerges a victor, and which victory is fully recognized by both of the parties to the proceeding. This mental struggle is usually the combat between the general mental powers of the two, without regard to special mental states induced at the time. But the man who is skilled in the art of dynamic mentation goes further than this, for he recognizes that he may concentrate his mentative energy into definite shape and form, and focus the force of his mental imagery direct upon the other person, with such force and power that the second person will feel the dynamic strength exerted.

This direct personal influence operates along the lines of both Desire Force and Will Power of course. I have explained elsewhere how the Will Power may be used to awaken desire in another; and how it may also capture the will of the second person. I have also explained how Desire Force induces a similar desire in the second person; and also how it is often used to captivate the will of the other person. It is not necessary for me to repeat these things—you are supposed to be fully acquainted with them, from your study of this book. And so I shall proceed to a consideration of the channels of expression of personal influence, and the methods usually employed by those using it.

THE INSTRUMENTS OF EXPRESSION.

These channels of influence may be classified as follows:

1. Suggestive channels, consisting of (a) the suggestive manner, and (b) the suggestive tone, and (c) the suggestive word;
2. The instrument of the eye;
3. The instrument of the touch; and all of these three forms are, of course, merely the channels or instruments by which, and through which, the Mind Power expresses itself—the channel through which pours the mentative energy. Let us consider them in the above order.

In the chapters on "Mental Suggestion," you will find stated the active principles of that phase of the subject, with which you should thoroughly familiarize yourself. You will see there that suggestion is the outward symbol of the inward mental state, and that it is the inner state that gives vitality to the suggestion. Get this idea fixed firmly in your mind, and always think of the force behind the suggestion. I have explained to you, also, that when one receives a suggestion through a physical agent, there is induced in him the mental state corresponding to the one originating that physical suggestion. For example, if you feel yourself filled with confidence, energy and fearlessness, your outward appearance will *reflect* that inner state, and the outer appearance will become a suggestion to others. These others will instinctively feel that your inner state is as I have stated. And, this being so, a physical suggestion made stronger than usual will produce a deeper impression on others than would any ordinary suggestion.

In view of the above, you will see why it is that those familiar with the subject deem it important to cultivate the suggestive channel instruments. Beginning with (a) the suggestive manner, you will see why it is that we are impressed with the manner of a man who manifests energy, self confidence, and power in every motion. And also, why we have confidence in a man whose manner indicates that he is a person used to being trusted by others—accustomed to having confidence reposed in him. And so I might mention hundreds of examples tending to show that if a man's manner conveys the impression that he is used to being treated in a certain way, and that he is accustomed to acting in a certain way, we are very apt to accept the suggestion of manner, and fall into line with the rest of people. And if the man happens to be a good actor, we may be imposed upon and fooled by his suggestive manner.

Not only does this law hold good in the case of the manner and appearance of success, strength, confidence, etc., but it also operates along the lines of the appearance and manner of failure, weakness, and distrust. Do you not know of cases wherein you have felt that certain persons were not worthy of confidence; or were not to be depended upon where strength of character was required; or were not likely to succeed? Of course you have, and you acted upon the suggestion, too.

In illustrating this point, I have frequently used the illustration of the two dogs, the one carrying himself in a manner betokening self respect and an ability to prevent and resent undue liberties, and the other carrying his tail between his legs, in a manner and appearance indicating that he expected to be kicked and cuffed. The first dog is almost invariably treated with respect, even by the most mischievous youngsters; while the second one almost always invites to himself the kicks, tin cans and brick bats of the young hoodlums of the neighborhood. And this illustration is as true in the case of people as in the case of dogs. Better take the hint!

But, you may say, how is one to acquire the proper suggestive manner? My answer is that there is but one sure way, and that is to begin to think out the part; visualize it; and act it out. In other words, if you wish to convey a suggestive manner of confidence, you must begin to *think* "Confidence" from morning until night. And you must also begin to visualize "Confidence" when you have the chance to do so—that is, you must make a mental picture of yourself as manifesting Confidence. And you must also begin to *act out the part*.

Now about this "acting out," I would say that I mean not only the "playing the part" in your interviews with people, but I also mean an *actual series of rehearsals* in private, just as you would perform if you were preparing to play a part on the stage, in public. You must form a mental image of how you would look and act if you were filled with confidence, and were approaching people. You will find that practice will improve you very much in this way, and that you will soon acquire a manner that will be like second nature and will really serve to give the suggestion of your manner to others with whom you come in contact. And, more than this, it will actually tend to build up confidence in yourself. Imagine yourself as approaching strange people, and then act out the part the best you know how, improving a little in ease, and smoothness of action each day. Think of how the actor on the stage impresses you—and then remember that the manner was acquired by constant practice, and work. And you may do the same, and may manage to impress other people just as the actor does you. And what is true in the case of "Confidence" is true regarding any character that you wish to play. Any and all characters may be played out in this way, and an appearance and manner acquired which will give the suggestion to others. I wish I could make you realize how much there is in this method. If you could realize how some men have used it to acquire qualities that have enabled them to prey upon the public, you would realize how important it might be for you for legitimate and honorable use.

In this acting out, you must remember that the practice will make you so perfect that the part will appear natural when you play it in public. But without practice, an attempt to play it in public will make one ridiculous. Remember the illustration of the real actor, and you will have the secret of acting out. And also remember this, that in the measure that you "throw your mind" into the part, so will be your success. When you practice, you must throw your mind into the acting, just as you would if you were in earnest. It is the mind back of it all, remember.

The second suggestive channel or instrument is "the suggestive tone." This, too, may be acquired by acting out. You must practice until you are able to express your meaning with "feeling" that all who hear may be impressed. You should begin your practice by choosing some simple words in everyday use—"Good morning!" for instance. Try it now, and see how roughly, clumsily and crudely you give the morning greeting. Then try to imagine that you are full of good cheer, energy, and brightness, and then throw your feeling into your "good morning," and see how different it seems. Practice this awhile and you will soon acquire a natural, cheery, bright, and invigorating tone when you say "good morning." You will not need a teacher in elocution to tell you how to do this. Try to *feel* the part, and you will express it naturally. Make your feelings more flexible, and your tones will reflect them. After you have mastered the simpler terms of expression, work up to larger sentences, and speeches. Try them on the chairs in your room, in imagining that people are seated therein; speak to them feelingly and with expression until you acquire the art. You will not realize how much you may gain by such practice until you actually try it. I wish that you could hear the testimony of some people who have acquired this art.

There is nothing more important in personal influence than a good suggestive tone. Think of the people whom you know, and then remember what an influence their voices have on you. Not only the quality of the voice, but the tone. You readily recognize the difference between the tone of the hesitating, timid, self doubting person, and that of the confident, self reliant individual. There is a subtle vibration about the tone of the latter that causes one to feel confidence and respect, and which exacts obedience in a quiet, calm way, devoid of bluster or rant.

If you will but think a moment, you will see that much depends upon the tone. You will see that when you say to a person, "You *can*!" the tone in which you say "*can!*" goes a long way toward producing the response. And so it is with the suggestive tone, no matter what it is made to express. It always impresses upon one that the speaker using it *means what he says*. And that is why many public men practice year after year in mastering this instrument of influence—the suggestive tone. Again would I refer you to the example of the actor—see how he manages to throw *feeling* into his tone. And you may do likewise, if you will but practice in earnest, and *throw your mind into the work.* Think of the thing you wish to express—visualize it—and then act it out in your tone. You will be surprised at the rapid progress that you will make. Remember always, though, the tone is but the instrument of expression of the mind back of it.

Many people make the mistake of "speaking with the muscles instead of with their nerves," as one writer has expressed it. In other words, they seem to throw *muscular force* into their tones, instead of *nervous energy*, and in so doing they make a great mistake, for the former has a dull, non penetrating effect, whereas the latter vibrates subtly and reaches the feeling part of one's mind. *Feel, feel, feel,* when you wish to speak impressively, and your tones will reflect the same, and induce a corresponding feeling in others.

The voice is a mighty indicator of the mental state within. Excepting the eye, no outward form of expression of character responds so quickly and fully to the inner mental state as the voice. The voice and eye are the two principal outward avenues of expression of the mental states within, and both register the subtle changes and degrees of the inner state. If you will stop to think for a moment and consider the different voices of the people you know, you will see that in nearly every case the voice gives one a clue to the character or prevailing mental states of the speaker. Not alone the quality of the voice but the tone. Every reader knows the difference between the tones of the hesitating, timid, self doubting person, and that of the confident, self reliant individual. In the tone of the latter there is noticeable that peculiar something that denotes power and authority, and inspires attention, interest and respect, without need of vulgar self assertion or blustering speech. Let us listen to the tones of our dynamic individual.

First, it is under the control of his will. It is loud or soft, as he wills it to be—it never runs away from him. If the person to whom he is talking raises his voice to a strident pitch, our individual does not follow suit. On the contrary he puts a little more force into his tone, but keeps the pitch the same, and before long, by his will, in his evenly pitched tone, he will actually force down the pitch of the other to a normal degree. I have seen many instances of this fact, and have noticed that the temper of the other person is toned down in accord with his decreasing pitch of voice. A calm, even positive tone, in which the will is apparent in self control and in forceful effect, will master the tones of others pitched in a fiercer key; and in the mastery of the voice of the other you will often effect a mastery of his will. By making captive the outer expression you often capture the inner man.

There are two very good reasons for one studying the voice of the dynamic individual, as follows: (1) Because it is by his voice that he manages to make some of the most powerful suggestions upon others; and (2) because by the expression in his voice, or rather the inner impulse causing the vocal expression, he causes to flow out strong mentative currents which affect and influence the other person. So in its inner, and outer, aspects the cultivation of the voice is quite desirable.

You will find that the dynamic individual particularly if he is engaged in an occupation necessitating his giving orders, and directions, or advice, to others, has developed a voice resembling in many details the "suggestive voice" habitual to the practitioner of mental suggestive therapeutics. The reason is plain. Both the man of business affairs and force, and the suggestionist, have accustomed themselves to speaking in a forceful, firm, positive manner, and thus fairly "driving home" their ideas expressed in words. The man of affairs does not know just why he does this, but his tone is the outward expression of his forceful mental state. And this is likewise true of the suggestionist, although he may have deliberately cultivated the suggestive tone at the beginning of his practice.

It is somewhat difficult to correctly define and explain the suggestive tone, although if one once hears it he will never forget it. But I will try my best to make it plain to you here. In the first place, the suggestive tone is fairly charged with the mental idea back of the words. Each word has an inner meaning, and the suggestive tone carries this idea with it, so that the hearer gets the full mentative benefit and influence of it. Do not imagine that this tone is theatrical, or tragic, or unnatural. It is none of these.

It is a forceful, natural tone. Its expression is that of "being in earnest" and meaning just what you are saying. You know how you would speak if you were earnestly telling some one to do some important thing, upon which much depended. Well, that's the tone, modified of course by the particular circumstances and necessities of each case. It must be in earnest—must be more or less "intense"—must have focused in it the "feeling" behind it, in such a way as to awaken in the mind of the hearer the feeling back of the words.

The voice of the dynamic individual is flexible, and adaptable to any mood or phase of feeling that he wishes to induce in his hearers. It may be positive and masterful, along the lines of suggestion by direct command, or authority. Or it may be subtle and insinuating, along the lines of suggestion by association or imitation. Or it may assume a teacher like tone, along the lines of suggestion by repetition, in which the statement is made in a quiet, convincing way, as a teacher makes his statements to his class, the repetition of which brings conviction to the mind of the hearer. Or it may take on that peculiar caressing tone which is noticed in magnetic men of a certain type, who allure, charm, fascinate and draw to them other people by reason of their subtle power of "charming." This power, which finds its expression largely in the voice always reminds me of a female leopard or tiger, for the feline is mingled with the feminine in a peculiar way. This tone of the voice can be best described as "caressing"—when it is exhibited by one well versed in its use every word seems to be a soft caress, and has a peculiar soothing effect upon the hearer, lulling his will to sleep and opening his emotive mentality to the suggestions and mentative currents of the speaker.

In short, the dynamic individual, in his use of the voice, has acquired to a certain degree the art of the actor and orator. He is able to express "feeling," real or assumed, by his voice, so that a corresponding mental state is set up in the minds of his hearers. And one may acquire this art. By practice a vibrant, resonant, expressive voice may be cultivated, and used, too, with the greatest effect in personal magnetism, As an instance of this let me cite you the case of Nathan Sheppard, the well known lecturer and authority on public speaking, Mr. Sheppard relates that when he first made up his mind to devote himself to public speaking he was told by his tutors that he would be a perfect failure in such a profession, because, as he says "My articulation was feeble; my organs of speech were inadequate; if I would screw up my little mouth it could be put into my mother's thimble." These facts were enough to discourage any man, but Sheppard rose above them, and determined to apply his will to the task of conquering these disadvantages, and mastering the subject of public speaking. And he succeeded marvelously. By pure will power he, as he says, "increased my voice tenfold; doubled my chest, and brought my unoratorical organs somewhat in subjection to my will." He became one of the best public speakers of his time. So there is hope for all of you, if you will but manifest persistency and earnestness in your application of the will.

The third suggestive channel is "the suggestive word." I may be able to explain this more clearly when I call your attention to the fact that "each word is a crystallized thought." In every word there is an imprisoned thought. And when you lodge a word in the mind of another person, the crystal covering is dissolved, and the released thought manifests itself. And, this being so, it becomes important for one to carefully choose the crystallized thoughts, or words, which he wishes to implant in the mind of another. You should study words until you are able to distinguish between those which carry a *live, active, feeling* thought, and those less strong.

Take the word "strong" for instance. Does it not make you feel strength when you hear it forcibly and feelingly pronounced? Take the word "*kind,*" and see what feelings it arouses in you. Pronounce the words "*lion*" and "*lamb,*" and see the different feelings you experience from the differing sounds. Take the word "*crash,*" and see how it suggests the crashing, crunching, tearing, startling thing for which it stands. Compare the sound of the words "*rough*" and "*smooth*"—and you will see what I mean. The only way that I can point out to you to acquire the use of suggestive words is to study words themselves. Listen to the words used by others, and note their effect on you. Take a small dictionary and run over its pages, and you will soon have a collection of good, strong, effective terms for handy use when occasion demands. A man does not have to be "highly educated" in the usual sense of that term, in order to use strong, suggestive words. Some instinctively choose vital words, charged with feeling, and such make their words *felt*. Think over this matter.

In the use of all the three suggestive instruments, or channels, remember that the object is to make others *feel* the mental state you are expressing. This is the whole thing in a nutshell.

CHAPTER 14

INSTRUMENTS OF EXPRESSION

Next in order in our list of instruments of channels of mentative expression is the eye, that most wonderful of all the human organs, and which is as much an instrument for the expression of Mind Power as it is an instrument for receiving the sense impression of sight. Let us consider it in its former aspect.

In the first place, the eye is one of the most potent and effective instruments of suggestion, although I have not included it in that class. The expression of the eye will induce mental conditions in others along the lines of suggestion, and those who understand and have mastered this art of using the eyes have at their disposal a wonderful instrument of suggestive influence. Those of us who have ever met a very "magnetic" man, or a "charming and fascinating" woman, have carried away with us a lively recollection of "the expression of the eyes" of such a person. Actors and public speakers, as well as those whose business it is to meet and impress people, often make a close study of eye expression in order to produce a heightened effect along these lines.

And what kind of an eye has our dynamic individual? Need you ask this question? What would you expect? Of all the physical avenues of expression of the mental state within, the eye is the most potent and nearest to the "soul within." The eyes have well been called" the windows of the soul," and they give a clearer idea of the inner man than all else combined. And, therefore, we may expect our magnetic man to have an eye that reflects the power within him. And we are not disappointed, for even a hasty glance will show that he has what people call "an expressive eye." It manifests every mental state, at the will of its owner. Now stern, now tender, now commanding, now loving, now masterful, now caressing—it is an obedient instrument of the will operating it.

And it produces the most wonderful suggestive effect upon those coming under its spell. As an inducer of mental states, the eye has no equal among the physical agents—even the voice, wonderfully potent though it be, must yield precedence to it. It is more than a physical agent—it is a direct avenue for the passage of mentative currents.

Very dynamic people, when aroused by deep interest, emotion or desire—combined with will—seem to have a constant stream of mentative energy flowing from their eyes, which is felt by those within their field of influence. I need not call your attention to the wonderful power of eye, for you are fully acquainted with it from personal experience. You know how power shows itself in the eyes of people. In cases where the will has been developed to a very high degree, it is true that the mentative energy can be so concentrated by a very earnest and powerful glance that an actual physical effect may be produced.

I have known and heard of cases in which a powerful glance halted people in their tracks. Cases of this kind are told of Napoleon, and others of developed Will Power. Andrew Jackson is said to have so paralyzed the will of a noted desperado by his glance that he surrendered meekly and accompanied his captor, although fully armed and heretofore deemed absolutely fearless and dangerous. The desperado afterward said that he could not understand just why he had not killed Jackson where he stood. It is related in some of the ancient histories, or tales, that one of the old Greeks paralyzed an enemy by a single burning glance. You have all seen people flinch and quail before the masterful glance of one possessed of a developed Will Power. You, personally, know how this feels.

Fothergill says: "The steady conflict of the eye is familiar to many of us. The boy looks at his mother to see if she is in earnest in her threat; when older he likewise looks at his schoolmaster to read his purpose. Two men or women look at each other steadily; no word is said, yet the conflict is over soon, and one walks ahead of the other ever after."

Oliver Wendell Holmes describes an "eye battle" as follows: "The Koh i noor's face turned so white with rage that his blue black mustache and beard looked fearful seen against it. He grinned with wrath, and caught at a tumbler, as if he would have thrown its contents at the speaker. The young Marylander fixed his clear, steady eye upon him and laid his hand on his arm, carelessly almost, but the Jewel felt it was held so that he could not move it. It was of no use. The youth was his master in muscle, and in that deadly Indian hug in which men wrestle with their eyes, over in five seconds, but breaks one of their two backs, and is good for three score years and ten, one trial enough—settles the whole matter—just as when two feathered songsters of the barnyard, game and dunghill, come together. After a jump or two at each other, and a few sharp kicks, there is an end of it; and it is '*Apres vous, monsieur*,' with the beaten party in all the social relations for all the rest of his days."

The following rules for the cultivation of eye expression were obtained from one of the leading authorities in this line in America. I herewith give them in detail, for those who may desire to practice them. I know of none better for the purpose.

EXERCISES IN EYE EXPRESSION.

"Begin by studying your eyes in a mirror. You will see that in the center of the eye ball there is a black spot; this is called the" pupil" of the eye. The larger circle surrounding the pupil is called the "iris." The white of the eye surrounds the iris. The upper eyelid moving over the eyeball produces a variety of expressions, each giving to the face a totally different appearance, or expression of suggestive meaning. All recognize the meaning of these different expressions, but very few of us understand the mechanism producing the impression. Standing before your mirror, study these various expressions. The following exercises may help you.

1. Hold the upper lid in such a position that its edge rests half way between the pupil and top of the iris. This gives an expression of Calmness.
2. Rest the edge of the upper eyelid at the top of the pupil. This gives an expression of Indifference.
3. The edge of the eyelid resting at the top of the iris gives an expression of Strong Interest.

4. The edge of the eyelid resting half way over the pupil gives an expression of Deep Thought.
5. The edge of the eyelid resting just above the edge of the iris, and thus showing a narrow strip of white between the edge of the lid and the edge of the iris, gives an expression of Emotional Activity.
6. The above position, exaggerated so as to show as much of the white "as possible between the edge of the iris and the edge of the lid, will give an expression of Emotional Excitement.

"Practice the above expressions and positions. With a little practice nearly every one may easily acquire the art of expression in the first four exercises, but the last two are more difficult of acquirement. The last exercise—Emotional Excitement—especially, is found to be quite difficult of attainment, and but a small percentage are able to produce the expression without considerable practice. Practice these movements until you can reproduce them without the aid of the mirror, just as a man may learn to shave without a mirror, by constant practice before one. The exercises will not only enable you to express the different mental states easily and freely, but will also tend to strengthen the muscles and nerves of the eyes themselves, providing that you proceed gradually and do not over task the eyes at the beginning. Do not scowl, or contract the brows in the practices. A few minutes at a time is all that you should use in practicing.

"When you have mastered the above exercises, especially Nos. 5 and 6, you may try the following, which is the most difficult of all:

"7. Rest the eyelid in the position of Strong Interest (No. 3), and then *at the same time* lift the edge of the *under lid* to the lower edge of the pupil. This position gives the expression of Close Scrutiny.

"You will be surprised at the added power of expression that the careful practice of the above exercises will give you. You will be able to manifest more suggestive feeling, and will induce emotional states of feeling in others. A little practice will give you such convincing proof of this that you will not need urging to further perfect yourself in them. The expressions of Emotional Activity and Emotional Excitement especially will produce a startling result if used on appropriate occasions when you wish to exhibit the appearance of the deepest emotional excitement and force."

DEVELOPMENT EXERCISES.

The following Development Exercises are highly recommended by the same teacher who has devoted years to study and experiment along these lines:

1. Open the eyes quite widely, but not so widely as to strain them, and hold them in that position for a few seconds, gazing into your mirror, which must be directly in front of you on a level with your eyes. While gazing open them a trifle wider still, without straining, and throw an intense expression into them. Do not move the eyebrows, but allow them to remain normal.
2. Resume the above position, and then change to the expression of Strong Interest (see previous exercises), looking at yourself in the glass just as you would in looking at another person with that expression.
3. Resume position 1, and then gradually change to the expression of Emotional Activity (see previous exercises), gazing at yourself in the mirror.
4. Resume position 1, and then gradually change to the expression of Emotional Excitement (see previous exercises), gazing at yourself in the mirror.
5. Resume position 1, and then gradually change to the expression of Close Scrutiny (see previous exercises), gazing at yourself in the mirror.

   "In the above exercises you must act as if the reflection of yourself in the mirror were in reality another person whom you wished to influence. The better you act this out, the better will your results be.
6. Practice the expression of Strong Interest on persons to whom you are listening, until you feel that you

have awakened a response in them, I may add that the expression of Deep Interest consists of but the same expression heightened by *more feeling* behind it; and the expression of Loving Interest is the same, "only more so." This "more feeling" may be either real or assumed, as in the case of the good actor.

7. Practice the expression of Close Scrutiny upon other persons upon appropriate occasions in which you desire to appear as taking a deep, critical interest in some proposition, undertaking, theory, etc. Many persons have built up a reputation for being 'good listeners' and 'keen observers' by this practice. I mention it for what it may be worth to you. I am merely giving you the 'rules of the game,' not necessarily advising you to play it."

And now I have reached thatpartof my subjectin which I must speak of the *power of the eye to convey mentative force*. Owing to some law of nervous mechanism not fully understood as yet, the eye is one of the most effective mediums for the passage of mentative currents from one person to another. I shall not attempt to indulge in any special theory on the subject but shall proceed to the description of the facts of the case. I may add, however, that advanced occultists inform us that portions of the human brain, during a manifestation of strong emotional effort, or exercise of will, resembles an incandescent surface, glowing and phosphorescent. And that also there are seen great beams of this incandescent energy streaming out from the eyes of the person, and reaching the mind of other persons. And more than this, these "beams" of energy transmit mental states, thoughts, etc., of the person, just as scientists have found that "beams of light" will carry waves of electricity, and have thus been able to send telegraphic, and even telephonic messages over such beams of light.

One who has mastered the fascination of the eye, is able to convey most readily to others the mentative currents which tend to produce similar mental states by mentative induction as explained elsewhere in this book. If you will but remember the above illustration of the "beam of light" along which the electric and magnetic currents travel, and will form a mental picture of these mentative beams from the eye, you will understand the process much better, and you will at the same time tend to give to your own mentative beams a substantial reality, along the lines of visualization. That is, when you wish to use these mentative beams; you should *imagine* them as actually existing in full force and reality, this will have a tendency to give them a material reality, and thus render them a highly efficient medium for the passage of your mentative currents.

And now, right here is the best place to instruct you in the proper use of the eye in what has been called "The Magnetic Gaze," but which would be more properly styled "The Dynamic Gaze." There has been much nonsense written on this subject, and in some of my own earlier writings I gave directions along these lines which I am now able to replace with more approved methods, and later discoveries coming from the study and experimentation of myself and others along these lines. I am willing to improve upon my own methods as well as upon those of others—I have no false pride upon this subject, and if tomorrow I find that I can improve upon my work of today, I shall do so and give my students the benefit of the change, instead of stubbornly "sticking to it," just because I had once stated a theory, fact, or result. There is no standing still in scientific work—he who stands still really goes backward.

The former instructions regarding the "Magnetic Gaze" told the student to concentrate his gaze "at the root of the nose" of the other person, that is, right between his two eyes. Now this was all very well, but there is a far better plan. This focusing the gaze between the eyes of the other person, really results in "crossing" your gaze, and thus robbing it of a portion of the direct electro magnetic power that it possesses. You may prove this by holding up a pencil before your eyes, and focusing your eyes upon it as you draw it nearer and nearer to your eyes. The nearer you get to the pencil, or to the other person, the more will your gaze be "crossed" and the effect impaired. A gaze from a pair of "crossed eyes" is not nearly so dynamic as one from a pair of straight eyes, giving out a direct, forceful impression.

The new "Dynamic Gaze" is performed as follows: You *do not* focus your gaze at a point between the two eyes of the other person, but, instead, you gaze directly and straightly into his two eyes with your two eyes. You will find this difficult, and tiring, if you perform it in the ordinary way—and herein lies the "secret." Instead of focusing your eyes upon his, as if you really wished to see the color of his eyes, you must so focus your eyes that you are really gazing *through him*, as if he were transparent and you wished to *see something beyond him*. A little practice before a mirror will show you what I mean better than I can explain it to you in words. Practice at "*gazing through*" objects will aid you in acquiring this gaze. Try for instance focusing your eyes upon the wall opposite you as you raise your eyes from this page. Then as you look at the wall slowly pass your hand before your eyes at a distance of about two feet, but don't change your focus—*don't see the hand plainly*, but keep your gaze focused on the wall, *as if you could see it through the hand.*

This gaze must not consist of a blank, vacant, stupid stare, but must be intense and earnest. Practice on objects as above stated, and with your mirror, will aid you in perfecting the gaze. It will help you if you have some friend with whom you can practice it.

The other person will not be aware that you are not "seeing" him, and are "*gazing through*" him—to him it will appear that you are giving him a very deep, intense, steady, earnest glance. He will see your pupils dilate, as they always do when looking at a distant object, and your "expression will be one of calm, serene power.

And another important point about this gaze is that you may maintain it a long time without tiring the eyes, and without the eyes watering or blinking. You may out stare another person, or animal, in this way, without fatigue, while the other's eyes grow tired and weak. So much is this true that the results of my own investigation of the subject have convinced me that the animals who manifest "fascination," really focus their eyes beyond the object in just this way. If ever you get a chance to observe an animal fascinating another, you will see that I am right in this theory.

This "*gazing through*," the other person is accomplished by a certain "accommodation" of the eye, as oculists and, opticians call it, and while you an performing it you cannot examine distinctly, or "see" distinctly the eyes of the other person, because your focus is different. To show you why you are able to maintain this gaze such a long time without tiring your eyes, I would remind you of the ease with which you may maintain the expression of being "wrapped in thought," "day dreaming," "lost in a brown study," "just thinking about things," etc., with which you all are familiar. In such a mental state you are able to "gaze into space" for a long time without the slightest fatigue, while a few seconds' focusing your eyes upon a near by object will tire them very much indeed. And then, again, you know how long you are able to gaze at an object far out at sea, or far across the desert, or far down or across the mountain, without tiring your eyes. The whole secret is that short range focusing upon an object tires the eyes much more than does "long range" gazing into space. This being the case, it will tire you far less "seeing through" a person, than gazing at him and "seeing" him at short range.

In practicing the maintaining of the gaze for a long time, I would advise against tiring the eyes by gazing at short range objects. Better practice at gazing at distant objects until you are able to maintain the gaze a long time, as you will be able to do after a little practice. In fact, I advise you to practice the "gazing into space," because proficiency in that will enable you to perfect the "Dynamic Gaze." After you have practiced this "gazing through" method a bit, you will be able to look at an object a couple of feet away, and gaze right through it—that is, you will not consciously "see" it objectively, although apparently staring hard at it.

Avoid all exercises tiring to the eyes, and proceed slowly working from trifling successes to more important ones. You will be surprised how a little intelligent practice along these lines will give you a penetrating glance, firm, earnest, and full of "magnetism" and "fascination," without the slightest sense of strain, fatigue or effort. You have long wished for such an expression—here it is for you.

CHAPTER 15

USING THE MENTATIVE INSTRUMENTS

In the use of the eyes for the purpose of conveying mentative currents, you should always remember that the *feeling* is the real power behind these currents of power, and that the brain is the dynamo from which the currents originate. The brain, you know, is the great transformer, or converter of the mentative energy, and acts just as does a dynamo in the direction of sending forth great waves of power. Consequently, if you wish to send out mentative currents for the purpose of inducing feeling in others, you must first have *feeling* generated in your mental dynamo.

It will be well for two people to practice the eye exercises together, but in the absence of a friend in whom you have confidence, you may obtain excellent results by practicing before your friendly mirror. In either case, you must first arouse in your mind the feeling that you wish to express in mentative currents. Put your feeling into your glance, and it will be felt.

Exercise 1. Look into the eyes of your friend (or your own in the mirror) and then say *mentally*: "I am stronger than you." Throw into your glance as much of the feeling of strength as you can.

Exercise 2. Say *mentally: "I am more Positive than you—I am outgazing you,"* throwing as much positivity as possible into your gaze, the same being inspired, of course, by our feeling.

Exercise 3. Say, and *feel: "You are afraid of me—I am making you feel my strength,"* throwing the feeling into your gaze.

After you have acquired the faculty of making your strength felt by above exercises you may use the same upon other people when the occasion renders it advisable. If you are addressed by some person whom you think is trying to master you mentatively, or whose strong influence you wish to ward off, you may use the above method on him. As a rule the person who is doing the talking has a slight advantage over the listener, all else being equal. The speaker is the more positive because he is expressing more power. But you may counteract this, if you are the listener, by simply sending him a glance, accompanied by the feeling of "*I scatter your force into bits—you cannot affect me!*"

In resisting an attack of this sort, keep your mouth closed, with the jaws tight, for this "bite" denotes strength and firmness, and brings into play the parts of the brain manifesting these qualities, and thus charges your mentative currents with these feelings. At the same time gaze firmly and steadily into the eyes of the other, using the "Dynamic Gaze." I would bid you remember that the person *standing* has an advantage over the one *sitting*. Avoid the sitting position when the other person is standing—do not give him this advantage, but take it yourself if you can.

In speaking to persons and requesting them to do something, you should accompany the verbal requestby a mental command. For instance, if you say "You will do this for me, *won't* you?" (this is the suggestive form of questioning, remember) you should accompany the question with the *command* (made mentally) with the proper glance, "You *shall* do this." If you are the person requested to do something that you do not wish to do, you should answer, "No, I do not care to do this," or "I do not see my way clear to do it," or "I am unable to oblige you," etc., etc., but at the same time you must send the *mental answer*, with its accompanying glance, "I will not do it, and *you cannot make me*."

A well known teacher along these lines several years ago, taught his pupils to gaze into the eyes of persons whom they wished to affect, at the same time saying mentally: *"I am looking at you. I am looking through your eyes into your brain. My will power is stronger than yours. You are under my control. I will compel you to do what I wish. You must do what I say. You shall do this. Do it at once."* It will readily be seen that this will generate a powerful mentative current, if there is a sufficiently strong feeling—will and desire—behind it. But right here I shall give you *an antidote for this kind of influence*. In all cases where you are attacked mentally in this way you may dissolve the Force by a positive denial.

The *positive denial* is the powerful force that scatters into tiny bits the force directed against one. It is *a destructive agent*, just as is the *positive statement* a constructive or creative one. One who understands the scientific use of this destructive force may undo the mentative work of others, to a surprising degree. *By a strong, positive denial, you may scatter and disintegrate any mentative influence directed against you.* This formula will give you a general idea of it. Suppose that you are repelling a statement such as given above. In that case you should say *mentally*, accompanying it with the proper glance, with feeling back of it: "*I deny positively* your power over me. *I deny it out of existence.* I *will not* do your bidding, and I *deny* your right and power to command me. I *deny your* power, and I affirm *my own*."

You may cultivate this power to use the *positive denial* by practicing on an imaginary person whom you may suppose is trying to influence you. Imagine the strong, positive person before you, trying to influence you and then start in to practice the positive denial on him, until you feel that you have beaten him off, and have sent him flying away in retreat. These imaginary mental battles will develop a great power of mentative resistance in you, and I advise you strengthen yourselves along these lines, if you feel that you are weak. You may improve on the above exercise, by imagining that after your enemy is in full retreat you follow him up and pour statement after statement into him, changing your position from a defender into an attacking force.

These imaginary rehearsals will do more for one than people think possible. They are like stage rehearsals that make perfect the actors. They are the fencing lessons from which the swordsman gains skill, and strength. Practice, *practice*, practice makes perfect in everything—in mentative work as, well as physical. There are good psychological and occult reasons behind this method and practice, but I shall not enter upon that field at present—this book is intended to give you the "how" of the subject, rather than the "why."

In personal conversation with another you will find it of the greatest value to see as clearly as possible a mental picture, chart or map, of what you are saying to him. By so doing you will impress most forcibly upon his mind that which you wish him to see, and feel. In this statement is compressed the secret of effective speaking. In the degree that *you* see and feel the thought that you are expressing in words, will be the degree of impression made upon, and mentative induction produced in, the other person. The secret of course lies in the power of visualization.

You may find an evidence of your increasing mentative influence by trying the psychological experiment of "willing" people to move this way or that way, by gazing intently at them. In this experiment it is not necessary for you to gaze into their eyes. Gazing at their back, preferably at the upper part of the neck, at the base of the brain, will answer. You may try "willing" persons to look around on the street, or in public places, etc. Or you may "will" that they turn to the right or left of you, when approaching each other on the street. Or, in stores you may "will" that a certain clerk, from out of a number, will step forward to wait upon you. These and many similar experiments have an interest to the majority of students, and are accomplished with comparative ease, after sufficient practice. The whole theory and practice consists of a steady gaze, and the *mental command*, and will, that the person will act so and so, together with the *earnest expectation* that he will obey the command, and the *mental picture* of his doing so. That is all there is to it.

In the use of the eye as a mentative instrument, remember first, last, and all the time, that *desire* and *will* are the phases of the mentative energy, and that in the degree that desire is kindled, and will is exerted, so will be the power expressed by yourself, and impressed upon others. Read this book over a number of times, until you have fully grasped the underlying principles. Then commit its exercises and instructions to memory. Then practice frequently, and perfect yourself in the methods pointed out, until you render them "second nature." You will be conscious of a gradual growth and development, along the lines of mentative power and influence. The flame of dynamic mentation once lighted, it will never die out—tend the flame carefully, keep the wick trimmed clean, and fill the lamp with oil, and it will ever burn bright and emit heat and light and power.

The last mentative instrument mentioned in a previous chapter is "the touch." There was a time, in my early stages of experimentation and psychological research, when I laughed at the idea of the touch playing any real part in the work of mental influence. Of course I saw the effect of the touch in certain phases of psychological work, but I believed that it was all "merely suggestion," but I soon learned that the touch was really a most potent instrument of mentative energy. I now explain it by the idea of the nerves being like the wires upon which the electric current travels. The brain is the dynamo, or converter of the energy, and while the latter travels in waves and currents without any wires (just as do the waves of the wireless telegraph) still *if there is a wire to be had*, then it follows the lines of least resistance and takes advantage of the nerve wire. Certain parts of the body have nerve cells very highly developed in them—are in fact miniature brains. In the cases of some persons of sensitive and trained touch, there exist little clusters of nerve cells at the ends of the fingers, that act like miniature brains. The lips are also highly developed in this respect, as the well known phenomena of "kissing" evidences. The fingers and hand are excellent polar mediums for conveying the mentative energy that pours down over the nerves from the brain, and through which it passes to the other person.

The use of the touch of the hands as a channel for conveying mentative energy depends greatly upon the development of the hands by the individual. Those who understand this matter, develop the conductivity of the hands by "treating" them, as follows: Think of your hands as excellent conductors of mentative energy, and imagine that you can feel the energy pouring down the nerves of your arms, and out of your hands, obeying your will, when you shake hands with people. You will soon develop your hands to such a degree that some sensitive persons will actually "feel" the current passing into them. Always accompany the passage of the current with the thought or feeling that you wish to induce in the other person, just as you do when you use the "Dynamic Gaze." In fact, the gaze and the hand clasp should be used together, when possible, for by so doing you double the effect.

When you shake hands with a person *throw mind and feeling into it*, and do not fall into the mechanical, lifeless method so common among people. Throw your feeling down to your hand, and at the same time make a mental command or statement appropriate to the case. For instance, grasp the person's hand with feeling, and interest, saying, mentally, at the same time: "*You like me.*" Then, when you draw your hand away, if possible let your fingers slide over the palm of his hand in a caressing manner, allowing his first finger to pass between your thumb and forefinger, close up in the crotch of the thumb. Practice this well, until you can perform it without thinking of it—that is, make it your natural way of shaking hands. You will find that this method of shaking hands will open up a new interest in people toward you, and in other ways you will discover its advantage. You never knew a "fascinating" person who did not have a good hand clasp. It is a part of the fascinating personality.

There are many persons, well grounded on the psychological principles underlying the subject, who use the hands as a medium for mentative energy, without shaking hands. For instance, they sit near the other person and place their hands so that their fingers will point toward him, at the same time *willing* that the current flow through the fingers and toward the other. They also use their hands in conversation so as to have the tips of their fingers pointing toward the other. This last plan becomes highly effective when used with the appropriate gestures, for it is akin to the mesmeric "pass" of the hands. In this connection I would say beware of the person who is always trying to put his hands on you—beware of the "pawing over" process. Avoid it in the ordinary way, if possible, or else deliberately practice the *positive denial* toward the person, holding the idea and mental statement that "I *deny* the power of your magnetism—I scatter it by my denial."

In concluding this chapter, I would especially caution young women, and older ones for that matter, against allowing men to be familiar with them in the direction of "holding hands," or similar practices. Not only does this "familiarity breed contempt" but there are good psychological reasons why the practice is to be condemned. You have seen what part the hands play in "magnetizing" as it is called, and is it not clearly discernible how one may use the hands in this "petting," and all that sort of thing, in order to psychologically affect another person? I am not speaking now of the caresses indulged in by honorable true lovers—for all the talk in the world would not change that sort of thing—but I am alluding to the indiscriminate "pawing over" on the part of strange men that some young girls allow. There is a danger in this sort of thing, and I want you to know it. If you have daughters, or young female relatives, warn them against this thing, and *tell them the reason why.*

And the same thing is true of the man who is always patting other men on the shoulder, or resting his arm around them, or else "taking hold of them" in a friendly caressing way during a conversation. Such men may not know the psychology of the thing, but they have found out that this sort of "patting up" makes other men more impressible, and amenable to their influence, and so they practice it. Make them stop it, either by moving away, or by *positive denial.*

Now, once more, remember the power of this *positive denial* as a disperser, and disintegrator of adverse influence. If this book taught you nothing else, it would still be "worth while" to you because of this one point of instruction. For this positive denial is a mentative armor that will protect you—a mentative sword that will defend you—a mentative lightning flash that will clear the mental atmosphere. Learn the secret of positive statement, and positive denial, and you are clad in an invulnerable armor and are armed with the weapon of power—and so you may, like the "Warrior Bold" go "gaily to the fray."

But, after all, the secret of influence in our dynamic individual lies in his mental states. The outer forms are but reflections of the inner. If you will cultivate the connection between your mind and the great Universal Will—the Universal Mind Power—then your will becomes so strong that the outward expressions will come of themselves. But in mounting the first steps of attainment, it becomes important for the student to pay attention to the outward characteristics, because by so doing he makes a clearer mental path for the acquisition of the desired mental states. By the very laws of mental suggestion he is able to imitate these outward expressions, and thus induce in himself the mental states, which, in time, become habitual. I do not mean that one should allow the suggestion of the other's appearance to move him in this way—this is not the idea. What I mean is that one may by auto suggestion so reproduce the outward characteristics associated with a desired mental state or, quality, and by acting them out actually materialize into reality the mental states themselves. Remember the rule—mental states take form in action—and action reproduces their associated mental states! It is a rule that works both ways. The voice makes the phonographic record—and the latter reproduces the sound! Remember this illustration, for it will help you to get the right conception of the psychological law underlying the phenomenon.

There is a certain point to which I would direct your attention at this stage. I refer to the well known psychological fact that "mental states express themselves in physical action." Every mental state has its associated physical action. And these actions when perceived by another person, are apt to induce similar mental states in that person, along the lines of mental suggestion. But there is another law, less understood by the public, and that is that "the manifestation of physical action tends to induce in the mind of the person performing it, the mental states generally associated with the production of the action."

Let us take a common example, to illustrate the operation of these two related laws. Let us suppose that you are holding a mental state of anger, fight, combativeness, etc. In that case you will find that your brows will frown; your jaws will be fixed in a savage "bite," and slightly protruded; and your hands will be clenched—the mental state has taken form in physical action. Very well, then—you all recognize this fact.

But there is the law reversed. If you will frown deeply; clench your fists savagely; fix your jaws in a fighting trim, etc., and will maintain that physical attitude for five minutes, at the same time allowing it to manifest in your walk, etc. (as it surely will) without interference, you will find yourself growing into a mental state of annoyance, combativeness, etc., and if you keep it up long enough, you will be "mad in earnest." So true is this that if you carry the thing far enough, and run into someone else, you will be very apt to "get into a row" with him. And, still more remarkable is the fact, the person that you "run into" will be very apt to take up the mental suggestion of your manner, and will also "feel fighty." It would not take much to stir up trouble between the two of you.

And, still more remarkable, if you continue this physical attitude until it produces the mental state, you will find that you are inducing similar mental states in those around you, by the agency of mentative currents. So you see the close connection between physical action, mental states, suggestion, and telementation! They act, and re act upon each other. What has been said of the mental state of anger applies equally to any intense feeling or mental state. Like begets like, along all the lines mentioned.

Now, all this means that the man who is possessed of a strong mental state will manifest, unconsciously, the physical actions which will affect others, along the lines of mental suggestion—he will not have to study the question of what suggestions to use, providing he "feels" sufficiently strong to automatically manifest the actions. But when a man does not "feel" sufficiently strong to manifest the suggestive actions, he may produce the same effect by "acting the part" (without being actually involved in it) by first reproducing the physical actions, which will thus induce a sufficiently strong mental state to manifest itself both along the line of suggestion, and also along the line of personal magnetism. Every good actor induces feeling in you in this way, along both these lines. And you may do the same if you want to—many dynamic people are doing it every day.

On this subject, so far as I have gone, I have given you a most important secret of psychological influence, in a plain, practical way—so simple in fact that there is a risk of many of you entirely overlooking its importance. Better go back over this part of the lesson again—many times—until you are able to catch its inner meaning, and are able to read between its lines. It's quite worth while, I assure you.

Of course, some of my kind critics will take me to task for teaching this "acting out" idea. They will call it "inculcating principles of deceit," etc., etc.—and will then go on their way admiring "magnetic" personalities, and regretting the absence of "tact" in other persons who have rubbed them the wrong way. I have noticed that these hyper critical people are generally hypo critical as well.

I have known many good men who were not "dynamic," and the world "turned them down," and often "jumped all over them." And I have known quite a number, not quite so good, who possessed quite a goodly degree of dynamic force, and the world received them with open arms, and showered its praises and rewards upon them. But this does not mean that one cannot be "good" and "dynamic" at the same time. There are plenty of "good" men who are highly "dynamic"—and there are plenty of "bad" men equally so. And there are plenty both good and bad, who lack "dynamic force." But, note this fact, please—that the good men, and the bad men, who are highly "dynamic," generally manage to "get there," along their own line of life. And both the good and bad who lack "dynamic force" are generally stranded along the wayside. Dynamic force is neither good nor bad—it is a natural force—and is used by all. In this respect it is like any other natural force.

And, then again, this book is not for the purpose of teaching the "bad" use of "dynamic force," rather than the "good." It states the principles and the law, as they are. It is true that the bad man may take advantage of the law and use it for bad purposes; but so may the good man take advantage of it and make himself a greater power for good, "dynamic force" is just as effective in the "preacher" as it is in the "confidence man"—and just as effective in the salesman and business man, and everyday person, as it is in either the preacher or the confidence man. It is a natural quality, and has nothing to do with "good and bad"—any more than has elocution, oratorical ability, or personal appearance.

If the good folk prefer to leave this important subject for the bad folk, that is their own concern, not mine. Personally, I feel like the old preacher, who was remonstrated with by some hide bound old parishioner regarding certain musical innovations that had been introduced in the church service. The old preacher looked kindly at the old veteran "conservative" of the flock, and said: "Well, brother, it may strike you in a different way, but to me it seems wrong to allow the Devil to monopolize all the good music—I believe in giving the Lord his share of it." And I say "Amen!" to this idea.

If "dynamic mentation" was as much used to further the interests of right, as it has been to further the interests of wrong, the old world would get down to a little easier motion. If the preacher would make his talks as "dynamic" as the actor does his plays, and the lawyer does his appeals to the jury, there would surely be "something doing" in church work, and the prevailing emptiness of the pews would be cured. If "goodness" was made as attractive as "badness," the Devil would be placed on the retired list.

CHAPTER 16

MENTAL SUGGESTION

Before beginning our consideration of the subject of Mental Suggestion; let me call your attention to the following general statements regarding Mentative Induction (in which general subject is included the sub divisions called Personal Magnetism; Mental Suggestion; and Telementative Induction) respectively:

1. Mental States may be caused by Mentative Induction.
2. Such induced mental states may be caused by the Mentative currents of Personal Magnetism; or by the Mentative currents of Telementation; or by Mental Suggestion.
3. Mentative currents are waves or streams of vibrant Mind Power, emanating from the minds of people, and carrying with them the vibrations of mental states; the vibrations tending to induce similar mental states in the minds of people within the field of induction.
   (*a*) There are two poles of Mind Power, i. e., the emotive pole, manifesting desire, feeling, emotion, etc.; and the motive pole, manifesting will, etc.; the acting force, affecting other minds, manifested by these two poles being called Desire Force and Will Power, respectively.
   (*b*) Desire Force tends to awaken similar vibrations in the minds of others, thus producing similar desires—or it charms the wills of others and causes them to carry out its desires—its action and nature bearing a strong resemblance to feminine mental power.
   (*c*) Will Power tends to awaken desire in the minds of others by sheer mastery and forcefulness—it also acts in the direction of combating and over powering the wills of others, and taking them captive—it also directs, masters, concentrates, or restrains one's own

Desire Force, on occasions—its action bears a strong resemblance to masculine mental power.

(*d*) When the mentative currents are emanated, and Mentative Induction is manifested, when the projector and recipients *are in the personal presence of each other*, we use the term Personal Magnetism. When the same manifestation occurs when the projector and recipients are *not in the personal presence of each other*, then we use the term Telementative Induction. But the principle employed is the same in each case—induction through telementation being the operative principle. In Personal Magnetism, however, Mental Suggestion usually assists in the induction of mental states. For this reason, Mental Suggestion should be studied in connection with Personal Magnetism, being supplementary thereto.

4. Mental Suggestion induces mental states, by reproducing the original mental states of others; or one's own previously experienced mental states, including the experience of the race ancestors, inherited and recorded in the sub conscious minds of their descendants.

Suggestion operates along the lines of acquiescence, imitation, association, and repetition, always acting through physical agents for inducing mental states.

In Personal Magnetism, the mentator pours out his mentative currents, generated by his will or desire, or both; either in a general way, or in a concentrated, directed manner; in a personal interview, and thus influences the mind of others by induction—this is usually, or always, accompanied by Mental Suggestion, using physical agents, such as the voice, eye, manner, etc., which heighten the effect produced.

And, now, with the understanding of the above stated general principles, let us proceed to a consideration of the subject of "Mental Suggestion."

Every student of psychology and mental science has heard and read much of that phase of mental phenomena called "Mental Suggestion." Much has been written and taught about it, and the term has been claimed by some teachers to cover all phases of mental influence. I do not entirely agree with these extreme advocates of suggestion, however, for I find much in the subject that calls for a further explanation. But, nevertheless, I feel certain that mental suggestion plays a most important part in almost every instance of this class of phenomena and must be seriously considered by all careful students of the subject. Combined with mentative induction by means of mentative currents, it accounts for nearly every phase of the phenomena of mental influence. Therefore I shall devote several chapters to the consideration of its underlying principles, laws and method of application. I feel that no one can be a successful practitioner of telementative influence or personal magnetism who is not a good suggestionist, because the very "knack" of projecting strong suggestions is necessary for the forceful projection of mentative energy and mental currents.

While all who have examined the subjectare aware of the force and effects of mental suggestion, few have found it possible to correctly define or describe the term, or to explain it to others. But I feel assured that my theory of mentative induction, and the two poles of Mind Power will enable you to form a very clear and comprehensive knowledge of the underlying laws of the subject, so that, understanding it, you will be able to apply its method of application to the best advantage.

"Mental Suggestion" is the term used to designate the process of inducing or exciting mental states or ideas, by means of the imagination, by the agency of words; actions; outward appearances; or other physical symbols.

I divide the phenomena of Mental Suggestion into two general classes or phases, i. e., (1) Active Suggestion, and (2) Passive Suggestion, as follows:

By Active Suggestion I mean the induction or excitement of mental state or ideas in others by means of positive command, affirmation, statements, etc., bearing directly upon the desired mental state. By Passive Suggestion I mean the induction or excitement of mental state or ideas by the subtle insinuation, introduction, or insertion of ideas into the minds of others, which insinuated ideas act in the direction of inducing the desired mental state. Active Suggestion is associated with the use of the motive pole of the mind of the suggestor; and Passive Suggestion is associated with the emotive pole of the suggestor. One is the masculine method and the other the feminine.

And here is a good place in which to direct your attention to a very important fact concerning the operation of suggestion in inducing mental states in others. I allude to the fact that suggestion operates along the line of "emotional mentality," "feeling," or "imagination," and has nothing to do with judgment, reason, argument, proof, etc. It belongs clearly to the "feeling" side of the mind, rather than to the "thinking" side. One's reason may be appealed to by clever reasoning, argument, logic, proof, etc., and an effect gained—but this belongs to an entirely different phase of mental action. The induction of mental states in others by means of suggestion has to do entirely with the "feeling" or "imaginative" phase of the mind. It deals with the production of "emotional mentality" rather than with "rational mentality." This is a most important point, and one that should be thoroughly understood by all students of the subject.

It is true that suggestion may accompany an appeal to the reason or judgment of the person influenced, and, indeed, is generally so used; but, strictly speaking, it constitutes an appeal to a part of the mind entirely removed from reasoning and judgment. It is emotional, and imaginative first, last, and all the time. And it operates along the same lines as the mental induction produced by mentative currents, as we shall see.

And now, with this preliminary understanding, let us pass on to a consideration of the meaning of the terms used. There is nothing like a clear understanding of the terms employed in treating of a subject. If one understands the "exact" meaning of the terms, he has progressed very far to an "exact" understanding of the subject itself, for the terms are the crystallized ideas involved in the subject. To understand the full and complete meaning of the terms of any subject is to know the whole subject thoroughly, for no one can understand a term thoroughly until he knows it in all of its relations—all that pertains to it.

Let us start with the word "suggestion" as used by the writers on mental suggestion. Some authorities give the broad, general definition of "anything that is impressed upon the mind through the senses," but this I consider entirely too sweeping, for this definition would make the term cover knowledge of all sort, no matter to what part of the mind it appealed, for all knowledge of the outward world is obtained through the senses.

Other authorities define the term as "anything insinuated into the mind, subtly, cautiously, and indirectly," this definition fitting nearly the one "favored by the dictionaries in defining the Word "suggestion" in its general sense, which is as follows: "a hint; a guarded mention; an intimation; something presented to the mind directly; an insinuation; etc." But this last definition of mental suggestion does not fit all the phases of the subject. It fits admirably into the phase known as Passive Suggestion, which operates by direct, forceful command, statement, etc.

And so I must give my own definition of the term to fit my conception of and understanding of its meaning. I, therefore, here define my use of the term"a Mental Suggestion" as follows: *A physical agency tending to induce or excite mental states or ideas through the imagination*. This is a broad definition, which, I think, will cover all the observable phenomena of Mental Suggestion.

I use the word "physical" to distinguish suggestive agents from the "mental" agents inducing mental states by the operation of mentative currents, telementation, etc. Of course this distinction will not please those who would claim all "mental" action as a form of the "physical," or vice versa. But as I have to draw the line somewhere, I prefer to draw it between the "physical" agent and the "mental," and I think that the majority of my readers will approve of this position. The word "agent" means, of course, "an acting power or cause," etc. The word "inducing," as I have used it, has been defined in the previous lesson. The word "excite" means "to call into activity in any way; to rouse to feeling; to kindle to strong emotions." The imagination is "that phase of mind which creates mental images, or objects, or sensation previously experienced."

In my use of the term "physical" in the above definition I include all words, spoken, written, or printed; mannerisms; physical actions of all kinds; physical; characteristics and appearances, etc., etc. All of these physical manifestations act as "agents" inducing mental states under favorable circumstances. By "mental states" I mean states of "feeling or emotion." By "ideas," I mean "images of objects conceived of by the mind."

It may be urged that the use of "words, spoken, written or printed," may be employed, and are employed, in every appeal to the mind of another, whether the appeal be along the lines of suggestion or argument, reason, etc. Certainly! And in that sense they act as suggestions. Arguments appeal to judgment and reason—but not to feeling, emotion or imagination which are, on the contrary, excited or induced by suggestions or other forms of emotional induction. One may present an idea to the mind of another, in a bold, forcible, logical manner, accompanied by argument or proof, but this is an appeal to reason and judgment" not to "feeling or emotion," which belong to an entirely different field of the mind. Then again, many personal appeals, which are apparently made to reason, are really made to the emotional side. One may subtly insinuate into an argument or conversation an appeal to the feelings or emotion of the hearer, in the shape of an idea in the nature of a hint, or indirect mention. Such idea will be "felt" by the listener, who will accept it into his mind, and before long he will regard it as one of his own thoughts—he will make it his own. He will think that he "thought" it, whereas, really, he simply "feels" it, and the "feeling" is induced. This is a case of "suggestion."

In ordinary social intercourse you will find that women are adepts in this subtle form of insinuative suggestion, as compared to men. Men will blurt out statements and ideas, and attempt to "prove" them, but the woman will gently "insinuate" the idea into the mind of the other person, so that, without having proven a fact, she will have managed to create a definite idea of feeling in the mind of the other by "suggestion." I think I need not give examples of this fact—it is apparent to all who have mingled with people.

And really this "suggestion" resembles the mental suggestion of the psychologists very much. It is true that the practitioner of mental suggestion, in his "treatments," often makes use of direct, forceful statements, such as: "You are strong, cheerful, well and happy," but you will notice even here that he does not "argue the point," or attempt to "prove" his statements. He simply affirms and asserts the fact, and by constantly repeated suggestions he finally causes the mind of the other person to accept the statement. So you see a "suggestion" may be either a subtle insinuation or a bold, positive statement—but it is never an argument, or process of proof.

The word "impression" is good, as applied to the effect of a suggestion, but I prefer to stick to my own terms, and therefore I shall consider that the effect of mental suggestion is caused by induction. "What," you may say, "I thought that induction was a term used when a mental state was set up in one by mentative currents from the mind of another?" Yes, this is true, but my last statement is true also. An induced mental state is one set up by outside influence of some kind, whether that outside influence be a mentative current or by suggestion through a word, a look, a sight or anything else. The word "induce," you know, means: "to lead; to influence; to prevail on; to effect; to cause," etc. And any mental state that is induced by an outside influence comes clearly under the term.

Any physical agent that tends to induce a feeling in the mind of another may be called a suggestion. Even the well known instance mentioned in the textbooks on psychology comes under this rule. In that instance it is related that a soldier was carrying some bundles and a pail to his barracks, when some practical joker yelled to him in an authoritative voice, "Attention!" Following the suggestion, which induced in him the "feeling" preceding certain habitual actions, he dropped his pail and bundles with a crash and stood at "attention," with eyes front, chin out, protruding breast, stomach drawn in, and hands at his sides with little fingers touching the seams of his trousers. That was a suggestion! Do you see the point?

The lives of all of us have been moulded largely by induction through suggestion. We accepted this suggestion, or that one, and it changed the whole current of our lives. Certain things induced certain feelings—called into activity certain mental states—and action followed close upon the heels of feeling.

There are varying degrees of suggestive power, just as there are varying degrees of what is called the "suggestibility" of persons—that is the tendency to accept suggestions. There are people who scarcely ever act from motives originating within themselves, but whose entire lives are lived out in obedience to the suggested ideas and feelings of others. The development of the Will Power regulates the degree of suggestibility. The man of the strong will is not so easily affected by a suggestion as is one whose will is weak, and who accepts without resistance the suggestions coming from all sides. But note the apparent paradox, persons of weak will may have their wills so developed and strengthened by scientific suggestive treatment that they may become veritable giants of will.

The careful student may feel inclined to ask me, at this point, why I speak of suggested "ideas," when I have said that suggestion has to do with mental states of feeling and emotion. Are not "ideas," he asks, something connected with thought rather than with feeling? The question is a proper one, and I must meet it. The word "idea" comes from the Greek word, meaning "to see." In its general use it means "a mental image, or a general notion or conception held in the mind." An idea is "symbolic image held in the mind." It is a symbol of something thought or felt.

Ideas are not formed by thought alone—feeling contributes its share of these mental images. To tell the truth, the majority of people scarcely "think" at all, in the highest sense of the word. Their reasoning and logical faculties are very rudimentary. They accept their ideas at second hand or second hundred hand—their thoughts must be pre digested for them by others, and the handed down "idea" is the result. The majority of ideas held in the mind of the race arise from feeling and emotion. People may not understand things, but they have experienced feelings or emotions regarding them, and have consequently formed many ideas and "ideals" therefrom. They do not know "just why" an idea is held by them—they know only that they "feel" it that way. And the majority of people are moved, swayed and act by reasons of induced "feelings," rather than by results of reasoning. I am not speaking of intuitional feelings now, but of the plain, everyday, emotional feeling of people.

Do you know what a feeling is? The word, used in this sense, means: a mental state; emotion; passion; sympathy; sentiment; susceptibility; etc." And "emotion" means an excitement of the feelings. "Feelings" belong to the instinctive side of our mind, rather than to the rational or reasoning side. They spring up from the subconscious strata of the mind, in response to the exciting cause coming from without. The instinctive part of our minds are stored with the experiences, feelings, emotions and mental states of our long line of ancestors, reaching away back to the early beginnings of life. In that part of the mind are sleeping instincts, emotions and feelings, our inheritance from the past, which await but the inducing cause to call them into activity. The reason or judgment, by means of the will, act as a restrainer, of course, according to the degree of development of the individual. And these outward agents, if of a "physical" nature, are suggestions of all kinds.

Look around you at the world of men and women. Then tell me whether they seem to be moved principally by reason or feeling. Are their actions based upon good judgment and correct and careful reasoning! Or are they the results of feeling and emotion! Do people do things because the things are considered right in the light of reason, or do they do them "because they feel like it?" Which produces the greatest motive force—an appeal to the reason of a number of people, or an appeal to their feelings and emotion? Which sways a gathering of people; the votes of a people; the actions of a mob—reason or feeling! Which moves even you, good student, reason or feeling! Answer the questions honestly, and *you will have* the key of suggestive influence!

CHAPTER 17

FOUR KINDS OF SUGGESTION

Mental suggestion produces its effect upon the minds of people along one or more of four general lines or paths of action. All the phenomena coming under this head may be placed in one or more of the four classes. These four paths, or lines of action, along which Mental Suggestion operates, are as follows:

1. Obedience;
2. Imitation;
3. Association;
4. Repetition.

I shall now proceed to consider these four paths, or lines of action, separately, in order, and in detail. Beginning with the first mentioned line of action, let us consider:

Suggestion Through Obedience—Suggestion operating along this line consists of the induction of mental states, etc., by the agency of a positive statement, assertion, assumption, authoritative attitude, etc., which so impresses itself upon the mind of the person suggested to that he sets up no opposition or resistance, but acquiesces quietly to the suggestion made to him.

The most common form of this first method of Suggestion is seen in the very general acquiescence to real or pretended "authority" on the part of the majority of people. When such people hear a statement made, positively and in a tone of conviction, by some person in authority, they accept the statement, and the feelings arising from the accepted statement, without resistance, and without any attempt to submit the matter to the exercise of their reason. And this is true not only when the person speaking has really a right to speak authoritatively, by virtue of his knowledge, experience, wisdom, etc., but also when some pretender sets up an appearance of authority, and speaking in a positive style, assuming the "Thus saith the Lord" manner, impresses his hearers with the idea he wishes to suggest to them. And then the good folk meekly acquiesce without Question and allow their feelings to be aroused accordingly, for the feelings are generally followed by actions in accord therewith.

It is astonishing, from one point of view, to see how obedient to this form of suggestion the masses of people are. They will allow their mental states, feelings and emotion to be induced by the impudent statements, and claims of cunning, shrewd and designing men, as well as by ignorant self deluded fanatics, who thus influence and sway them. These self constituted authorities utter their oracular statements and opinions in a tone of absolute certainty, and the crowd takes them at their own valuation. It seems to be only necessary for some positive man to attract the attention of the people and then make some bold claim or statement, in the proper manner and tone, and with their appearance of authority, and lo! some of the people, at least, fall into line.

Did you ever think that people as a rule are "obedient animals?" Well, they are, providing you can manage to impress them with your authority. It is much easier for them to acquiesce than to refuse to do so. They find it easier to say and think "Yes" rather than "No." Their will is not often called into action by their reason and judgment, it being too often entirely under the control of the feeling and emotional side of them.

There is a fundamental law under this phase of suggestive action, and in order to find it we must go back to the beginning of the race, perhaps farther. In the earlier days among animals and men, there were natural leaders, who ruled by force of might of body or mind. These natural leaders were implicitly obeyed by the masses, who had learned by experience that it was better for the tribe, or herd, as a whole, to be governed by their strongest and sharpest witted members. And so gradually this dominant idea of acquiescence and obedience to authority developed and became a fixture in the race mind. And it is firmly planted in the mind of the race today, so much so that only the strongest minds are able to free themselves from it to any great extent. It is authority here, and authority there, in law, letters, religion, politics, and every other field of human endeavor. People do not begin by asking themselves: "What do I think about this matter?" but instead start off by saying: "What does So and So think of it?" Their "So and So" is their authority, who does their thinking for them, and they take their keynote from him or her. The authority induces their mental states for them.

If these leaders and authorities were really the wisest of the race, it would not matter so very much, although even then it might prevent the development of individuality in the masses. But the worst feature is that the majority of these "authorities" don't know, and know that they don't know, but the people haven't found them out. They assume the manners, air, appearance, etc., of "the real thing," and the people being accustomed to these symbols of authority, and mistaking the imitation article for the real, are impressed by the authoritative utterance and accept the suggestion.

This fact is well known to the classes that prey upon the public. The "confidence men" (in and out of the criminal class) assume this air of authority, and their suggestions are accepted by the people. They are good actors—that is one of the requisites of the suggestionist, and these people understand the law. They proceed upon the theory accredited to Aaron Burr—that remark, you may remember, was that "the law is that which is boldly asserted and plausibly maintained." And so these folk keep on "boldly asserting," and "plausibly maintaining," and find that "it generally goes."

To see a principle in its naked simplicity one should look for its operation in extreme instances. And the extreme instance in this case is the hypnotic "subject" who has surrendered his judgment entirely to the mind of the operator. The "subject" will acquiesce in the most absurd suggestions from the operator and proceed to carry them into effect. And suggestion, you know, is the active factor in hypnotism, the hypnotic condition being only a psychological condition in which the effect of suggestion is heightened.

But one does not have to go to the ranks of the somnambules for striking illustrations, for such are to be found in all walks of life among people who have no individuality of their own, but who seem to live and act entirely upon the "say so" of others. They have no quality of initiative, but must always be told just what to do, and how to do it, by others. These people will accept almost any kind of suggestion, if made by others in an authoritative tone and manner. They do not have to be persuaded by argument, but are fairly driven and ordered to do things by stronger willed persons. They are impressionable and "sensitive," and seem to have no wills of their own. These people are very suggestible, and every day's history records many startling cases of the effect of suggestion through acquiescence on the part of such people.

The key note of this form of Suggestion is a positive statement or command, given with the air and appearance of authority. The secret of the effect is the tendency upon the part of the majority of people to acquiesce in an authoritative statement or command, rather than to dispute it, and the tendency toward thinking "Yes" rather than "No!"

This form of suggestion is to be observed in the highest degree among those who have always depended upon others for orders, or instruction, and who have not had to "use their own wits" and resources in life. Unskilled laborers and the sons of rich men belong to this class as a rule. These people seem to need someone to do their thinking for them, even in the smallest events of their lives, and are most suggestible along these lines. Then the degree of suggestibility along these lines decreases as we ascend among people who have had to "do things" for themselves, and who have not depended upon others so much. It is the slightest among people who have had the ordering of others to do, or who have had to depend upon their own wits in getting through life—the men of marked degree of initiative have scarcely a trace of this form of suggestibility. "Initiative," you know, is a term for "doing things without being told"—using one's own wits and resources—the true "American Spirit" (which so many Americans lack).

The degree of power in giving this form of suggestion depends materially upon the development of will on the part of the suggestor, and also upon his assumption of the appearance, manners, air and tone of authority, the latter requisites being the outward symbols. If one has the Will Power strongly developed, the symbols will appear of themselves as a natural consequence. But to those who have not the developed Will Power, and whose authority is more or less "counterfeit," the assumption of the outward symbols becomes a matter of great importance, and these people devote much study to the cultivation of these outward forms. And these "counterfeit" symbols—the art of the actor—serve their purpose to impress and suggest to the crowd, and their assumers set up a very brave front and obtain a very fair degree of success in the part they are acting—that is, until they come in contact with a man of real Will Power, when they gracefully retire after the first clash of mentative swords.

To those who are negative and who are too susceptible to this form of suggestion, I advise the cultivation of Will Power, which will be fully taught in the later chapters of this book, entitled "Mental Architecture," etc. Nothing but the cultivation of the will will render one positive and impervious to suggestive influences of this sort.

The second line of action of Mental Suggestion is that called:

Suggestion Through Imitation—This form of Mental Suggestion is very common—perhaps the most common of all the forms. Man is essentially an imitative animal. He is always copying the actions, appearances and ideas of others, thereby going to prove his descent from the monkey like ancestors, in whom this trait of character was largely developed. Personally, I believe that those traits of imitation may be traced back to the early days of the race, or before, when animals and men were in a wild state, and exposed to constant danger of attack of enemies. Then a motion of fright on the part of one would be communicated to the others of the tribe, and gradually the trait of instinctive imitation was developed, the traces of which are still strongly with the race, even to this day. We may find instances of this trait all around us. When we watch a tight rope walker, our bodies instinctively sway in imitative motion. When we watch the faces of actors on the stage, our own faces work in sympathy, more or less. And so it goes on all around us, and in us—ever the tendency toward imitation. Children manifest a great degree of this trait and copy and acquire the mannerisms of those around to a surprising degree of detail

This form of Mental Suggestion is very common. People are constantly taking up the suggestion of the mental states, feelings, and emotions of those around them, and reproducing them in their own acts. The majority of people are like human sheep, who will follow a leader everywhere and along all sorts of paths. Let the old bell wether jump over a rail, and every sheep in the flock will do likewise—and they will keep on jumping over the same place, at the same height, even if the rail be removed before the whole flock gets over. We are constantly doing things simply because other people do them. We are constantly aping after others. In our fashions, styles, forms, etc., we are servile imitators. Larry Hehr shows a vest button hung by a thread and all the young apes in the land follow suit. Funny! isn't it?

This law of imitation plays an important part in the phenomena of Mental Suggestion along these lines. Somebody does a certain thing and at once other people take up the suggestion and copy the original actor. Let the newspaper record a certain crime and many others of the same type follow closely after. Let there be a suicide, and many others follow, usually adopting the same methods. Let there be a number of cases of some kind of folly and dissipation, and immediately there is "an epidemic" of the same thing. Let the papers say much about the appearance of a new disease, and at once a number of people manifest symptoms of it. Diseases get to be quite the fashion in this way. The feelings and emotions of the instinctive part of the mind are called into sympathetic action along the lines of imitative suggestion, and physical effects follow shortly after.

Shrewd men take advantage of this tendency of the human mind, and, by getting a few people interested in certain things, they manage to set the fashion, and the crowd follows like sheep. Get people talking about a thing, and the contagion spreads until everybody is interested in the matter. The majority of people are more or less susceptible to this form of suggestion, the degree depending upon their habit of thinking, judging and acting for themselves. The man or woman who has ideas of his, or her, own, is not so apt to be impressed by every wave of popular fashion, style and thought as those who maintain a more negative attitude toward the minds of others. The method of curing an undue tendency toward imitative action is to start in to build up your individuality, and to develop positivity, along the lines mentioned in the concluding chapters of this book.

The third line of action of Mental Suggestion is:

Suggestion Through Association—This form of Mental Suggestion is very common. It is based upon the acquired impressions of the race, by which certain words, actions, manners, tones, appearances, etc., are associated with certain previously experienced mental states. Mental States take form in physical action and expression, as we know. A man feeling in a certain way is apt to express himself by certain actions or in certain words. These actions and words thus become symbols of the mental state producing them, and consequently they produce upon the mind of the person seeing or hearing them the mental image connected with that mental state. And this mental image is calculated to induce a similar or corresponding state in the mind of the person seeing and hearing. So that these symbols are really Mental Suggestions, since they tend to induce mental states.

I wish to remind you that every written, printed or spoken word, or words, is the outward and physical expression of some inner mental state of the person uttering or writing the words. The words are the "outward and visible signs" of an "inward feeling"—remember this always. Mere words, in themselves, have no suggestive value—the value depends upon the meaning impressed upon them by the mind of the person using them accompanied by an understanding of their meaning by the person hearing or reading them. The word "horror," for instance, or "uncanny," has a definite meaning to persons familiar with it. It bears a direct relation to a mental feeling, or emotion, and is the physical and outward expression of the same. One may say the word over and over again to a person who has never heard it, or to one of another race who does not understand the term, and no suggestive effect follows. But speak the word to one who is accustomed to connect and associate it with a definite feeling that they have experienced, and the feeling will be produced, or "induced," if the circumstances of the use of the word be favorable. The word "love," used properly, will awaken in the mind of its hearers feelings corresponding with the term. And these feelings must have been experienced before, either directly or indirectly, before they may be induced by suggestion. Feelings experienced by one's ancestors leave a record in one's subconscious mentality, which may also be induced by the appropriate suggestion.

Personally, words seem to me to be like the wax record of a phonograph. The record is covered with minute impressions produced by the sound waves entering the phonograph. Place this record in its place in the phonograph and start the latter in motion and lo! the minute impressions on the record will reproduce or "induce" in the diaphragm the same kind of sound waves that originally caused the impressions. In this way a word, which is the physical symbolic record of feeling, will produce its associated feeling in the mind of the person hearing or reading it.

And, as I have said, the feeling produced will depend largely upon the understanding of the meaning of the word held by the person receiving the impression. For instance, in the case of the word "love," let us suppose that the term is strongly and feelingly suggested to a number of persons at the same time, and in the same way. You will find that the feeling induced in the one person will be that of love of parents; in another love of children; in another love of husband or wife; in another love of God; in another an exalted affection for some person of the opposite sex; in another the low animal passion for one of the other sex; and so on, each experiencing a feeling occasioned by his or her association of the word with some feeling previously entertained. The same word may induce a feeling of the greatest pleasure in one person, and the greatest horror or disgust in another—the difference depending upon the association of the word in the mind of the two persons.

I have dwelt upon these facts in order to make clear to you that there is no magic power in words in themselves, and that all their force and effect depends upon the associated feeling of which they are the crystallized physical and outward former symbol. The word is the body—the feeling is its soul.

And so it is with the suggestion of appearance, manner, surrounding, etc. Each of these depends for force and effect upon some accustomed association with some inner feeling, which feeling is reproduced or induced by the outward symbol of the thing. We associate certain things with certain feelings, and when we see these things we are apt to experience the feeling indicated. People have been overcome by the sight of a picture, or a scene in a play—a song—a poem—or suggestive music.

And here is where the art of the suggestionist comes into play. He watches closely and discovers that certain words, tones, manners, appearances, actions, motions, etc., are associated in the minds of people with certain feelings and ideas. And so when he wishes to reproduce, produce, or induce in others these ideas or feelings, he simply reproduces the associated physical symbols, in words, manner, motion, or appearance, and the effect is produced. The conjurer makes certain motions with his hands which you have always associated with certain actions, and you feel that the action itself has been performed—but the conjurer omits the action, and you are fooled. The "confidence man" assumes the appearance, manners and actions which you have always associated with certain qualities of character and you feel that he is what he seems to be—but he isn't, and you are fooled. This "play acting" of people is all a form of suggestion, and you are fooled because you accept the symbol for the reality, unless you understand the game. The actor assumes the actions, tones, dress and words of certain characters, and if he is a good actor you forget the reality and laugh and weep, and otherwise feel that what you see is reality, although you really know underneath it all that it is only a play. And all this is mental suggestion remember.

Remember, now and always, that a mental suggestion operates by the presentation of the outward symbol associated with the feeling to be induced. Put the right record in the phonograph and the corresponding sound is produced or induced. Do you see? This law underlies all the phenomena of Mental Suggestion—

understand the law of suggestion and you have the master key to the phenomena.

Oratory, and other forms of appeal to the feeling by spoken words, gives us a typical example of the operation of this form of Mental Suggestion. The orator; the lawyer; the preacher; each uses words calculated to induce mental states, feelings and emotions, in the minds of his hearers. Such a one soon begins to learn the suggestive value of words, tones, and expression. He avoids the use of cold, abstract words, and drifts into the use of those which are symbols for deep feeling and emotion, knowing that these word symbols uttered with the proper tone and expression will induce the feelings for which they stand in the minds of the hearers. The hearers' emotions and feelings are played upon, in this way, like an instrument. The emotion or passion, whether it be love, fear, hate, greed, patriotism, courage, jealousy, sympathy, etc., etc., is awakened by the skillful use of the words, tones, and expression which stand as symbols for these feelings.

If you will remember how you were touched by an address that afterward seemed to you to be hyperbolic and flamboyant—without argument, proof or sense—then you will realize how you were made the subject of Mental Suggestion through association. The skillful salesman operates upon you in the same way. So does his twin brother, the advertising man. The revivalist has this art reduced to a perfect science.

Words—words—words—inciters to action; inducers of feeling; symbol of mental states, and reproducers of mental states—despise them not; sneer not at them, for they have brought down low the mightiest of minds, when properly used. Even when written, their potency is great. Countries have often been made captive by a clever phrase, which when analyzed meant nothing in reason—merely an awakener of feeling. Let me make the catch phrases of a country, and I care not who makes its laws!

The man best adapted to employ this form of suggestion is he who is more or less of an actor—that is, who possesses the faculty of throwing "expression" and "feeling" into words, actions and manner. Good orators, pleaders, salesmen, and others have this faculty largely developed. It belongs to the feminine side of the phenomena, for it has the "charming," drawing, leading aspect, and works by the employment of the emotive pole of mentation, rather the will or motive pole, as in the case of the first mentioned phase of suggestion—that of authoritative statement or command. It operates not by beating down the will of the other person, but rather by inducing a sympathetic rhythm of feeling and emotion, which overpowers his own will, and causes it to act accordingly.

One should ever be on guard against this kind of influence. The best way to escape it, is to adopt the policy of never acting immediately in response to an appeal of this kind. Rather wait until the effect has worn off, and then submit the matter to the consideration of your reason and judgment. Of course, the cultivation of will power will act as a shield or armor, protecting you from the subtle vibrations of this kind, for this form of suggestion is usually accompanied by strong mentative currents from the mind of the speaker. Fence yourself off from a too ready response to sympathetic appeals along the emotional lines. Let the head stand by the heart, ready to prevent its running away with you.

Men should have the reason in the ascendant, not the emotional nature. When you feel yourself being carried off of your feet, by some emotional excitement, steady yourself and ask your mind this question: *is this a mental suggestion?*" The question will tend to bring you to your state of equilibrium. When you know what a Mental Suggestion is, then you wilt learn to recognize them, and be on the lookout for them. This state of mind will act as a strong neutralizing agent for the most skillfully put suggestion. Have your torpedo nets out, no matter how secure you may imagine yourself to be. One caution more—be especially cautious, and slow to accept a suggestion when you are worn out, tired, or in a passive, pleasurable state—that is, whenever your will is resting; or else exhausted. On these occasions, "when in doubt, say No!" You will save yourself much regret by remembering this bit of advice. It is based on a proven psychological law. I have learned this law by bitter personal experience. *Remember it!*

Let us consider the fourth line of action of Mental Suggestion:

Suggestion Through Repetition—This form of Mental Suggestion is quite common, and the study of its manifestations is quite interesting, for it brings into operation a well known psychological principle, which has its correspondences in the physical world—"constant dripping will wear away the hardest stone."

You know the story of the man who told his favorite lie so often that he believed it himself! Well this is a psychological fact. People have started in to make a certain appearance of truth, in words, or manner, by assuming something to be true that was not so. Then they kept on repeating the thing, adding a little here, and a little there, until the thing got to be "a fixed idea" with them, and they actually believe it. And if a person can suggest himself into accepting a false belief in this way, you can see how it will operate on others.

The secret of the operation of this form of suggestion lies in the psychological facts of weakened resistance through repetition of the "attack," and the "force of habit." The first time an unaccustomed suggestion is made, the mind sets up an active resistance; but the next time it is presented, the suggestion is not quite so unfamiliar as before, and a lessened resistance is set up; and so on, until at last no resistance is interposed, and the Suggestion is accepted. You know the old verse:

"*Vice is a monster of so frightful mien,*
That, to be hated, needs but to be seen.
But seen too oft, familiar with her face,
We first endure, then pity, then embrace."

And this rule holds good with suggestions. We first resist them; then endure them; then accept them—unless we understand the law.

The psychological fact involved in this form of suggestion is that impressions upon brain cells become deepened by constant repetition. It is like sinking a die into a cake of wax—it goes deeper at each pressure. The mind is very apt to accept as true anything that it finds deeply impressed upon its records. It has become accustomed to finding these deep impressions only when they have been made by repeated efforts of its own intellect, or judgment, or experience, and so when it finds these deep impressions that have been placed there by repeated Suggestions of others, it is not apt to discriminate. It finds itself "feeling" these things that have been repeatedly impressed upon it. Like the cuckoo's egg in the robin's nest, these illegitimate mental impressions are nurtured as one's "very own."

There is a constant struggle for existence upon the part of the ideas, or mental images impressed upon me. The strong crowd out the weak. And in the majority of cases, the strongest ones are those which have either been impressed in a vivid manner, or else by repetition. The second time you meet a man, you may have trouble in remembering him; but the third time it is easier; and so on, until at last you forget that he ever was a stranger. And so it is with these suggested ideas—you grow familiar with them through repetition; they lose their strangeness to you; and at last you cease to concern yourself about them. A strange thing is generally inspected, examined, viewed suspiciously, etc., but after the strangeness has worn off you cease to exercise the former caution. "Familiarity breeds contempt." and also lack of caution. Suggestion gains force by each repetition. This is one of the fundamental laws of suggestion, and one that all should remember.

If you would take mental stock of yourself, you would find that you entertain a vast number of feelings, ideas and opinions, which you possess simply through this law of repeated suggestion. You have heard certain things affirmed, over and over again, until you have come to accept them as veritable facts, notwithstanding that you possess not the slightest personal knowledge of any logical proof, concerning them. Shrewd moulders of public opinion employ this law, and constantly repeat a certain thing, in varying words and style, until at last the public accepts it as a proven and unquestioned fact.

Many a man has gained a reputation for wisdom, merely because his friends repeatedly affirmed it, and the public accepted the suggestion. Many a statesman has had a reputation built up for him by friendly newspaper correspondents, whose constantly repeated suggestions have caused the idea to crystallize into a material form in the public mind. And many a reputation has been destroyed by the repeated shrugs, sneers, and insinuations of gossips and evil wishers.

Advertisers understand this law, and keep the repeated suggestion of the merit of their wares constantly before the public mind, until it becomes gospel with the people. "If at first you don't succeed," and "Never take No! for an answer," are two axioms very dear to the heart of the man who uses suggestion "in his business."

Do not be deceived by this subtle form of suggestion. Do not imagine that an untrue thing becomes true because it is repeated often. Do not allow your judgment to be lulled to sleep by this drowsy repetition of the slumber song. Keep awake—keep awake! An understanding of this law of suggestion will throw light on many things that have puzzled you heretofore. Think over it a bit, when you have time.

CHAPTER 18

HOW SUGGESTION IS USED

Let us now consider the various forms of application of suggestion in everyday life. They are several and for convenience I separate them into three forms, or groups, i. e., (1) Involuntary Suggestion; (2) Voluntary Suggestion; and (3) Auto Suggestion. Let us now consider the first form:

Involuntary Suggestion.—By this term I mean the use of suggestion involuntarily; without a particular purpose; or unconsciously. We are giving suggestions of words, manner, action, etc., every moment of our lives. And these suggestions are constantly being accepted by those around us. We are constantly influencing those with whom we come in contact, the greater part of the work being performed unconsciously by us. We are acting as living inspiration for some, and living discouragement for others, according to circumstances. Our moods, actions, words, appearance, manners, etc., act as suggestions to those around us. I am not now speaking of the effect of mentative currents, etc., but of mental suggestion, pure, and simple.

A business house is permeated by the personality of its head, and his personal characteristics impress themselves upon those under him, by the means of suggestion. He sets the gait of the place. If he is active, and enterprising, so are the workers employed by him; and if he is careless and shiftless, so will they be apt to be. We affect those around us by our mental attitudes, manifested in action, and they affect us—if we allow them to do so.

Children are quite amenable to suggestion of this sort, being natural imitators, and they soon take on the mental attitude of the parents toward them. If the parent treats the child as being beyond control, the child will respond; if the child be considered obstinate, etc., he will take on the suggestion, and the original trouble will be magnified. People talk before their children, little realizing that the little minds are very suggestible, and are constantly taking suggestive color from those around them. People should endeavor to present to their children only the best, positive, helpful, uplifting, and encouraging mental states. They should avoid giving the child the impression that it is "bad," or "mean," or "deceitful," or "shy," or anything of that sort. The child will be apt to accept the suggestion coming from a source that it naturally looks to for information, and it will be very apt to proceed to act upon the suggestion and make the words of the parent come true. I have heard of children who had become so impressed with their parents' suggestion that they "would come to some bad end, yet," that they had to fight against it the balance of their lives. Sow the suggestive seeds that you desire to sprout into reality—be careful to select the right kind. This subject of suggestion to children can be merely alluded to here, for it would fill a book of itself. I felt impelled to say a few words about it in this lesson, because my experience has taught me its extreme importance.

This is the rule of Involuntary Suggestion: *Our words, actions, manner, tones, appearance, and general personality convey suggestions to those around us, inducing mental states in accordance therewith.*

Therefore, act out only the character that you wish to impress upon the world—and act it the best you know how. The world will connect you with the part you are playing, according to the suggestions thus made—sometimes you will get a better verdict than you really deserve; sometimes a worse one, but in either event, your mental attitude, reflected by your involuntary suggestions, will have caused the verdict, whatever it may be. Therefore, form a correct mental attitude, based upon some ideal of the part you wish to play—and then play it out to the best of your ability. Observe the outward appearance of the part you are playing, for this is what the world sees first, last and all the time—and you are judged by your suggestive "make up," and stage action. Act well your part, for thereupon rests the verdict of the audience.

The second form of the application of suggestion is:

Voluntary Suggestion.—This form of the application of suggestion is manifested in cases in which the suggestion is deliberately and purposely made with the end of impressing other persons. Its manifestations may be grouped into three classes, as follows: (a) Suggestive Treatment; (b) Hypnotic Suggestion; (c) Suggestion in the form of Personal Influence.

By (a) Suggestive Treatment I refer to the practice of Mental Suggestion used as a form of "treatment" for physical ills, or mental deficiencies, etc. The treatments for physical ills come under the term of "Mental Therapeutics," and will be spoken of in the chapter bearing that title. Treatment by suggestion for mental deficiencies, etc., is a branch of science that is rapidly coming to the fore. For some time it was clouded by its mistaken connection with hypnotism, but now that it has been divorced therefrom it is being used to a much greater degree by scientists in all parts of the world. Its principle rests on the fact that brain centers and brain cells may be "grown," developed, and increased by properly directed suggestions, so that one may be practically "made over" mentally. New qualities may be induced, and objectionable ones decreased. Objectionable habits and traits may be eliminated, and desirable ones substituted or newly induced.

The wonders of this form of practical psychology are being unfolded rapidly, and a great era is before us in this branch of science. The broad principle of the "treatment" lies in the fact that the mental states induced by the proper suggestion tend to exercise and develop the portion of the brain in which they are manifested. Hence the theory once understood, and the best method adopted, the rest of the treatment becomes as simple as developing any muscle of the body by the appropriate exercise. I call this form of treatment "Brain Building," by suggestion, etc.

(b) Suggestion in Hypnotism is a subject that I shall merely refer to here, for this is not a manual of hypnotism. Sufficient it is to say that hypnotism is a combination of the use of mentative energy in a certain form, coupled with suggestion. It is a proven psychological fact that in the hypnotic condition, all suggestions have a greatly exaggerated effect, and a suggestion that would scarcely be noticed in the ordinary state becomes a strong motive force to one in the state of hypnosis. In this state the most absurd suggestions are accepted, and acted upon—the most extraordinary delusions are entertained—and the suggestions of future action, or post hypnotic suggestions, are made effective. I wish to caution my students against allowing themselves to be hypnotized for experimental or other purposes. It is conducive to negative conditions, and I heartily disapprove of the practice. I would not allow anyone to hypnotize me, and I would urge upon my students a similar attitude toward "experimenters." The best effects of suggestion may be obtained without hypnosis—the latter is merely an abnormal and morbid state, most undesirable to normal people. Let it alone!

(c) Suggestion in Personal Influence is referred to in other parts of this work, and appears more fully in the chapters treating of Personal Influence, for it belongs to that phase of the general subject.

The third form of application of Suggestion is what is known as:

Auto Suggestion.—By this term is mental self suggestion, or suggestions given by one to his own mind. This is a most interesting and important phase of the subject, and will be dealt with fully in the chapters on Mental Architecture, etc., under which head it falls. It is by auto suggestions that so many people have "made themselves over," mentally, and have become that which they willed to be. Its principles are precisely the same as in the other forms of suggestion, except that the treatment is given by one's self instead of by another person.

The vehicles of suggestion, i. e., the voice, the manner, etc., have been alluded to in other chapters as we proceeded.

An eminent teacher of the use of suggestion in commercial pursuits, in speaking of the effect of suggestion in inducing mental states, says: "You can make a man think with you if you work on his feelings or higher nature, even though you run counter to his ordinary judgment. If in this way you can dazzle his reason sufficiently, you can spur him to almost any action of which man is capable." And this teacher is perfectly right in his statement, although he follows the old "subjective mind" idea and identifies "feeling" with the "higher nature," instead of treating it as belonging to the emotive pole of mentation. And, if I may be pardoned, I would suggest that the above statement would be a little nearer the true state of affairs if he had said: "You can make a man *feel* with you if you work on his emotive mentality," etc.

The teachers of Business Psychology very ably instruct their pupils in the art of suggestion in the process of making sales. They instruct the salesmen to first gain the prospective customer's "attention," then "arouse his interest," then awaken "desire," and then—close the sale. These steps in the psychology of salesmanship apply equally well to the science of advertising, or any other appeal to the minds of people, and are logically correct. The attention once gained, the mind becomes more or

less receptive; the mind once receptive, interest is aroused and a greater degree of receptivity is induced; interest is gradually led to desire, induced by the subtle suggestion of words and the exhibition of the article to be sold; and at last, when the proper psychological state is aroused, the trained salesman gently but firmly gives the positive suggestion of authority, or demand, pointing to the place where the customer must sign his name, thus using suggestion along both the lines of acquiescence and imitation—and the order is taken. Did you ever subscribe to a book at the solicitation of a good book agent? Well, if you did, and will let your mind run backward over the proceeding, you will see how the above rule works in practice. (1) Attention, (2) Interest, (3) Desire, (4) Sale—these are the steps of salesmanship by suggestion; and advertising sales as well. Great is suggestion in business!

I have known salesmen to gently suggest the closing of a sale by handing the customer a fountain pen, placed at the "suggestive slant," at the same time pointing to the space on the order blank, with the "take it for granted" tone and utterance: "Sign right here, please!"—and it was signed.

The largest employers of agents have regular training schools, in which the new agents are given the benefit of the experience of the old hands at the business—and some of these old hands could give a professional suggestionist points on his own science. The agent is told how the different classes of people act, the objections they will be likely to raise, and how the trained agent may overcome these obstacles by clever work, including, of course, an intelligent use of suggestion. The average person would be surprised at the ideas advanced and the knowledge of suggestion possessed by some of these men.

One of these agents once told me that one of the first things he learned when starting to work was that the agent should never permit the customer to take his "prospectus," or sample pages, in his own hands. He said to me: "I always keep the prospectus in my own hands, for if I let it get away from me I will have lost the power of controlling the attention and interest of the customer. He will then have the matter in his own hands, and will have gotten away from me—he will then do the leading, instead of my doing it. I always keep the upper hand of my man or woman. I do the leading, guiding, directing and influencing myself—I keep the controlling gear in my own hands, always."

And, in the science of advertising, also, there is a constant use of suggestion—usually conscious and premeditated. This is taught in the "courses" and "schools" of advertising, and the "ad. men" are well grounded on the subject. The use of the "direct command," as the "ad. men" call it, is very common. People are positively told to do certain things in these advertisements. They are told to "Take home a cake of Hinky dink's Soap tonight; your wife needs it!" And they do it. Or they see a mammoth hand pointing down at them from a sign, and almost hear the corresponding mammoth voice, as it says (in painted words): "Say, you! Smoke Honey Dope Cigars; they're the best ever!!!" And, if you manage to reject the command the first time, you will probably yield at the repeated suggestion of the same thing being hurled at you at every corner and high fence, and "Honey Dope" will he your favorite brand until some other suggestion catches you. Suggestion by authority and repetition, remember; that's what does the business for you! They call this "the Direct Command" in the advertising schools.

Then there are other subtle forms of suggestion in advertising. You see staring from every bit of space, on billboard and in newspapers and magazines: "Uwanta Cracker," or something of that sort—and you usually wind up by acquiescing. And then you are constantly told that "Babies howl for Grandma Hankin's Infantile Soother," and then when you hear some baby howling you think of what you have been told they are howling for, and then you run and buy a bottle of "Grandma Hankin's."

And then you are told that some cigar is "Generously Liberal" in size and quality; or that some kind of cocoa is "Grateful and Refreshing"; or that some brand of soap is "99.999% Pure"; and that some pickle man makes "763 Varieties"; etc., etc., etc. Only last night I saw a new one—"Somebody's Whisky is smooth," and every imbiber in the car was smacking his lips and thinking about the "smooth" feeling in his mouth and throat. It *was* smooth—the idea, not the stuff, I mean. And some other whisky man shows a picture of a glass, a bottle, some ice and a syphon of seltzer, with simply these words: "Oldboy's Highball—That's All"! All of these things are suggestions, and some of them very powerful ones, too, when constantly impressed upon the mind by repetition. They "get in their work" on you.

A writer on the psychology of advertising advises, among other things, that advertisements of articles to eat or drink should contain the words calculated to induce the feeling of "taste" in the minds of the readers. "Sweet," "refreshing," "thirst quenching," "nourishing," etc., etc.—how suggestive they are! And how effective! How do they act? you ask. How? Well, this way—just you read these words: "*A nice, big juicy lemon—tart and strong—I can taste it now!*" Just imagine these words accompanied by a picture of a man squeezing the juice of a lemon into his mouth, and where are you? I'll tell you where—your mouth is filled with saliva, from the imagined taste of the tart lemon juice! Now, isn't it? Tell this to some of your friends and see how it works. I once heard a story of a bad little boy, who would stand in front of a "German band," with a lemon to his mouth, sucking away vigorously. Result: The mouths of the musicians became filled with so much saliva that they could not play on. Exit boy, with Professor Umpah, the bass horn player, in full pursuit, the air being filled with "Dunner und Blitzen!" and worse. Just suggestion!

I have known of dealers in Spring goods to force the season by filling their windows with the advance stock. I have seen hat dealers start up the straw hat season by putting on a straw themselves, their clerks ditto, and then a few friends. The sprinkling of "straws" gave the suggestion to the street, and the straw hat season was opened. Business men understand suggestion. Even the newsboys understand it. The best ones are above asking as the novices do, "Want a *paper*, mister?" or worse still, "You *don't want* a paper, mister, *do* you?" The good ones say, instead, boldly and confidently, "*Here's* your paper, mister!" sticking it under your nose—and you take it. Let me tell you a tale about a "barker" at a pleasure resort in Chicago, several years ago. He was the best I ever heard. Here is the story—it's a true one:

This man was the "barker" or "spieler" for one of the attractions of the place, the "pony ride" attraction. Many were the ponies lined up to carry the children around the ring, for a nickel a ride. The "spieler" would wait until a crowd of children, with or without their parents, would enter the place and then he would begin in the strongest, most strenuous, rasping, suggestive tone: "Ride, *ride* ride! *Have* a ride, *take* a ride, *have* a ride, *take* a ride! Anybody, everybody; *anybody*, everybody! Ride, ride, *r r r r r ride!!!! Anybody* rides, *everybody* rides—rides, *rides*, rides—rides, *rides*, rides—*r r r r r rides*! *Take* a ride, *have* a ride, *take* a ride, *have* a ride, take a ride, *have* a ride? Anybody, everybody, *anybody*, everybody—*ride, ride r r r r r r r r ride! R r r r r r r r r r ride! R r r r r r r r r r r r r ride!*" He would keep this sort of thing up for several minutes, apparently without taking a fresh breath. The very air seemed to quiver and vibrate in the rhythm of his "r r r r r r ide, r r r r r r ide!" And every child within hearing who could raise a nickel would surely *ride!* The word "*ride!*" positively, authoritatively and constantly repeated, was one of the most startling exhibitions of this form of suggestion that I have ever seen or heard. I have heard many imitators of this "spieler," but have never met his equal. Perhaps he has now passed on to some higher form of usefulness—he was worthy of it. He was a master, surely.

I have seen men in bowling alleys caused to make false plays by some bystander suggesting the false shot. The same thing is true in shooting galleries, etc. You have but to look around you and see these, everyday instances of suggestion, in some form or other. Induced feeling, remember! That is the key of all manifestations of suggestion. Look out for it! And, in conclusion, I know of a little boy who exemplified the law of suggestion one April Fool's Day by placing a sign on the coat tail of another boy. The sign read "kick me!" And they did!

The skillful lawyer uses suggestion in his work in examining or cross examining witnesses. He suggests things to a suggestible witness, and coaxes and leads him on to admissions and statements that he did not intend making—sometimes statements that are not strictly correct. Such a one will say, "You *did* so and so," or "You *saw* so and so, didn't you?" etc., the direct statement made in an authoritative manner, causing the suggestible witness to acquiesce. Look out for this confident, authoritative manner, in a lawyer or anyone else. It is calculated to lead one into acquiescence, for man is "an obedient animal," and it is "so much easier to say Yes! than No! when you see that Yes! is expected."

It is charged that police detectives have worked false "confessions" out of suggestible criminals in this way, by keeping hammering away at them until their wills are worn out, and they would say "Yes!" to escape further questioning, like the girl who finally accepted the lover's repeated proposal in order to get rid of him. This firm, decided, authoritative statement or demand, when allied to the law of repetition, has caused much mischief in the world, and many have "given in" to it, to their sorrow. I trust that these warning words will save some other trouble of this kind. When the law is once understood it is comparatively easy to escape the suggestion. The strength in the suggestor of this kind lies in the ignorance of the person suggested. Forewarned is forearmed, in this case.

I have heard of business men who would instruct their clerks to ask questions of their customers in this way: "You like *this* pattern, do you not?" or "This is a *beautiful* shade, is it not?" etc., etc., etc. Do you see the point? The statement is made first, and the question is asked right on top of it. Isn't it easier to say Yes! than No! to this kind of a question? (See there, now, I asked the question in that way, myself, although I had no intention of doing so. I took my own suggestion.)

In this connection I may add that it is a well known psychological fact that, when two persons are conversing, the one standing, or sitting higher than the other, has the advantage of a certain positive attitude or position. And the person seated below the speaker is forced into a relatively passive or negative condition, or position. That is, everything else being equal, the person elevated will be positive to the other, and the one seated on a lower level will be passive, relatively. The raised platform of the teacher, speaker, preacher, etc., has a good psychological basis. And the power that a lawyer feels when "talking on his feet" to the jury seated in front of him is a manifestation of a law that he may not be aware of—but the judge has the best of the lawyer, for the latter must look up to him when he talks.

Try the experiment of practicing the above position with some friend, first one being seated and then the other, and see how you can actually feel the difference between the two positions. The raised position of clerks in the large stores, and the low seats so accommodatingly placed for the customers, have good reasons. If you ever feel that some one is placing you in a negative or passive condition, rise to your feet, and you will feel doubly strong and forceful. This is a little hint that may be worth many times the price of this book to you, some of these days. Look over the foolish things that you have been talked or influenced into, and see if you were not seated and the other person standing, or seated higher than you. This is a little thing—but it works big results, sometimes. Better heed it.

There is a great difference in the suggestibility of persons, some being almost immune from suggestion, while others are so suggestible that they have but to be told a thing in a positive, forceful, confident, authoritative tone and manner, to accept the suggestion, particularly if it be repeated several times. They will likewise readily absorb the suggestions of imitation and association. But I have told you about this elsewhere in this lesson. Study those around you, and you will soon discover the different degrees. The hypnotic "subject" is at the extreme negative end of the scale.

I now wish to call your attention to what may be called "future suggestion," or, as the hypnotists call it "post hypnotism," etc. Future suggestions are like seeds planted in the mind, which grow, blossom and hear fruit at some future time. The hypnotists produce this phenomena by giving the subject, while in the hypnotic condition, the suggestion that at a certain time, either in a few minutes, or hours, or days, he will *do* certain things, or *feel* certain things. But the newer school of psychologists have discovered that these future suggestions may be made in the ordinary receptive state, just as is the case with any of the other forms of mental suggestions, and the result will be the same as that obtained by the hypnotists, in spite of their theories and methods.

I do not purpose going into detail regarding this class of phenomena, because all that is necessary to be said can be comprised in the following two statements: (1) That, generally speaking, all the phenomena of the ordinary immediate mental suggestion may be produced as future suggestion; and (2) that all the phenomena of future suggestion, produced by the suggestor upon another person, may be likewise produced by auto suggestions, that is, by the person inducing suggestions in himself.

Many foolish suggestions are given in everyday life along the lines of future suggestion, and alas! many of them are accepted carelessly, owing to a lack of knowledge of the principle. How many times has it been said to an impressionable young bride, "Never mind, you'll grow tired of him *after a while*," etc. Or to a man, "Wait *until the novelty wears off* and you'll see how sick of the job you'll get." Or, "You'll lose your interest and enthusiasm, *by and by*." Or, "You'll find him out *after a while* and will see that he's not what he seems." And so on—you may add to these instances from your own experience. And too often these suggestions are recalled and have a tendency to cause the person to "make them come true." Many fortune tellers' prophecies have been made come true in this way by impressionable and ignorant people. I have given you a key to this principle now—heed the lesson! If you feel that an attempt at future impression is being made on you neutralize it with a mental *"No, I won't"!* That is the antidote for the bane.

The second principle in the statement made several paragraphs further back—i.e., that all the phenomena of future suggestion may be duplicated by auto-suggestion, or suggestions made by oneself—is true and worthy of consideration. You make up your mind that you must awaken to catch a train at four tomorrow morning and you awaken in time. You have set your mental alarm clock. If you have an engagement at three this afternoon you may set your alarm as follows (talking to yourself, of course): "Now, see here! Remember that you must see Smith at three this afternoon—three, *three*, I say! Remember now, *three, I* say"! And if you impress it sufficiently strong upon your mind, a little before three you will begin to feel uneasy, and then suddenly your Smith engagement will "pop" into your mind from your sub conscious region, and you will reach out for your hat and overcoat Mental alarm clock, remember! That tells the whole tale.

You see, the experimenter giving future suggestions simply sets the mental alarm clock going along the lines of suggestion. He makes the mental suggestion and attaches it to the mental alarm clock—when the alarm goes off the suggestion emerges into the field of consciousness and acts just as if it had been freshly made. That's the whole story in plain, homely terms.

But don't be frightened, you timid people. Remember this, that you will not accept a future suggestion unless you would also accept a present suggestion—the degree of "suggestibility" is the same in both cases. The only reason a future suggestion has the advantage over a present one is that it is more subtle, and people are not as much on guard about future things as they are about things to be "done right now." You will resent a suggestion that you "Do this thing *right now*," while you pay but little attention to the earnest suggestion that "*in a year from now* you will feel so and so about this matter," and dismiss the subject with a shrug of the shoulders, instead of saying, at least mentally, *"No, I won't"!*

The present suggestion is apt to attract your attention the more forcibly, because it is more apparent—while the future suggestion is more "insinuating." But now that you know the facts of the matter you may laugh at them both, and *take the sting out of them* by your little "*No, I won't"!*

And, just one word more. If you feel that you are harboring any future suggestions made on you in the past, but upon which the alarm has not yet gone off, you may kill them by direct self suggestion, or auto suggestions to the contrary. That is, you may say "I *shall not* act upon any adverse suggestions that may have been made to me—I *will* them out of my mind—*I kill them* this moment by the power of my *will*." And at the same time make a mental picture of the suggestion being obliterated by the action of your will, just as the chalk mark is erased from the blackboard by the passing over it of the eraser. Try this plan and be free!

CHAPTER 19

INDUCED IMAGINATION

There is a form of suggestion which tends to arouse activities in the imaginative regions of the minds of people. Of course, the imagination plays a part in all manifestations of suggestion, but in this particular form its action is especially apparent. I call this class of phenomena "Induced Imagination."

The term "imagination," you know, means "the power of the mind to create mental images of objects of Sense; the power to reconstruct or recombine the materials furnished by experience, memory or fancy; a mental image formed by the faculty of imagination," etc., etc. The word is derived from the English word "image," which in turn has for its root the Latin word "*imatari*," meaning "to imitate."

The imagination is creative in its nature and works with the plastic material of the mind. The writers usually make a distinction between what is called "imagination proper," on the one hand, and what is called "fancy" on the other. By "imagination proper" is meant the higher forms of activity of the image creating faculty, such as is manifested in the creation of literature, art, music, philosophical theory, scientific hypothesis, etc. By "fancy" is meant the lighter forms of the manifestation of the image creating faculty, such as the ideal fancies and day dreams of people; the arbitrary and capricious imaginings; fantasy, etc. "Imagination proper" may be considered as a positive phase, and "fancy" as the negative phase, of the image creating faculty.

Imagination in its positive phase is a most important faculty of the human being. It lies at the basis of active mental manifestations. One must form a mental image of a thing before he can manifest it in objective form. It is distinctly creative in its nature, and really forms the mould in which deeds and actions are cast—it forms the architect's plan, which we use to build our life of action and deeds. And, *mind you this*, it is the faculty used in "Visualization," which is spoken of in other chapters. Positive imagination is very far from being the fanciful, capricious, light, whimsical thing that many suppose it to be. It is one of the most positive manifestions of the mind. Not only does it precede, and is necessary to, the performance of objective acts, and the producing of material things—but it is also the faculty by which we impress our mental images upon the minds of others by mentative induction, and by the uses of desire and will. Positive imagination is the mother of "ideas." An "idea" is but "an image formed in the mind"; and the imagination is the faculty in which the "image" (or "idea") is formed. And in proportion to the activity of the imagination, so is the strength of the image or idea. And as is the strength of the image or idea, so is the degree of its power to impress itself upon the minds of others. So you see, imagination, in its positive phase is a strong, real thing. But it is largely with its negative phase that we shall have to deal with here.

You know that your negative imagination, or fancy, may be aroused by outward persons or things. You hear a piece of music, and before you know it your fancy is running along painting all sorts of pictures in your mind, and inducing all sorts of feelings. A picture may affect you in the same way. A piece of poetry, or poem, may lift you out of yourself on the wings of fancy. A book may carry you along in a world of fantasy and unreality, until you forget the actual world around you—have you not had this experience? And, more marked than any of the above mentioned cases, is the effect of a perfect stage performance, in which the world and characters of the play take such a hold upon you as to seem reality itself, and you laugh and cry with the characters of the play. You scowl at the villain, and tremble at the danger of the heroine. You glory in the hero's success, and shed tears at the sorrows and trials of the suffering characters. And you feel these things in proportion that your negative imagination or fancy is called into activity by induction. But remember this—the actors, poet, writer, composer, or artist *created* his effect by the exercise of his or her *positive* imagination; while the effect upon you is induced in your negative imagination. The first is an act of positive creation, while the second is merely a *reflection* impressed upon your mind, by either the suggestion; or the mentative energy of the actor.

In your consideration of the above, remember what I have said about suggestion, in an earlier chapter. Suggestion is merely the presentation of the outward symbol of the inner feeling.

The radical wing of the school of suggestionists pooh pooh at the idea of mentative energy having anything to do with the phenomena which we are now considering. They claim that "suggestion" is sufficient to account for it all. Without going deeply into a discussion of this matter, I would ask these gentlemen: *Why is it that the same words, uttered in the same tone, by two different suggestors, produce widely different degrees of effect?* Also: What is that peculiar personal force that we *feel* when certain persons suggest, that is absent in the suggestions of others? My answer is that the difference lies in the degree of feeling called into activity in the mind of the suggestor—*the degree of mentative energy released by him.* And I think that any careful investigator will agree with me in this, if he will open his mind to all the impressions received during his investigations, instead of tying himself to a previously conceived theory.

The theories of suggestion are not contrary to those of mentative energy and induction, when properly understood. The facts of the suggestionists are undoubted, but they make the mistake of ignoring the mental states of the suggestionist. They think that their effects are produced by suggestion alone, and forget the mental state behind the suggestion which is the real motive force. If their theories be true, why is it that two men using the same words of suggestion, upon the same subject, produce varying degrees of effect? It is because the mental states or dynamic mentation of the two men vary in quality and degree.

In connection with this subject of negative imagination or fancy, I would call your attention to a class of phenomena, along the same general lines, in which certain states of imagination, or fancy, are *self induced.* Nearly all races of men have discovered that there are means possible to people whereby they may produce in themselves abnormal conditions, known as the "trance," "dream states"; "transcendental condition"; etc. And men, from the dim past to the present time, have seen fit to indulge in these deplorable practices. The means by which these states are obtained are various, the favorite methods being the gazing at a bright object; fixing the gaze at the root of the nose; staring at the umbilicus, staring at a drop of ink; inhaling vapors; listening to weird music, etc., etc. Much mock occultism, which is really "psychism," depends upon these methods for its results, manifestation and phenomena. The Hindu" fakirs" and the Arab dervishes indulge freely in these methods, and produce results which while highly esteemed by themselves, are viewed with disgust, horror and repulsion by true occultists of all lands, who regard these practices as harmful, and the phenomena resulting therefrom as bogus and misleading.

And much of the latter day western psychism is also based upon the same practices, and brings about like results. In this connection I would say that some of the practices adopted by some of the "New Thought" people belong to this class. I have seen certain methods advised for "Going into the Silence," in which the student is advised to focus his gaze on the root of his nose, etc., which is the identical method used by Braid to produce hypnotic conditions, and which is also used by the Hindu "fakirs" to produce "trance" conditions. Is it not time that the truth regarding these things should be known?

This "trance" phenomena, whether produced by mesmeric processes or by other means, are abnormal, unhealthy, and undesirable phases of mental condition. I cannot speak too strongly against the encouragement of, and instruction in, the development (I had almost said the "Devil opment") of these abnormal states, either by self practice or by means of hypnotic or mesmeric methods. It is high time that someone should call the attention of the public to the dangers of this so called "psychism." I *know positively* that this kind of "psychism" is not the desirable thing that it is supposed to be. I know, also, that *it is very far from true occult development*. This kind of "psychism," when compared with true occultism, is but as the baleful glare of the moon, as contrasted with the bright, warm, life giving rays of the sun. This false occultism, which is not occultism at all, but merely a negative form of "psychism," has deluded many into its folds, and has led its followers on to planes which are akin to mental quagmires and swamps, following the *ignis fatuus*, or "will o' the wisp" of this pseudo spirituality which is but a negative form of psychism.

These self induced abnormal conditions may be produced by hypnotic methods, by leading the subject into the "deeper stages," which some authorities speak of as if they were "highly spiritual," but which are nothing more than the miserable, abnormal, deplorable "trance" conditions just referred to. These conditions may be produced by hypnotic methods, simply because *any mental state may be so produced*, and not because of any mystic process, or knowledge, or connection. They resemble the so called "sleep conditions" of hypnotism. The only difference is that the operator induces the condition by mental influence, and suggestion, just as he would induce any other mental state—instead of the subject inducing it in himself. It is the same old abnormal, harmful practice, in another guise. And anything that is said against the self induced condition is equally applicable to the operator induced one. They are the same thing! It is all hypnosis, or auto hypnosis.

I shall not describe the conditions at further length, nor shall I give any instructions in the production of them. I consider them essentially harmful, and my object in speaking of them here is to warn off and caution people not to allow themselves to be placed in this condition by experimenters. The practice is weakening to the will, for the reason that it depends upon the tiring of *the attention* by straining the eyes or other organs of sense. Practitioners of mental influence in all ages have recognized this fact and have employed objects calculated to tire out the attention. Bright objects to stare at and thus tire out the sense of sight have been employed; monotonous sounds ending in "*um m m m m*" are used by the Orientals to tire out the sense of hearing by its monotonous and soothing sound; vapors and perfumes and incense are used to overcome the sense of smell—all tending to tire out the will, and to reduce it to a passive, non resisting stage. Then when the will has been rendered passive, or tired, the mind becomes receptive and impressionable, and, in extreme cases, becomes as wax in the hands of the operator.

Let me urge upon you to avoid this abnormal "psychism"—put it away from you as you would a poisonous cobra, for it seeks to strike at the heart of your will, and would thus paralyze your mentality. Beware of all that tends to make you weak. Beware of the claims of "soul development" or "spiritual unfoldment" that are accompanied by these methods, for they are but psychism masquerading as occultism or spiritual development. Remember my test: *"Does this, make me strong?"* Apply the touch stone, and then govern yourself accordingly.

Concluding this, part of the subject, I would say that if any of you are disposed to question the correctness of my above statement, then you have but to examine the types of "psychics" seen on all sides. Are they not all hyper impressionable; excessively sensitive; neurotic; hysterical; passive; negative people? Do they not become as mere psychic harps, upon which the passing mental breezes play, producing weird sounds? Remember, now, I am speaking of genuine psychics, not the bogus psychics, who "are out for the money," and who are a shrewd, cunning lot, far from being impressionable, and in reality using their mesmeric power to impress and influence the credulous persons coming under their influence. I am not alluding to these people, but to the poor, frail willed, negative sensitives, who are as impressionable as the photographer's "negative"—and to whom also the "development" means but the bringing out of impression from outside. I pray you, be a *human positive*, not a *human negative!*

CHAPTER 20

INDUCED IMAGINATION IN INDIA

At this point I wish to call your attention to a feature of the subject that has received but scant attention at the hands of western writers. I allude to the wonderful manifestations of induced imagination displayed by some of the magicians of the orient, particularly of India and Persia. These feats are being performed today in those lands and are equal to any of the wonderful instances related of the ancient Persian or Egyptian magicians.

Without going into an extended consideration of the subject in question I will mention a few of the recorded instances of induced imagination among the oriental people, in order to give you an idea of the degree of power possible to an adept in the practice. One writer describes an exhibition of this kind in India, witnessed by himself. The writer was a profound skeptic, who believed that it was all "hanky panky" along the lines of sleight of hand or similar methods—that is, he so believed until he actually witnessed the demonstration. He goes on to relate that the magician was a native Hindu, of dignified and imposing appearance, surrounded by a number of assistants of his own race.

The magician seated himself on the ground, with several jars, boxes, implements, and other paraphernalia before him. He opened the seance by the production of a number of tiny snakes, which he lifted from one of the boxes, and placed on the ground before him, in full sight of the audience, after allowing the latter to examine the serpents and thereby satisfy themselves regarding their reality. An English naturalist present identified the snakes as belonging to a well known native variety. The magician then began a slow, mournful, droning, monotonous song, the predominant sound of which was "*um m m m m m m m,*" like the droning of a bumble bee or a distant saw mill. The snakes reared themselves up and moved their heads from side to side at the sound of the chant, the magician touching them softly with his wand from time to time. To the eyes of the audience the snakes seemed to gradually grow from their original tiny proportions until finally they appeared as immense boa constrictors, which caused great alarm among the audience, both Englishmen and native. The magician bade the audience remain quiet and assured them that there was no danger—then he reversed the process, and the snakes were seen to gradually decrease in size until they vanished from sight altogether.

The next act was equally as wonderful. The magician placed one of his assistants in the center of a circle described on the sand, and with appropriate gestures and ceremony went through some magical incantation. The boy was then seen to spin around, faster and faster, like a large top, and then began to gradually ascend in the air, still spinning around, until he vanished from sight. Then the magician reversed the process and brought him down from the aerial heights, the boy appearing like a small speck at first, gradually growing larger as he neared the earth, until he stood before the audience, bowing and smiling.

The next act was the placing of some mango seeds in the sand, building a tiny hillock around them. The magician then began his chant and waved his hands over the hillock. In a moment a tiny shoot was seen to appear, and then a little bush which gradually grew up until a mature mango tree was seen, bearing leaves. Then blossoms were seen, and the ripe fruit appeared, which was passed among the audience. Then, reversing the process, the tree disappeared gradually, and at the end the magician dug up the original seeds and showed them to his audience. And, wonderful to relate, the fruit that had been distributed among the people also disappeared.

The concluding act was as startling as those preceding it. The magician produced a coil of real rope, which was passed around for examination. Then he knotted one end of it and then tossed the knot into the air. The rope rapidly uncoiled itself, and the knot was seen away up in the air, and still ascending. When the rope was completely uncoiled, and the end left dangling on the ground as if supported by some hook holding the knotted end hundreds of feet up in the air, one of the assistants approached the rope and took hold of it. At a shout from the magician he began climbing rapidly up the rope, and in a short time disappeared from view, after appearing as a tiny speck in the air. Then at another word from the magician the rope itself flew up in the air and vanished from sight.

This concluded the performance. But here is a remarkable sequel An Englishman present took a snap shot with a pocket camera, just as the boy began to climb the rope. *When the negative was developed there was no trace of rope, boy or anything else appertaining to the manifestation.* Even the magician was absent from the center of the scene and was shown on the plate as sitting down on one side, with an amused smile on his face. This fact demonstrated that which similar tests have also proven; i. e., that *the feats were not really performed at all, but were simply illusions produced by impressions upon the minds of the audience.* In fact, they were examples of induced imagination. I shall give you another proof of this in a moment or two, after I have related a few more instances of this wonderful manifestation.

Another writer, a correspondent of an American paper, relates that he was once on a steamer plying up one of the rivers in India, when, at a stopping place, there scrambled up the side as nimbly as a monkey a native Hindu, clad only in a loin cloth and having a tight rolled red bundle fastened at the back of his neck to keep it safe from the water while swimming from shore. There was nothing about the man to distinguish him from the ordinary fakirs, but he soon showed his quality.

Passing along the deck he picked up a ball of thin rope which was lying there, and, unwinding an end, he knotted it and tossed the knot up in the air, where it ascended, rapidly unwinding the ball, until the whole of the rope disappeared in the air, just as in the instance previously related. Then passing a sailor who was holding in his hand a broken cocoanut shell containing the liquid or "water" of the nut, he lifted the shell from his hand and holding it high up over a ship's bucket standing nearby he emptied the liquid until it filled the bucket, and repeated the process upon another bucket, and so on until twelve buckets had been filled from the half cocoanut shell. Then he picked up one of the buckets filled with the liquid and, holding it in his hand, he caused it to gradually shrink until it completely disappeared. Then a moment later he exhibited a tiny speck in his hand, which gradually grew until it was again the bucket of water filled to the brim with the liquid, which he then poured out on the deck.

Witnessing the strange performance was a young mother with her babe beside her and a young nurse girl several feet away. To her horror the mother then beheld the nurse girl rising a few feet in the air and moving rapidly toward the babe, reaching down for the infant as she glided over it, and then rising high into the air with the child clasped in her arms, until both were lost in the clouds. The mother burst into frantic cries and shrieks and gazed upward; and as she gazed she saw a fleecy cloud appear, which gradually took the shape of the nurse girl, who grew larger and larger as she descended, until she finally reached the deck again and handed the babe to the rejoiced mother. The mother, after clasping her babe close to her bosom, cried out, "How dare you take my child away?" when to her surprise the girl answered, "Why, ma'am, the baby has been asleep all the time and I have not touched him." And then the fakir smiled and said, "Mem Sahib has only been dreaming strange things." It was merely an instance of induced imagination of a remarkable degree of power, produced by the Mental Imagery of the fakir; and his previous feats were also so performed.

But this was only the beginning. The fakir then untied his red bundle, and, extracting therefrom a cocoanut he exhibited it to the passengers, passing it around for inspection. Then, placing the nut on the end of a bamboo stick, and, balancing it there, he commanded it in *Hindi* to spout as a fountain, and immediately a great Jet of water sprang from it, falling over the deck in great showers. He then caused it to stop flowing, and it obeyed; then he restarted it. This is repeated several times. Then he materialized a cobra from the air and caused it to disappear at his command, after he had terrified the passengers with it. Then he materialized several human forms in broad sunlight in full view of the passengers, and afterwards caused them to melt away gradually until they disappeared like a cloud of steam. Then taking up a collection, which was quite liberal, he jumped over the side and swam rapidly to shore.

The natives among the ship's passengers smiled at the wonder of the Europeans present and laughed at the latter's talk of jugglery or magic power, informing them that it was merely an instance of Hindu Telepathy, or Mental Influence, and that those among them who resisted the spell saw nothing except the fakir with glistening eyes showing every evidence of a powerful and concentrated exercise of his Imagination. These feats are quite common in some parts of India, but they are known to be but mental illusions, for all attempts to catch the exhibition on photographic plates have failed, the plate showing nothing but the magician in a state of mental concentration. The magicians have developed the power of causing many persons at the same time to have the illusion of seeing, hearing, tasting and smelling things that have no material existence. It is induced imagination in a developed degree, but differs only in degree from the phenomena more familiar to the Western World.

In this connection I would like to add the testimony and explanation given to me personally by a greatly esteemed friend of mine—a Hindu sage traveling in this country, who in addition to his Oriental learning has received the highest English education and who is "a highly educated man" in both the eastern and western meanings of the term. This gentleman told me that when a youth he had witnessed exhibitions of the kind just related in his native land. At first he was puzzled and mystified by them, but his naturally scientific turn of mind caused him to seek for the solution. He began experimenting, and soon at least was able to classify the phenomena as pure mental illusion. He found that the crowd would gather close around the magician in order to see what was going on, although all were required to keep a certain number of yards away from the wonder worker by the latter's instructions and requirements. My friend found that if he retreated a few yards beyond the outer edge of the crowd *he could see nothing but the magician*, all the "magical doings" disappearing. When he would join the crowd the mystic appearances were again plainly seen. He tried the experiment in several ways, with the same result. Then he tried a riskier one and pushed nearer to the magician than was allowable—and with the same result. In short, the influence was confined to a certain area and the mental influence was doubtless increased by the "contagion" of the different minds in the crowd. My friend tested the well known "Mango feat" and the "Rope disappearing feat" (as related in these pages) in this way and determined that they came well under the rule of mental illusion, instead of being an occurrence defying the established laws of Nature. The testimony of this gentleman corroborated the opinion that I had already formed to that effect, which opinion agrees with that of the best authorities.

In closing this chapter I wish to point out to the students of the work an erroneous idea that has crept into some of the Western works along the lines of hypnotism, etc., and which I shall now mention and explain. The Hindu magicians, or mesmerists, frequently sit in a squatting position during their "enchantments," droning a monotonous, soothing chant, as has been described, and at the same time moving the body from the waist upward, in a circling, twisting motion, from the hips, at the same time fixing their gaze firmly upon their audience. This motion and twisting is merely an accompaniment to the droning chant akin to the motions of the Oriental dancers who twist their bodies in a similar manner in rhythm to the music. The motion is merely a custom among these people and has nothing to do with the production of the phenomena, as all Hindu occultists know and will tell you. In fact, the higher magicians among the Hindus do nothing of the sort, but maintain a dignified, calm, standing position, or the firm "yogi" seat," in which the body is evenly and firmly poised in a position of dignified rest, the hands resting on the lap, the back of one hand in the palm of the other.

All native Hindus understand the above matter, but western visitors jump at the conclusion that this gyrating circling of the body from the hips has something to do with the "power" manifested. And, as I have said, some of the western works on the subject have gone into considerable detail regarding this wonderful "Oriental Magic," which they assert is accomplished because of this twisting of the body. They might just as well point out some physical trick of motion of each leading western hypnotist and assert that the motion was the "secret of his power." I do not think that further comment is necessary in this case. The motions and attitudes, etc., are merely part of the setting of the piece, or possibly bits of "stage business," designed to heighten the impression of mystery. That's all.

I have been informed by an authority whose word is entitled to the greatest respect, and who has spent many years in India and other oriental countries, that the following method is used by these oriental magicians in developing within themselves the power to induce these strong mental images in the minds of those witnessing their performances: The magician starts when a youth and practices mental imagery in his own mind. This process is akin to Visualization, as mentioned by me in other chapters of this work. The magician at first uses his will in an endeavor to form a clear and distinct mental image of some familiar object, a rose, for instance. He practices until he is able to actually *see the thing before him "in his mind's eye,"* just as certain eminent painters have acquired the faculty of "visualizing" the faces of persons they meet, so that they can reproduce them on canvas without further sittings. Then he experiments upon larger objects, and then upon groups of objects, and so on to more complex pictures.

After years of constant experimentation and practice a few of those undertaking the work find themselves able to picture any of the scenes described in this chapter as "feats"—thatis, they are able to clearly picture them in their own minds. And this being accomplished, the magician is able by his highly developed concentrated will to project the mental image into the mind of those around him. It is induced imagination raised to a high degree of manifestation.

The people of the west will not devote the time and attention to the cultivation of such faculties, while the oriental will willingly give up half of his life for the attainment. But, on the other hand, the western man will devote his time to the acquirement of Will Power and concentration in the direction of becoming a ruler of men and a general of finance. Each to his taste and temperament—and neither would "trade" places nor power with the other. They are both dealing with the same force, however, as little as they realize it.

CHAPTER 21

THE OCEAN OF MIND POWER

You will see by reference to previous chapters thatthe term "Telementation" is used by me in the sense of "mentative influence at a distance," the word being derived from the Greek word *Tele*, meaning "afar off"; and the word "mentation," which I use in the sense of "mental activity." You will also remember that the word "mentation" implies activity of the Mind Power, which I hold to be universal in its character. You will also remember that the action of telementation depends upon the production of induced mental states by mentative currents. Mentative induction, you remember, operate's along the same lines as magnetic or electrical induction, that is, a mental state may be reproduced in another mind by mentative induction operating by means of mentative currents.

I have explained how mental states may be induced by suggestion, as well as by mentative currents, and shall not allude to this phase at this place, but shall consider mentative induction in its phase of manifestation by means of mentative currents. This mention of technical terms may seen somewhat "dry" to you, but you should acquaint yourself with the intelligent use and meaning of the terms, for thereby you will be enabled to hold the ideas firmly in your mind. Terms are "pegs" upon which you may hang thoughts and ideas, so that you may find them when you need them. Otherwise they are scattered around in confusion.

In order that you may more fully understand the wonderful phenomena of telementation, I think we would better take another look at the fundamental principle or Mind Power itself. By understanding the nature of the force employed, you may better understand its effect and laws of operation. You will remember that I have postulated the existence of a universal Mind Power, which is imminent in, and manifested in, all form of life, energy and mind. I have also held that all personal manifestations of Mind Power, in ourselves and others, are but centers of power in the great Ocean of Universal Mind Power. You will remember also, that I have claimed that the brain was not a "creator" of Mind Power, but rather in the nature of a "converter" or "transformer" of the universal Mind Power into usable forms and phases. Well so far, we understand the matter. Now let us pass on to the consideration of the mentative currents.

In the first place, the currents must be set into motion somewhere and somehow. Where and how? Let us see! We must see that the mentative currents have their origin, or rather, their initial impulse, in and from the mind of some individual. How? In and from his brain, of course. Why? Because the brain is the "transformer" or "converter" of the Mind Power into usable shapes and phases. What is the nature of the brain's action? Science, as well as the occult teachings, inform us that in all brain processes there is a "burning up" of brain substance and nervous matter, just as there is a corresponding "burning up" of the elements in an electric battery. The process is very similar in both cases.

Both brain and battery "convert" or "transform" an energy already existing in an universal form, which energy cannot be created, added to, nor taken away from. And both use up material in the process. And both generate "currents" of force which are capable of affecting changes in other substances, etc. Science shows us that there is a production or generation of "heat" in the manifestation of Mind Power in the brain. The temperature of the brain rises when it is employed in active thought work, or other forms of mental activity, or excitement. And even the temperature of a tiny nerve increases when it is used. This fact has been fully demonstrated by Science.

What causes the brain to manifest this energy? Mental states! What is a mental state! You know what "mental" means—and "state" means "a condition." So a mental state is "a mental condition" Then upon what do mental states, or "conditions," depend, and why do they vary? Upon the degrees of vibration of excitement of the mental apparatus! Mental apparatus? Must a thing have a Mental Apparatus, before it can manifest mental states, original or induced? Yes! but remember this, *everything* has its mental apparatus, even down to "the atom, and the particles that compose atoms; everything "feels" and "responds to feeling," even among the most material forms—Science states this emphatically; and everything that "feels" and "responds," must manifest desire and will, if only in an elementary way, and must have mental apparatus in order to do this; there is mind, and the machinery of mind, in every atom, and all that is evolved therefrom. This is not my personal statement alone, but is the last word of Modern Science, as voiced by her most advanced advocates.

"Vibration of excitement," I have said. What is a vibration? It is a state of intense, rapid movement of a particle. Science informs us that everything is in vibration, always; and that the differing nature of things depends upon their respective rate of vibrations. And what is "excitement," as I use the term? It means "aroused activity." So, then, there is to be found a condition of "aroused vibrational activity" underlying all mental states? And this aroused vibrational activity communicates motion to the mentative currents, and starts them toward others in whom they induce similar mental states. That is the story in full.

Then if we have a mental state of "aroused vibrational activity" of an individual, how is it passed on to other individuals without direct contact? By mentative currents or waves! What are mentative currents or waves, and how do they operate? Now we are right up to the question with a full understanding of what it means. Then let us answer it in the light of modern Science.

There is a great misapprehension in the minds of the majority of people about "currents" and "waves" of light, magnetism, electricity, heat, etc. They are aware that waves of heat and light, for instance travel over millions and millions of miles from the sun to the earth, and are then felt here, although originating there millions of miles away. They know this fully, but they seem to think that the heat and light are substances that actually "travel" in waves over the distance. But this is not the teaching of Science, which, on the contrary, holds that light and heat do not so travel, but that the original heat and light vibrations set up "waves in the ether." The ether is a suppositious fine form of matter, filling all space, even between the atoms, as well as between the worlds—nobody knows anything "actually" about the ether, but Science has been forced to postulate its existence, in order to account for certain phenomena.

Science holds that these "waves in the ether," once set into motion, travel on until they come in contact with matter capable of taking up their vibrations. When this kind of matter is found, it takes up the ethereal vibrations, and reproduces them in the shape of heat and light. In other words, the original light and heat of the sun does not "travel" to the earth to be then experienced by the latter, but, on the contrary, the original solar heat and light set up the "waves in the ether," which travel along until the earth is reached, when meeting with the proper material they are reproduced or "transformed" into heat and light vibrations similar to those of the original impulse, and we of the earth feel the heat and see the light. Electricity and magnetism are reproduced in the same way. It is just like the sound vibrations setting up electrical vibration in the telephone, which travel along and then are re transformed into sound vibrations again at the other end of the line. When you think of this, please remember that the receiving end vibrations are "induced."

There is something else just as much generally misunderstood. People think that these "waves" actually travel, just as they think that waves in water travel, when we drop a stone in the pond. But they are mistaken in both instances. The force of the motion of the stone produces the elevation of the water, that you call a wave. Then the motion is passed on and another wave is formed. Then another, and another, until you have a series of waves that apparently travel toward the shore. But the waves don't travel. They merely communicate their motion to the particles of the water next to them and a continuous moving effort is exhibited. The real motion of a wave is "up and down" only. Place a cork in the water and then create waves and you will see that while the wave motion travels outward, the cork merely bobs up and down and does not move with the waves. Here is how Science illustrates the motion: It bids you take a rope and tie one end of it to a post or wall, etc., the loose end being retained in your hand. Now slacken the rope a little and begin to agitate it up and down. You will then see a wave motion generated, a series of waves passing over the rope from your hand to the post or wall. And yet you know that the rope itself has not traveled, but has merely moved up and down. It is not a matter of *travel*, but of communicated and induced motion. All waves are alike in this respect—light waves, heat waves, electrical waves, magnetic waves and mind waves. All communicate vibrations, which move on in a wave motion. But these heat and light waves are "waves in the ether," which ether is a material thing. Do I hold that Mind Power waves are the same? Not exactly. I hold that Mind Power is higher even than the finest ethereal substance, and that it pervades the latter. And I hold that we are all centers in a great Ocean of Mind Power. And, therefore, I claim that the mentative currents and waves are really currents and waves in that Great Ocean of Mind Power. And the vibrational activity set up in your mind, my mind, or the minds of thousands, pass on their vibrations to the great ocean of Mind Power, and produce "waves" or "currents" of energy, which travel on until they reach the mental apparatus of other individuals, in which they tend to reproduce the original vibrations or mental states—by induction, remember. In other words, I hold that these "waves" and" currents" are like the ocean's waves and currents—not only *of* the ocean, but also *in* it. My idea of the mentative currents or waves are that they are not only manifestations of the Universal Mind Power, but also that they travel *in the Ocean* of that universal principle. And that great Mentative Ocean is full of currents, and waves, and eddies, and swirls, and whirlpools, and gulf streams, and other forms of activity.

Picture to yourself a great Ocean of Mind Power. If you are unable to grasp the idea, then do the next best thing, and think of this mental ocean as a great sea of energy. Or if you prefer, think of it as the great Universal Ether filling all space. At any rate, the picture must show this Mind Power filling all space, even in between the atoms and even *in* the atoms themselves. Perhaps you had better commence by forming the picture of all space as being empty of all forms and shapes, and containing nothing but this pure Mind Power—an Ocean of Mind Power must be thought of as an energy or force, capable of setting into operation all kinds of manifestations when started. Then think of a tiny center of power being formed in this great Mind Power Ocean—a little whirlpool, so tiny that the strongest microscopes can scarcely distinguish it. Then see countless numbers of similar whirlpools being formed in this Ocean. These little whirlpools we will call centers of power. They combine and shapes begin to appear. Atoms of matter appear, being composed of combination of these tiny centers, which thus become larger and greater centers. Then come combinations of these atoms and the various forms of matter result, for all substances, you know, are composed of atoms, in various combinations; all the atoms, seemingly being composed of little particles called electrons, which seem to be like tiny units of force, but which are attracted and repelled by each other, and seem to have their "likes" and "dislikes," thus showing the elements of mind within them.

And then these shapes and forms of matter become more and more complex, and the centers of power more potent. And the forms of living things begin to appear, mounting from the lowly microscopic cell on to combinations of cells, in plant life, then animal life, and then human life. And each form, as it mounts higher, displays more and more Mind Power. Until at last we see Man with his wonderful mind, as a great center of power. But, remember this always, that all these shapes and forms, and cells, and plants, and animals and men, have as their inner essential substance this same Mind Power principle, of which the Ocean itself is composed. They are Centers of Power in this Mind Power Ocean, but are composed of the same substance as the Ocean itself. You may think of them as vibratory whirlpools of Mind Power if you like—and you will not be very far out of the way if you do. All things are centers of activity and energy, in the Great Universal Ocean of Mind Power. These centers of power are of varying degrees of activity. We will call the strong ones "positive," and the weak ones "negative." So according to their varying degrees of power and vibration, each center is positive to some others, and negative to others still. Each has its degree of positivity. Now think of these centers as human minds, and you will be able to fill out your picture in detail.

Then picture each one of these centers manifesting vibrational activity, and thus converting and transforming the mentative energy from the Ocean of Mind Power. And then see them sending out waves, and currents of mentative energy, which induce similar vibrations or mental states in other centers. Then see some of the strong, positive centers, setting up great rotating currents, resembling whirlpools in the body of the Mind Power Ocean, which extend further and further out from the center, and affect other centers far away from it. If you will examine your picture more closely, you will see that these rotary currents are continually drawing to the centers the things, and persons, and ideas that they are attracting by reason of their particular rate of vibration, while things of different vibrations seem to be comparatively unaffected by the currents. This and other things you may see in your picture as it grows clearer to you. And, in addition to these currents, you see great waves traveling out in certain directions, toward certain objects to which they have been directed. In short, you see all the phenomena of the ocean of water reproduced in this Ocean of Mind Power. You see the picture of the circulation of Mind Power. You see the forming and growing and evolution of centers of activity and mentative energy.

And when you come to look a little closer at your picture, you will see that each one of these centers of energy seems to have two poles of activity, one of which acts in the direction of impelling, driving, pushing, forcing, urging, directing, etc., the action being always "outward"; and the other acting in the direction of drawing, pulling, attracting, coaxing, alluring, charming, leading, etc., the action always being "inward." One seems to be a masculine force, the other a feminine force. One seems to act as Will Power; the other as Desire Force.

These two poles of Mind Power possessed by each center are called the motive pole, and the emotive pole, respectively. I have described their characteristics several times as we have proceeded in these lessons. But, once more, let me call your attention to the meaning of the terms applied to them. "Motive" means, of course, "that which moves; that which incites to action." "E motive" means "that which moves or excites the feelings." You will remember that "excitement" means "aroused activity." So then, "emotive" means "that which arouses the feelings into activity." And the emotive side of the mind always has to do with "feelings," and the "motive" with willing. And the best results always arise from a combination of both feeling and willing—desiring and acting. As in all other things, a combination of the masculine and feminine qualities and characteristics produces the best results. Each has its strong and weak points—but together they are irresistible along all lines or work, physical, mental and spiritual.

And now the broad outlines of our mental picture have been drawn, and the general details filled in. But our picture is more than this. It is a moving picture in vivid action and spirited motion. It will show us the varied phenomena of telementation in a series of moving, acting, realistic, thrilling scenes. And yet all will occur on and in the picture itself, without going outside of it for material. The mental picture contains the material for an infinite variety of action and combination—it is a world within itself. And now, I will set the machinery into operation and show you your mental picture of this Mind Power Ocean and its centers of energy in full motion and activity. Kindly give me your full, attention while I describe the moving scenes to you!

CHAPTER 22

A GLIMPSE OF THE OCCULT WORLD

In the preceding chapter, I have asked you to form a mental picture of the Ocean of Mind Power. Let us now proceed to examine this picture in detail—let us observe the activities and manifestations that present themselves.

In considering this Magic Mental Picture I must imagine that you are a highly developed occultist and that consequently you are able to "see" on what occultists call the "Second Plane." Without going into the subject in detail here (for it forms no part of this present work) I will say that occultists recognize Seven Planes of Life, all of which have their own laws and phenomena. The First Plane is our ordinary material plane, the phenomena of which may be observed by all having their physical senses. This First Plane is the plane of matter, and all of its phenomena is that of matter. All that can be seen on that plane is the movement or presence of matter. Even when we say that we see the manifestation of some force (on this plane), we really mean that we see that force as it produces a movement or change in matter—we do not see the force at all; all that we see is the matter moved by the force.

The Second Plane is the plane of forces, on which operate energy or force in all of its forms. Occultists who have reached the second degree of unfoldment, are able to sense the phenomena on this Second Plane—that is, they are able to witness the phenomena of the forces on their own plane and independent of the presence of matter. To illustrate this I would say that on the First Plane (the plane of the majority of the race) the phenomena attaching to electricity can be sensed only through the agency of the matter in which the electricity operates—you can see material objects moved by electricity, but you cannot see the electricity itself. The same is true of magnetism—you may see the needle drawn to the magnet, but you cannot see the current of magnetic vibrations themselves. You cannot see the vibratory light waves, but you can see the manifestation of light when these waves strike upon a material object.

But, on the Second Plane, those who have attained the second degree, report that the "vibratory waves" of electricity, magnetism, light, heat, etc., are capable of being sensed by them without the presence of the material vehicle. They report that they are able to see the vibrations themselves—for instance, they can see the waves of electricity or magnetism as they pass through the ether and before they reach the material objects which they affect in a way visible to the ordinary eye. They report that even the vibratory waves of the X Ray are visible to them, without the agency of the fluorescent screen used by scientific men before the X Rays become apparent to them. You know, of course, that these X Rays, and in fact also the higher rays of ordinary light, are invisible to the human eye, although capable of being recorded by instruments, photographic plates, etc. And these Second Plane people report that the vibrations of the Mind Power waves, or currents, are plainly perceptible to them. But remember, they do not see "Mind" itself—they see merely the "waves" of energy emanating from Mind.

The remaining five planes, that is the third, fourth, fifth, sixth, and seventh planes, respectively, are subjects that belong to the higher degrees of occultism, and form no part of the subject of this book. I merely mention them so that advanced students may recognize that I am aware of their existence and importance, and am not misled by any erroneous belief in there being only two planes. These chapters belong to the Second Plane teachings, and do not deal with the Third Plane or those still higher. They deal with the "energy" phase of Mind—that is Mind in its aspect of Mind Power. Some day I may write of the "Higher Planes"—but not now.

So, to return to our Mind Power Picture, I will assume that you are able to sense the Second Plane phenomena, and thus actually see the passage and existence of the mentative waves and currents. By giving you the teachings in this way, I will be able to picture the phenomena much clearer than if I held to the First Plane method. I want to show you the forces, themselves, as well as their effect upon material forms.

The first thing that you will see in our Mind Power Picture, is the presence of great clouds of vapory substance, somewhat resembling the fleecy clouds of a summer day, although some of the clouds are much heavier and darker looking. And, you will note the presence of color in these clouds, some of them being a dull grey, and others being tinted like the clouds at sunset or sunrise. It is a beautiful sight, this ever changing mass of colored clouds of all kinds, shapes, forms, and degrees of density. Let us consider just what these various colors mean—for each has its own meaning, the color being dependent upon the degree of vibration and the degree of vibration depending upon the *feeling* which started the waves into motion. I had not intended to mention this in these chapters, but I now see that I cannot omit it without causing a loss to my students. When one gets talking about Second Plane phenomena, it is hard to refrain from telling the story through to the finish.

Let me give you the "Emotional Colors," that you may recognize them as you see them in the picture. Here they are: *Blue* is the vibrational color pertaining to spiritual feeling, and represents the various religious feelings, and emotions, the shade growing lighter as the religious concept rises toward true spirituality. Light blue represents a high, unselfish, spiritual feeling; a beautiful violet representing the highest religious feeling; and a peculiar shade which may be called "ultra violet" representing a spiritual unfoldment of a very high order. *Yellow* is the vibrational color pertaining to the feelings and emotions associated with intellectual power, the shade growing clearer as the intellect mounts to higher conceptions. A dull, dark yellow is the color of the ordinary intellectual state, while the brilliant intellect shows itself in a beautiful golden hue. There is a shade still higher than this, although most rare among the race. I allude to that shade of true primary yellow, which belongs to those who have attained a high degree of true occult unfoldment—the spiritually illumined. The highest occult teachings inform us that the vibrational shade belonging to "Spirit" or the "Essence of

Being," is a pure white light, of an unusual brilliancy. *Orange*, which is a combination of yellow and red, pertains to those possessing the pride of intellectuality, or intellectual ambition, of a marked degree. *Brown* is the vibrational color of avarice and greed. *Red* is the vibrational color of passion, in all of its phases. Dull, deep red betokens the animal passions, and sensuality. A dark bright red betokens anger and hate—when mingled with black it is anger or hate arising from malice, or envy; when mingled with green it relates to anger from jealousy or envy; when shown without the mingling color it denotes "fight" for some supposed right, or ordinary cause. When this color is seen in the shade of *Crimson*, it betokens a higher form of love, the shade becoming lighter and clearer as the degree of the feeling advances in the scale of character. A gross, selfish love shows as a dull crimson, while a higher form of love displays a clearer shade, terminating in a shade approaching a soft rose color when the character of the attachment is on a high plane. *Green* is a peculiar vibrational color, and betokens a number of odd phases of feeling and emotion. A peculiar dull dirty green betokens jealousy or envy. A greyish green indicates deceit, which shade becomes clearer and brighter as the quality of the "deceit" rises in the scale. A bright clear shade of green is seen when there is a manifestation of "tact"; "diplomacy"; "politeness"; "adaptability," etc., etc., *Grey* is a negative vibrational color, which in its dark shades indicates gloom, depression, or melancholy, etc.; and in a bright clear shade indicates selfishness; and in a certain pallid shade indicates fear or terror. *Black* is the vibrational color of hate, malice, revenge, and similar states of feeling.

These vibrational emotional colors, of course, combine, and blend into each other in countless combinations, but the above will give you a key to the same.

The vibrational colors of the two mental poles can scarcely be called colors at all, for their colors and shades are derived from the character of the feeling inspiring them, which gives to them the degree of vibration and color indicating the motive or emotive impulse. But there may be seen a difference even in these two; that is, the emotive pole, in its currents of Desire Force, shows a scintillating effect, as if there were a multitude of minute sparks, or stars in the current; and the motive pole, in its currents of Will Power shows an effect something like a multitude of tiny and minute lightning flashes, playing in the stream or current.

In addition to the shades mentioned above, there is another that should be mentioned while we are considering the subject. I allude to what might be called the "vitality vibrations," which radiate from the living body, and which are caused by the "vital force" which permeates the body during life, and makes possible the running of the physical machinery—some prefer to call it nerve force. These vibrations show no special color, although when near, or in the body, they manifest a faint reddish tint. But when seen away from the body they show a lack of color, like clear water, and resemble the heated air arising from a stove, lamp, or heated ground—that is to say, they look like a colorless, vibrating body of air. The degree and strength of these vibrations depend upon the state of physical health of the person manifesting them.

Now, as we gaze upon our Mind Power Picture, and see moving thereon the shapes and forms of human beings, we may see that each being is surrounded with an "aura" or egg shaped "atmosphere" of these Emotional Vibrations—radiations emanated from his mental states. This aura extends out from the body for a distance of about one yard, and gradually fades away as the distance from the body is increased. And the aura of each person is seen to be colored according to the vibrations belonging to his prevailing mental states.

Each mental state shows itself in its appropriate shade, in the proper combinations, blendings, etc., and therefore, the trained occultist is able to read a person's character like an open book, from these emotional colors. And even though one may not be manifesting any special mental state at the moment, his aura will still be colored because of his prevailing mental state—his "character," as it were. And of course, these vibrations composing the aura of a person will affect those coming in contact with, or near him, or her. That is the reason why we feel the "personal atmosphere" of people when we come near them. Even beyond the visible aura, the vibrations continue in a fainter degree. And so, on our picture we can tell just what kind of people are passing before us—their mental states are revealed by the Emotional Colors.

And now we shall see how people affect others. We see one man approach another. The degree of dynamic positivity of the first man is superior to that of the second, and we see, as we watch, that the coloring of his aura gradually interpenetrates that of the weaker man, and the coloring of the latter's aura gradually grows to more closely resemble that of the first man. We may watch the process, and thus become aware that the following things are happening, *viz.*, the mental states of the first man are inducing similar feelings and emotions in the second man, by means of the currents of mentative energy that are flowing toward him. The first man is making no effort to impress the second man, but being the more positive his "magnetism" affects that of the other man and induces similar states. The second man "takes on the states" of the first man, as we may see by the change in coloring. This is the way that people unconsciously affect other people, and the latter are unconsciously affected. Simply a case of unconscious mentative induction, you see.

The second man moves on, feeling more depressed, or elated, as the case may be, by reason of his contact with the first man, and also carrying away with him a little of the other man's general feelings, and "character." This second man, a little later on, meets another man, and we may see how this new man affects the "second man" by the suggestion of his manner and words. He does not seem to be sending out such strong currents as the man first spoken of, but his outward symbols of voice, words, manner, etc., are well acted out, and we soon see our "second man" having mental states induced in him by suggestion. You have now seen two stages or phases of mentative induction.

Our positive man has gone on his way, and soon he spies another man whom he wishes to influence in certain matters. Watch him now, and you wilt see something interesting. The positive man's aura seems to be disturbed, and great tongues of color seem to leap from it, and lap around the other man, the whole process resembling the action of tongues of flame or fire. These tongues of Mind Power wrap themselves all around one other man and some seem to scintillate as they, manifest the action of fairly "pulling" him toward the positive man, while others seem to be beating upon him like a rain of tiny flashes of lightning—the one is the play of Desire Force, and the other the action of Will Power. This gives us a good illustration of personal influence in an interview, or a phase of personal magnetism.

As the action grows more spirited, you may see the Will Power of the positive man darting out in straight, sharp flashes, like great sparks from an electric battery, and you may see the process by which he beats down, and neutralizes the Will Power of the weaker man, until he seems to exhaust it and take it captive, and the man acquiesces in the statements and demands of the stronger willed man. This process is hastened by the fact that the Desire Force of the weaker man has become so impressed by the stronger will that it becomes dazed, or fascinated; the effect being strongly increased by the Desire Force of the stronger man by setting up mentative induction a corresponding vibration in the desire pole of the weaker man. And a fourth element in the attack is that the strong Desire Force of the strong man also tends to "pull" the will of the weaker one toward it and away from its natural mate, its own desire pole. This is a case of a combined, determined attack. It is true that the positive man may not know a single fact regarding Mind Power, but he has learned the process of affecting and influencing others, and bending them to his will and desire, although he is ignorant of the scientific explanation of the process. Every positive dynamic individual understands this, instinctively, and his knowledge increases as practice gives him more confidence in himself.

These people pass from the scene, and we may see in their place men and women "charming," "alluring," and "drawing" others by reason of their Desire Force operating along the lines of so called "love," but which is but little more than selfish animal passion, in some cases grosser than that manifested by the animals, because it is abnormal in its manifestations, and inordinate in its demands. We see much of this in our picture but we notice here and there that some people seem able to repel these attractions easily, and are not affected by the currents of desire. Their general mental state is so different that great resistance is interposed, and the attacking current is deflected and defeated, even without the use of a great effort of the will. You see many instances of this in all forms of mentative influence. "Like attracts like" in this mentative work, and those who are attracted are generally those whose mental states correspond to a great extent with those of the person affecting them. There are, of course, exceptions to this rule, owing to ignorance and lack of experience, coupled with confidence and trust—but the rule is true in general.

Passing before you in the picture, you see preachers influencing their congregations. You see the great currents of mentative energy rolling over the hall, or church. The congregations being in a receptive and passive attitude, with wills relaxed, they actually draw out the force of the preacher. You may judge just what grade of religious feeling the preacher is pouring out, by examining the shade of his "blue emotional color." You will be apt to see a better shade among the poorer churches and denominations, and a very repulsive dark purplish blue among the "fashionable" churches, as a rule. You will notice also the waves and currents arising from the congregation, which establishes the "atmosphere" of the church, and which will be immediately felt by a stranger entering its doors. You will see similar things at the theaters, and political meetings, and all gatherings of people, the color always giving you the key to the character of the meeting, and the people attending it.

Next you see the hypnotist and his "subject" in a public hall. You will notice that the hypnotist's Emotional Color is not attractive. You will notice the neutral grey color of the aura of the subject, who seems to have squeezed every bit of his own mental states out of him—he is a "professional subject," and is a slave of the "professor." You will see the hypnotist's magnetism pouring into the subject, and filling his mind completely. You will see how the will of the hypnotist supplants the will of the subject, and dominates him absolutely. You will notice that both the desire pole and the will pole of the subject seem to show no energy of their own, but are moved entirely by the personality and mind of the operator. This is an extreme case, of course, but it better illustrates the phenomenon. And, by its effect upon the audience, you may determine just how far advanced mentally they are, the color giving you the cue.

Of course, Mental Suggestion is playing its part in all of these cases, but we cannot see that because it is not a current or wave, but is merely the operation of outward symbols in the direction of inducing mental states in others—we may see the induced mental states, but can learn the nature of the suggestion only by watching and listening at what is said and done. I am mentioning only a few of the many cases that you are witnessing in the picture, but these few cases will illustrate the different phases of the principle and operation of the force. But all of these cases have given you merely an illustration of telementation at "short range"—now let us proceed to examine the instances of the operation of the same force at "long range," in all of its many and wonderful phases.

Before doing so, however, let us take a quick look at the "mental atmospheres" of the towns, cities, and villages, as well as of the buildings, localities, etc., passing before us on the picture. This is most interesting and instructive. In the first place, you will notice the great clouds of mentative energy permeating every place, and every corner, each showing its own shade of vibrational color, indicating the vibrations arising from the prevalence of certain mental states. I have spoken of the causes of this in a previous chapter, and shall not repeat the details here. You will remember that I have explained to you how the various currents of mentative energy, of all kinds and degrees, come in contact with each other, and often blend, combine, or else act in the direction of neutralizing each other's force. Currents of a similar degree of vibration harmonize, and form combinations, or blendings. Opposing vibrations in currents tend to antagonize each other, and neutralize each other's force.

In this way are the "mental atmospheres" of places formed. You may see them in the picture.

But, you may ask, why do these clouds persist after the person has sent them forth? The answer is that force once set into motion persists for a greater or lesser time, depending upon the intensity of the original impulse. Just as the light of a star, or rather, its light waves, exist and move on centuries after the star has ceased to be; just as the heat vibrations continue in a room, when the producing cause has been removed; just as odors remain when the cause moves away; so do the mentative vibrations, and their corresponding thought forms, continue long after the original feeling has passed away—yes, for years afterwards, in some cases.

In this way places, houses, stores, etc., maintain "atmospheres" imparted by the vibrations of people long since moved away, or passed away. Stores are "unlucky" because of the negative mental states of some people who have occupied them. Houses are "haunted" by reason of the vibrations arising from intense desire or feelings, or horror and fear of some one participating in a crime, either as criminal or victim. The "atmospheres" of prisons are quite noticeable even to the ordinary visitor, who feels the vibrations with which the place is saturated. The atmosphere of places of low pleasures is equally noticeable. I know of a place of this kind in which the vibrations continued for years after the original tenants had departed and the building had been used for business purposes. Hospitals have a very depressing influence upon the majority of people. Of course these negative effects can be removed by mentally "treating" the place or room, and sending forth streams of mentative energy of a positive stimulating character.

On the other hand, the presence of an active, energetic, successful man, or set of men, in a place, will permeate the place with positive vibrations that will stimulate all who abide there. I have in mind a certain large office building in a large city, which is filled with these vibrations, originally arising from a few leading men who built and occupied it, and then attracted to themselves others of the same kind, the result being that the combined influence now renders the place an "inspiration" for those having offices in it. I have heard people say that after moving in that building their business doubled itself, and their energy increased in the same proportion. There is a law underlying these things, and if people understood it they would take advantage of its positive sides, and avoid its negative phases. I think that I have given you a good strong hint in this direction.

These great clouds of vapory manifested Mind Power, often constitute what are called "Thought Forms," which I shall proceed to describe to you. Follow my explanations of these things as they appear on the picture, please. These thought forms are really "feeling forms" remember, although I use the more familiar term. These thought forms although all generated or "created" in the same manner differ very materially in their characteristics, and details. Let us consider some of these details and characteristics, and "appearances." By "appearances," I mean of course, their appearance to those who can sense on the Second Plane. But whether one can so sense, or not, the effect of these thought forms manifest upon them just the same. It is not necessary to "see" a thing in order to "feel" its influence. But, you understand this, of course, from what has been said already. The most common form is that of a series of undulating waves, or ripples of a vapory cloud like substance, passing out from the mind of the person experiencing the mental state originating them, the waves manifesting a ring like form, moving out in every direction from the common centre, just as do the rings caused by a stone having been dropped into a pond. The distance traveled, and the rate of speed manifested, depends upon the intensity of the emotional impulse. The speed diminishes according to the distance traveled, but long after the actual motion seems to have ceased, there exists an almost imperceptible motion that causes the outer wave to drift on, in a lazy, listless manner.

Another variety of thought forms manifest like a volume of smoke being blown from the lips of a cigar smoker. Such forms pour out in long streams, then spread out and broaden, although maintaining the direction originally imparted to them. This form arises when the mental state arises directly in connection with some other person or thing, and when the attention of the mentator is centered, consciously or unconsciously, upon that person or thing. In this case, the motion of the thought form is in the direction of the person or thing being directly considered by the mentator. Akin to this form, is a series of forms resembling a puffing forth of smoke from a huge smokestack, great "puffs" of mentative thought forms being sent out in a certain direction, as the jerky repeated mentative impulses are originated and manifested in the mind of the mentator.

Other kinds of thought forms pour forth steadily, but lazily, in the direction of the object thought of. Others, still, are ejected in all directions from the mentator, like the steam escaping from the lid of a tea kettle which is being lifted by the force of the steam within. Still another form appears like a "streak" of light flashing from a mirror held in the sun. Certain particular forms of Will Power manifest as vivid lightning flashes. Other forms travel and seem to enfold the object thought of, and which being impelled by the strong desire of the mentator act as if they were trying to "draw" back to him the objects desired. In fact, that is exactly the nature of the action of this class of thought forms, the effect produced depending, of course, upon the positiveness of the mentator, and the strength of the desire. The effect of course also is materially influenced by the degree of positiveness of the person affected, and other attractions which prevent the yielding to the "pull" of Desire Force.

In the case of a strong desire on the part of the mentator, provided that the "ruling passion" is being manifested day after day, there appears a combination of thought forms which resembles a huge octopus of dense structure, with enormous vapory tentacles or arms reaching out in all directions seeking the thing desired, and endeavoring to draw it back to its centre. In the case of a high aspiration, backed by a strong and active will, this combination will appear tinted with a color and shade of vibrational color corresponding with the character of the mental state, while, in the case of a low character of desire the darker colors will likewise manifest themselves.

Still another kind of thought form acts as if it were trying to push back the object in some particular direction, while others seem to hold back the object. In both of these cases, the action and direction of the thought form depends upon the nature and character of the desire or will of the mentator at the time of the conception of the mentative current. A most peculiar kind of thought form appears when the mentator is desirous of obtaining information regarding some certain subject; and is earnestly sending his Desire Force in all directions in order to draw it to him, the mentator generally being unconscious or at least in ignorance of the nature of the actual process. In this case the thought form maintains a thin connection with the mind of the mentator, and darting here and there it attracts to itself the thought forms emanating from the minds of others, which may happen to contain the desired vibrations. It even reaches out to the presence of other mentators, and absorbs the mentative vibrations emanating from them, and literally "steals their ideas," if they have not properly guarded the same by their will.

In this connection, I may call to your attention the well known fact that persons thinking along the same lines, although in different parts of the world, are often brought in close *rapport* with each other in this way, as many people know by their own experience. In this case, the thought forms seem to act as a sort of "Mentative Wire;" conveying the vibrations from one mind to another. Very much akin to this last mentioned kind of thought form, is another which occurs in instances of direct telemental communication between persons. In this case the thought form proceeds in a long straight line, from the one mind to the other, and then acts as a "direct wire" conveying the mentative currents, or vibrations, from one to the other.

There is another variety of thought form that spreads out in gradually widening sweeps, the thought form having a rotary motion. The sweeps are in a constantly widening circle, and reach out further and further each day, according to the impulse imparted to them by the mentator. But the most peculiar feature of this thought form is a strange movement towards its own centre, by which it "sucks in" all that it attracts to its vortex. This phase is manifested by men of strong positivity whose enterprise and schemes are spread over large areas, and who set themselves up as centres of these mentative "whirlpools," and draw to themselves all that come within the sweep of their influence. They make things "come their way," in fact.

I have described but a few of the manifold appearances and varieties of the thought forms that you see before you in the picture. But we shall consider a few more in detail as we proceed with the subject. In thinking of these thought forms always picture them as, having shape and form, like any material substance, for by so doing you will better realize the nature of their workings. Some thought forms indeed are not only "things," but become so infused by the intense desire and will of the mentator that they become almost like "living forces." Such thought forms carry the characteristics of the mentator to such an extent—are infused with his "nature" to such a degree—that when they are felt they seem almost like the actual presence of the mentator himself, that is as if he were present urging his claims or statements in person.

Such cases are of course rare, so far as conscious production is concerned. They may be good or bad. A strong desire on the part of a dying person has often caused an actual "appearance" by a loved one or friend, although the soul had not left the body. And in cases of dire distress or need people often so "draw" upon those who care for them that the latter will send to them a powerful thought form of help, advice and assistance. Trained occultists can do this voluntarily, and consciously, but very few others have reached this stage.

CHAPTER 23

SELF PROTECTION

And now let us return to the consideration of the various forms of the practical operation of telementation. You will of course realize that even in the case of mentative influence in personal interviews there is a passage of mentative currents and a manifestation of telementation. The distance between the two minds is slight, but the principle in operation is precisely the same as when the distance is hundreds of miles—and the process is identical.

And you will remember that when I speak of Desire Force, and Will Power, I am speaking of the force of the respective Two Poles of Mind Power—both of these forms being but phases of the same energy or force. So do not imagine that there are three distinct forces—there is but one force, and that is Mind Power, of which Will Power and Desire Force, respectively, are but manifestations, the difference depending upon the two respective poles of force, the motive and emotive, respectively. I trust that you will remember this.

I will divide the manifestations of telementation into two general classes, *viz.* (1) Direct telementation, that is, that use of the Force with the *direct purpose of influencing a certain person or persons*; (2) Indirect telementation, that is the use of the Force with only a *general purpose* of effecting the desired result, *without special direction toward any particular person or persons*. We will now consider these two classes of telementation, in their different phases.

First in considering the subject of direct telementation, we see the cases in which personal influence is exerted in personal interviews, and under circumstances in which the mentator and the other person or persons are in close contact—that is, within each other's sight. Under this sub class falls the phenomenon of fascination, personal magnetism, personal influence, persuasion, charming, inducing, etc., etc., in all of their many and varied phases. We have seen these several manifestations as we have proceeded in these chapters, and we need not stop to further consider them at length in this place. You understand that the effect is caused by the outpouring of the Mind Power, in the forms of Will Power and Desire Force, to the end that similar mental states are induced in the minds of others and the desire or will of the mentator is satisfied, to a greater or lesser degree, or completeness according to the circumstances of the case.

The second sub-class includes those in stances of telementation at a "long range," which produces the phenomena of mental influencing, will projection; and other forms of influencing, under many names and disguises, including, of course, the employment of the force for the benefit and advantage of the person "treated" or influenced, as well as the repulsive and deplorable uses alluded to as having been practiced by all peoples in all times, for the purpose of injury to others and selfish profit and advantage to the users.

This includes what is known as White Magic, or use of the force in an unselfish and justifiable way, and with worthy ends in view; and Black Magic, or the use of the same force for unworthy ends, and in selfish and unjustifiable ways. But, as I have said in the early part of these lessons, this force is like any other great natural force, and is capable of being used for good or for evil, according to the moral state of the user. It is true that the Black Magician is always entangled in his own web, sooner or later, and falls a victim to the forces he has aroused—but that does not alter the statement that I have made.

In this form of telementation, the mentator usually concentrates upon the person or thing that he wishes to affect, and then consciously, and by the use of his will, he sends to that person or thing a current or currents of Desire Force or Will Power, or both. It is known to occultists that the degree of effect so produced depends largely upon the degree of concentration employed by the mentator. The degree of concentration depends upon the will, and is manifested in the form of attention. The usual plan is to use the concentrated will to form a clear mental image of the person or thing to be affected, and then to proceed as if one were in the actual presence of the person. The clearer the image, the greater the degree of concentrated will employed, and consequently the greater the degree of the projecting power of the current. Underlying all the phenomena of "adverse treatments," witchcraft, etc., etc., is the same form of telementation. But, here, I wish to say an important word, and that is that the generally claimed effect of these forms of adverse influence is greatly exaggerated, and all real occultists know that the principal reason of the unquestioned effect of this power lies in the mental state of belief, faith, and fear of the persons affected. That is, if one "believes" or "fears" that another has the power of adversely influencing or affecting him, then the effect will depend largely upon that degree of faith or fear.

The persons who are affected by "adverse treatments" or "witchcraft" or similar forms of adverse influence, invariably "believe" and "fear" that these influences are effective against them. By their mental states they render themselves negative, and receptive to the influences directed against them. This is an occult truth, and one that should be made widely known. It is the "antidote" to the "bane" of "adverse treatments" of which we hear so much in modern times, as well as in ancient history, under various names. If people would only assert their individual power as centers of power they would surround themselves with such a positive protective aura that the waves of adverse vibrations would beat against them without ever reaching within their mental structure. We hear of many cases of people being "treated" in this way, in these latter day of pseudo occultism. We hear of "treaters" making "denials" regarding people, and thus sending them adverse telementation. These people will assert, and work themselves up, into a corresponding feeling of "I deny that So and So is well; or prosperous, etc., etc.," some even going so far as to "deny" that the other person "*is*." You may, imagine the effect of currents of this feeling reaching a mind rendered negative by "belief" and "fear" that the other person can so affect them. The suggestion of the "fear," or "belief" (and that is just what it is, "suggestion") renders the mind of such a person a fit receptive agent for the adverse" treatment." I tell you, if you will but assert your Individuality, and assume the fearless attitude, you will be able to laugh in the faces of these "adverse practitioners" of Black Magic, for that is just what it is, no matter how much they may try to disguise it by pious names.

These modern "adverse treatments" are nothing less than forms of the old witchcraft which so worried our great grandfathers; nothing more than the Voodoo practices, or "conjure business" that so affrights the poor negro to day. The principles are the same—the practice is the same—and the practitioners are the same at heart—black hearted Black Magicians, all of them, and subject to the same inevitable fate which overtakes all such people, no matter how high their pretenses. The physical and material agencies used by the Voodoo men, and the "witches" of old,—the wax images, and pith balls, and all the rest of the tom foolery, were nothing but the agencies upon which the will of the practitioner could concentrate—an aid to concentrated will. Of course, besides, they served to terrify their victims by suggestion. I do not deny that material objects "take up" and absorb the "magnetism" of the people, good and bad—for that is a well established occult truth, and the efficacy of "charms," sacred relics, etc., etc., depends upon this fact, together with the aid of suggestion. But *I do say that all the charms in the world—all the witchcraft and Voodoo material agencies—can produce no other effect than is allowed them by the minds of the persons sought to be affected. Fear and belief determines the degree of receptivity to such influences*. The *Kahuna* or "prayer man" of Hawaii prays people to death, unless they buy him off—*but it is the fear and belief on the part of the people that render his work effective*. If they would say "scat" to him, mentally, by asserting their individuality as mentative centers, they would be absolutely immune. I need not recount the many instances of this kind of telementation, for adverse purposes, for the pages of history are full of them, although the historians sneer at the whole subject, deeming it a myth, and laughing over the credulity of our forefathers, notwithstanding the fact that "witches" and "conjurers" went to the scaffold and stake, confessing their guilt. It is all very well to attribute it all to the "imagination" of the persons affected, but why do they not tell us a little about this strange "imagination" that produced such real effects upon people. The cause may have been "imaginary" but the effects were certainly very "real."

I will relate but one instance, which will serve as a type of these forms of telementation. It is cited by an old German physician. He relates that he was consulted by a farmer who complained of being disturbed at night by strange noises which sounded like some one striking iron. The noises occurred between the hours of ten and twelve every night. The physician asked him if he had any enemy he suspected of thus influencing and annoying him. He replied that there was no one but an old village blacksmith, an old enemy whose power he feared, and who lived several miles from the farmer. The physician bade him return the next day, and in the meantime visited the blacksmith, and asked him what he did between the hours of ten and twelve at night, accompanying the question with a glance of a strong will and power. The blacksmith, now somewhat frightened, replied. "*I hammer a bar of iron every night at that time, and all the while I think intently of a bad enemy of mine, who once cheated me out of some money; and I will at the same time that the noise shall disturb his rest.*" The physician ordered him to desist, and at the same time made the farmer pay over the money due the blacksmith, and there was no more trouble. If you wish further instances of this sort, turn over the pages of any old book which treats upon the "Witchcraft Delusion," and note the similarity. But one instance is enough to illustrate the matter—they are all "cut out of the same cloth." You will note the two necessary elements present in every case *viz*., (1) the use of the force by one person; and (2) the belief or fear, or both, on the part of the second person. Now you have the whole story.

And, also remember, this that I have told you—the same Force that is used in such cases for evil purposes, may also be used, and *is* used for the most beneficial and worthy purposes. The "treatments" for good things practiced by the "practitioners" of the various schools of Mental Science, and other New Thought people are along the lines of direct telementation. People have been encouraged, helped, healed, reformed, and otherwise aided and benefited by telementation. Do not lose the recollection of the good in considering the bad. The good belongs to the phase of

White Magic, and its use can result only in good to the practitioner of it; whereas the Black Magician must reap the whirlwind of the wind that he has sown. These things "come home to roost," always, according to their kind—and they bring their friends home with them.

In addition to the selfish and evil use above mentioned, there is another selfish use of direct telementation that is quite common of these late years. I allude to the use of mentative influence, by telementation for the purpose of influencing people to fall in with the schemes and plans and enterprises of the mentator. The principle involved is the same as in all these "treatment," good and bad. And the practice is the same. The mentator forms the mental image of the other person, and then floods him with currents of Desire Force, or Will Power, or both, at the same time earnestly willing and desiring that he will do as the mentator wishes him to do. The mentator usually uses his will to make the other do this in the mental picture—in imagination—thus forming a mental matrix, to which he then tries to make the other conform. This is a form of "Visualization," of which I shall speak presently. Of course, this practice like any other of the kind, may be defeated by one asserting his individuality and will.

Of course, you will not feel disposed to put into operation many of the methods herein described, yet, from your very acquaintance with what has been mentioned in these pages, you will be enabled to *see* the operation of the principles in the everyday life around you. You will see them in operation on every side, now that you are familiar with their laws of operation. And you will find yourself instinctively guarding against its influence, just as you would guard against a threatened physical blow. And you will be surprised, and perhaps pained sometimes, at seeing people trying to influence you in this way, whom you would not have suspected of doing so. On the whole, you will be a much wiser and stronger man or woman by reason of the information herein given you. And you will have the advantage of knowing how to resist, defeat and dispel the adverse influences that may be used to influence you. Remember the assertion of the positive will, and the use of the positive denial!

The person wishing to influence another at a distance, just as he would in the case of a personal interview, forms a mental image of the person whom he wishes to influence, and then proceeds just as if the person was actually before him. I know of at least one teacher who advises his students to "treat" prospective customers, and others with whom they expect to have dealings, or relations, as follows: "Imagine your prospective customer, or other person, as seated in a chair before which you are standing. Make the imagined picture as strong as possible, for upon this depends your success. Then proceed to 'treat' the person just as you would if he were actually present. Concentrate your will upon him, and tell him just what you expect to tell him when you meet him. Use all of the arguments that you can think of, and at the same time hold the thought that he *must* do as you say. Try to imagine him as complying with your wishes, in every respect, for this imagining will tend to 'come true' when you really meet the person. This rule may be used, not only in the case of prospective customers, but also in the cases of persons whom you wish to *influence in any way whatsoever*."

Now, all this is very plain to the student of this book, for the principles employed are familiar to its readers. The result of a practice like the above would undoubtedly tend to clear a "mentative path" in the other person's mind, and make easier the effect of a subsequent interview. For the other person would be thus accustomed to the idea, thought or feeling, and the work of clearing away the mental underbrush would be done in advance. But, fortunately for us all, we have the antidote for this bane, if we have acquainted ourselves with the underlying principles of the subject. So important do I regard the subject of self protection in connection with direct telementation, that I have thought it well to add to this chapter the following general rules which I trust you will read carefully, and with which you should fully acquaint yourself. The bane is well known—the antidote is known to but few. For this reason I attach much importance to the study of the latter at this place.

In connection with the following rules and advice you should also acquaint yourself with what I have said elsewhere regarding protection against suggestive impressions; and also with my advice regarding the cultivation of a positive mentality; and with the chapters which take up the subject of establishing a mentative center, etc. Here are the rules:—

I. In the first place, steady your mind, and calm your feeling. Then pause for a moment, and say the words "*I Am*," calmly and forcibly, at the same time forming a mental picture of yourself as a center of Force and Power in the Great Ocean of Mind Power. See yourself as standing alone and full of power. Then mentally form a picture of your aura, extending about a yard on all sides of you, in an egg shaped form. See that this aura is charged with your Will Power, which is flowing outward, repelling any adverse mental suggestions that are being sent to you, and causing them to fly back to the source from whence they came. A little practice will enable you to perfect this picture, which will greatly aid you in creating a strong positive aura of will, which will prove to be a dynamic armor and shield. The affirmation, "*I Am*" is the strongest known to occult Science, for it is a positive statement of actual being. You may use the following affirmation also, if you please—it has helped many: "I assert my individuality as a center of force, power and being. Nothing can adversely affect me. My mind is mine own, and I refuse admittance to unwelcome suggestions or influences. My desires are my own, and refuse to admit undesirable vibrations by induction or otherwise. My will is my own, and I charge it with power to beat off and repel all undesirable influences. I am surrounded by an aura of positive

"Will, which protects me absolutely."

The following denial has proved of the greatest value to many: "*I deny*, to all or any, the power to influence me against my best interests—I am my own master." These words may seem simple, but if you will use them you will be surprised at their efficacy. You realize, of course, that it is the mental state aroused by the words, that "does the work," rather than any special virtue in the words themselves.

II. Guard yourself from acting upon "impulses." When you feel a sudden or unaccountable "impulse" to do this thing, or that thing, stop and assert your positive individuality, and then drive out all outside influences, by repeating the affirmations, etc., given above, and by creating the proper mental picture. Then, when you have recovered your balance, consider the impulse, and decide whether it is to your best interests, or otherwise. You will be able to see this clearly, by reason of your "mental housecleaning" a moment before. Then, if the impulse seems to be against your best interests, drive it from you, saying: "I drive you away from me—you do not belong to me—return to those who sent you," or other words to that effect. This may be rendered more forceful if you will but create a mental picture of the discarded idea flying away from you in the shape of a tiny thought wave. These mental pictures aid one very materially in such matters, both in the sending forth of an idea, as well as in the discarding of one.

III. Cultivate the picture and idea of a positive aura, and always think of yourself as being encased in such a one. See yourself as a strong positive "I"—a center of power—encased in an impregnable sheath of auric force. You will thus be able to build up yourself into a mighty center of defence. You will be surprised at the confused manner of people who try to influence you, when they come in contact with this aura, and find their suggestions and mentative currents being cast back upon themselves. Such people find themselves "all broken up" when they meet a condition like this, which they do not understand, for very few of them are practical occultists. The mental picture of yourself as a center of power, surrounded with a positive aura, will, if persisted in, render you extremely positive, so that your influence is sure to be felt by the world with which you come in contact.

You will often be amused by occurrences following after the rejection of these "stray impulses," etc. You will find if you have had an impulse to buy a certain thing, or sell a certain thing at a sacrifice, that in a day or so, perhaps an hour or so, you will be approached by some person who will advise you personally to do that same thing, the person being likely to be benefited by the scheme or plan. I do not mean that such person has necessarily tried to influence you by mentative currents, for he may not have consciously done so, but nevertheless that is just what has happened, and his desire or will has caused these currents to flow in your direction, and you have felt them. Now that your eyes have been opened to this fact, you will be amused and surprised to see how many corroborative proofs you will receive. But always assert your individuality as a center of power, and all will be well with you in these matters.

A man's Mentative Force is immensely more powerful when he uses it to protect his individuality than when he uses it to attack the individuality of another. In fact, if *everyone* understood the laws of mentative defence, and would avail himself of the information given under this head, there would be almost a total absence of mentative attack, for the futility of the same would soon be recognized. The only reason, that the strong individuals are able to affect the weaker ones so frequently is because the others do not know their inner power, and make no defense—in fact, the majority of people do not know of these laws at all; and, if one tells them, they sneer and smile knowingly, tapping their foreheads to indicate that their informant is "just a little off." Poor sheep, and geese, they are so happy in their ignorance and conceit that it almost seems a pity to disturb them.

But to return to my subject. You will find that it requires a much less effort of will to protect your individuality than it does to attack the individuality of another. You will find that the law is on your side when you say, "I *won't* be influenced—I *deny* the power of another to weaken my individuality," for you have then called into operation that law of Nature which is always in operation, and which she gives to her creatures in the way of an instinctive protective force. So there is no occasion to be afraid—you are immune from attacks if you will but assert the force within you.

In passing on to the other phases of telementation, I would again remind you that in these instances of direct telementation the force may be used both consciously, or unconsciously. Those who know the laws of the use of the force may propel these telementative currents direct to those whom they wish to influence, just as they may consciously give mental suggestions in a personal interview. But, even where these laws are not understood, the currents or the suggestions are sent forth by the strong desire or will animating the person. Of course the person who understands the subject will be able to direct his force with greater precision and *effect*, but in any event the effect is produced in the same way.

CHAPTER 24

INDIRECT INFLUENCE

Let us now pass on to a consideration of the second class of Telementation, which I call "Indirect Telementation," or the use of the Force with a *general purpose* of affecting the desired result, *without special direction toward any particular person or persons*. This form of manifestation of telementation may be grouped into two sub classes, *viz*., (a) in which the general desire or will of the individual to attain certain results manifests itself in personal interviews, and induces mental states in those with whom he comes in contact; and (b) in cases wherein the general desire and will manifest in telementative currents, or waves, or whirlpools, affecting all persons and things who are interested in any way in the enterprise, scheme, plan or undertaking of the individual, and tending to cause them to "fall into line" and obey the will or comply with the desires of the general plan of the individual.

This last form of telementative influence is far more common than one would suppose. Strong, positive men start into motion waves and currents that sweep over the country, gathering force with each added impetus, and using the principle of "mental contagion" to increase its influence. Great "leaders of men" are centers of these mentative whirlpools, and similar forms of mentative influence, and draw in, or suck in to themselves persons, things, and objects conducive to their plans and ambitions. They do not have it all their own way, of course, for there are many influences at work which tend to neutralize their efforts. Other men have conflicting schemes which interfere with and often destroy the influence of these great mentators, and people are becoming educated regarding the nature of the forces they employ, and will not accept adverse suggestions or allow their vibrations to influence them. Still the force is still used to great effect by many politicians, and other persons who reach out toward large numbers of people.

Leading "generals of business" also make use of the force in this manner, and draw things "their way." In fact nearly everybody who does business with people scattered over a large territory, employs this force more or less, generally unconsciously. And many of these uses work no harm upon those affected, because many of these people are engaged in legitimate enterprise, and want always to give a "square deal," and a "good dollar's worth." I am not holding up this manifestation of telementation as reprehensible—I am merely stating its general laws and forms of manifestation. One may repel these mentative waves in the same way, and by the same methods mentioned in the preceding chapters in reference to the repelling of direct telementation. The rule is the same in both cases, for the principle involved is the same.

Before leaving this branch of the subject, I would remind you that one may take advantage of this last mentioned form of telementation for his own good, in a perfectly proper and justifiable way. One may wish to gain certain information and knowledge about certain subjects. If so, if he will hold a strong desire that the desired knowledge shall come to his notice and attention, and if at the same time he wills that the mentative currents flow forth in search of persons, things, and objects capable of imparting the knowledge or information, he will get results. He will find that after a while he will run across people who will be glad to give him the information he wants; or he will pick up a book that will either tell him what he wants, or else will refer to some other book or subject that will point out the path to him. These instances are quite common, and afford wonderful proofs of the laws herein stated. In this way no one is harmed, and mutual benefits are obtained. People are attracted to each other in this way, and each finds his own.

The above manifestation results from the operation of what has been called the "Law of Attraction," by the workings of which each person is continually drawing to himself the people, things, objects and even "circumstances" in harmony and accord with his prevailing mental states. Like attracts like, and the mental states determine that which one draws to himself. If you are not satisfied with what is coming to you, start to work and change your mental attitudes and mental states, and you will see a change gradually setting in, and things that you want will begin to "come your way." This law of attraction has been much written about in works on Mental Science during the past ten years, so it is not necessary for me to go into details about it here. I have given you the general principles in this chapter, and you may apply them accordingly.

A most important fact about the effect of mentative vibrations upon people lies in the principle that one is more affected by vibrations in harmony with his own accustomed feelings and mental states, than by those of opposite natures. A man who is full of evil schemes, and selfish aims, is more apt to be caught up by similar vibrations than one who lives above that plane of thought. He is more easily tempted by evil suggestions and influences, than one to whom these things are abhorrent. And the same is true on every plane.

A man whose mental attitude is one of confidence and fearlessness, is not apt to be affected by vibrations of a negative, pessimistic, gloomy nature, and vice versa. Therefore, if you wish to receive the vibrations of the thoughts and feelings of others, you must place yourself in a mental attitude corresponding with those vibrations you wish to receive. And if you wish to avoid vibrations of a certain kind, the best way is to rise above them in your own mind, and to cultivate mental states opposite to them. The positive always overcomes the negative—and optimistic mental states are always positive to pessimistic mental states. The sense of individuality, and one's relation to the Universal Mind Power, is the strongest and most positive mental state one can attain. Therefore cultivate it, first, last and all the time.

I now come to a phase of the subject that underlies all of the phenomena of telementation, and really gives the "key" to much of its wonderful effects. I allude to what occultists know as "Visualization." This visualization is to telementation what the pattern is to the maker of objects; what the plans of the architect are to the builders; what the "mould" or "matrix" is to moulders of metal. It is the skeleton around which the materialization of thought forms occurs. It is of the greatest importance to you to acquaint yourselves with its laws and effects.

To "visualize" means to "see mentally"—that is, to form a mental image of a thing—to "see it in one's mind," etc., Visualization, along the lines of one's daily occupation is a most important thing, but one that is very poorly appreciated because little understood. The best workmen, writers, inventors, composers, etc., are those who are able "to see the thing in the mind," and then reproduce it in materialized form. Sir Francis Galton, one of the best authorities upon the subject, has said: "The free action of a vivid visualizing faculty is of much importance in connection with the higher processes of generalized thought.…A visual image is the most perfect form of mental representation wherever the shape, position, and relations of objects to space are concerned.…*The best workmen are those who visualize the whole of what they propose to do, before they take a tool in their hand*.…Strategists, artists of all denominations, physicists who contrive new experiments, and in short, all who do not follow routine, have need of it.…A faculty that is of importance in all technical and artistic occupations; that gives accuracy to our perceptions, and justice to our generalizations; is starved by lazy disuse, instead of being cultivated judiciously in such a way as will, on the whole, bring the best return. I believe that a serious study of the best means of developing and utilizing this faculty, without prejudice to the practice of abstract thought in symbols, is one of the many pressing desiderata in the yet unformed science of education."

And all that Sir Francis Galton has said above is equally true of the cultivation of the art of visualization in connection with telementation. The trouble with the majority of people is that they *do not know just what they do want*. They are not able to form clear mental images of that which they wish to "create" or "materialize." The men who obtain the greatest and most wonderful results through mentative influence, particularly in the form of telementation, are those men who are able to "*visualize*" most clearly the things that they wish to "materialize"—who are able to form the mental image of the things they wish to manifest.

The secret of visualization lies in the occult and psychological principle that "as is the mental matrix, so is the mental form; and as is the mental form; so is the physical materialization." In other words, the visualized mental image is the matrix or mould into which the Mind Power is poured, and from which it takes form; and around this mental image the deposit of materialization forms—and thus does the ideal become the real. If you wish to get the best effects from Mind Power you must create a mental image around which the material or physical materialization is formed—and the way to form the proper mental image is by visualization, which thus builds up the matrix or mould in which the Mind Power pours. And as is the matrix so is the image, and as is the image so is the materialization.

Before you can draw to you the material needed for building up the things or conditions you desire you must form a clear mental image of *just what you want to materialize*—and before you can make this mental image, you must *realize mentally* just exactly what you *do* desire. And the process of this is called visualization. That is, you build up a mental matrix or mould, little by little, until you have it before you clearly—until it stands out clearly formed as a mental image, just as you would see it if it were actually materialized. Then you must hold this mental image before you constantly, regarding it not as a *mere imagination*, but as a *something real* which you have created in your mind, and which will proceed to surround itself with the material necessary to give it material objectivity, or materialization.

If you cannot see the whole thing at first, as a mental image—that is, if you are not able to build up a complete matrix by visualization, then do the next best thing—which is the *very best* thing for the majority of people—and build a matrix of the *first step* toward the whole thing, that is, the first thing that is needed. Then concentrate upon this first thing until the mental image stands out sharp and clear, and you will find that things have been started in motion. Then, you may add little by little to your matrix, and build up your mental image a little larger and in greater detail.

And here is an important thing. You must mentally *see* the thing as actually existing, *right now*, and not as "going to exist" later on. You must realize that the mental image exists right now, else it will lack clearness and effectiveness.

You must pour into that mental image a constant supply of strong, positive Desire Force, and Will Power, all of which will spread out in the proper directions and affect the material needed to materialize your mental image. By so doing you impart to the mentative currents the necessary impetus and direction, and they will operate along these lines, and will proceed to materialize your mental image for you. Things will come your way; people will appear who are necessary to your plans; information will come to you from strange sources, and in unexpected times and places; opportunities will open themselves up to you. But remember this, that you must be prepared to act upon, these openings, and opportunities. You must be alert and watchful, and *expectant*. You will have to do the work, remember, yourself, although the forces you have started into operation will supply you with the material. The door will be opened to you, but you must step in yourself; the tools and materials will be provided you, but you must use them; the information will be laid before you, but you must make it your own. Even Mind Power will not avail the lazy man. You must learn to "do things" yourself.

This subject of visualization would fill a book by itself, but I hope that I have been able to give you a clear idea of its *working principles*. Remember always this rule—this Triple Key of Attainment, as I have often called it: (1) You must *desire* a thing most intensely; (2) then you must *earnestly expect* it: (3) then you must use your *will* in the direction of *action* tending to bring it about. But first of all, as I have said, you must *know just what you do want*, and then proceed to create the mental matrix or mould by *visualization*—that is, you must proceed to *mentally* see it as already existing.

This chapter must be read and studied in connection with the chapters preceding it, for they blend into each other, and the information "laps." I have given you certain principles, in plain, practical form, which may seem so simple to you as to be passed over without the proper consideration and examination. Do not make this mistake, I pray you. Do not long for high sounding terms and mystical verbiage. The truth is capable of being expressed without these fancy trappings or drapery. I have tried to tell you the principle of these things—but you must study carefully in order to grasp every point. I have boiled down, and condensed a great deal of information into this lesson—be sure that you do not allow any of the points to escape you. You cannot expect to acquaint yourself fully with this subject in one hasty reading. You must read and re read many times, with careful study and thought. You must do some thinking on your own account, in order to apply these general principles to your own "symptoms" and needs. You must read carefully, and then think a little. There is no royal road to Mind Power, or anything else. I have tried to make the road a little easier for you—but you must do the traveling yourself. You cannot reach the heights by proxy. You must digest these things yourself—predigested ideas will do you no good.

Underlying all of these wonderful manifestations of telementation, there is just the simple principle that I have pointed out to you—induction of mental states by Desire Force and Will Power. Everything occurs by reason of this principle. You may think that the book that you needed, and which came to you so wonderfully, must have arrived in some other way. Not so, the book was placed here, and moved there, by *people*, and these people have minds capable of being moved by vibratory waves, and so when once the thing was set into operation, all things worked together toward the given end. Even the present book reached you under the law of attraction. There is no chance in these matters—there are laws in operation everywhere, and always—and over all there is the Great Law.

And, now in concluding this chapter, I would remind you to always realize that you are centers of living mental energy in the great Ocean of Mind Power. And that you are strong in the degree that you are *positive*. And that you are positive in the degree that you are an individual. And you are an Individual in the degree that you realize that you are a "center of living will." There is nothing to fear but fear—you are capable of asserting your individuality always, and everywhere—your only chains are those you forge for yourself—you are free right now, here, and always. Do not be deluded by the petty things of personality, that pass away and perish over night—but rest serene and firm in the consciousness that you are an individual living will center; and fear not to assert the individual "I." There is no Devil but fear—nothing but fear can keep you from your own heritage and birthright. Assert the "I" and banish fear.

CHAPTER 25

MENTAL THERAPEUTICS

"Therapeutics" means "the healing art," therefore "Mental Therapeutics" means "the art or science of Mental Healing."

If I were writing this lesson from the standpoint of twenty years ago, I would think it advisable to fill page after page with a recital of the many claims of mental healing, but no such necessity exists at the present time. People have heard much regarding mental healing, and while they may differ in their theories and opinion regarding the nature of the cures performed, still nearly all of them will acknowledge that cures *have* been made and *are* being made by mental healing methods.

The history of mental healing extends away back into the past, and the earliest pages of history treat it as if it were a long established and well accepted method. In fact the history of mental healing is the history of Mind Power, so far as the older peoples and races are concerned. The ancient Magi used their mental powers in the direction of healing the sick, and restoring natural, healthy conditions. People were brought to the temples to be healed, and after the customary incantations, and ceremonies, designed to affect the imagination and respect of the primitive people, they were found to be benefited, and actually cured in time. But under and back of all these ceremonies and rites, the principle effecting the cure was the same principle that is being used today by all forms of mental healing, under whatever names it may be disguised and masked. There is but one mental healing principle, and that has always been used; is being used now; and always will be used, so long as the race exists.

And this principle is the application and employment of Mind Power. Mind Power is positive to both force and matter, as we have seen in these chapters, and the negative always yields to the positive when the latter is properly and intelligently applied.

Mind Power really builds up the body from a single cell, and is inherent in every part and particle of the body. Every cell has its supply of Mind Power—the cell, and combination of cells, and the whole body in fact, is the result of conditions of manifestations of Mind Power. The body is *all mind*, at the last analysis. Mind Power manifests itself in countless ways in the universe, and the physical bodies, and the cells of which they are composed are simply certain forms of manifestation of its force. And, this being so, mental healing is not a case of "mind over matter," as is often taught, but is *a manifestation of positive mind over negative mind*. The central mind of man is positive to the mind in the body of man, and hence the healing effect.

Every cell has its share of mind, and science shows us that each cell can and does live its life as a separate entity, always, however, subordinate to the whole system of cells, and the mind controlling it. And the mind in each cell, or system of cells, may be reached by the positive mind of a person, when properly applied. In order to fully grasp the significance of this statement, you must remember that every organ, part, bone, nerve, vessel, tissue and everything else in your body, is built up of cells which have formed certain combinations. There are individual cells in your blood and other parts of the body; and there are cell communities in your body, which perform certain functions and which you call "my liver"; "my heart"; "my stomach"; "my kidneys," etc., etc. And there is mind in every one of them. And the mind in every cell, and in every organ may be reached by Mind Power applied by the mind of oneself or another person.

And in this simple statement, I have embodied my idea of mental healing, which idea is based upon years of earnest study, experiment, and investigation, aided by personal acquaintance with and association with some of the most celebrated mental healers of this age. I have discarded fanciful theory, after fanciful theory, as unnecessary to account for the facts observed by the leading investigators of mental healing, and have at last "boiled down" the matter to this point and idea of *Mind in the cells and cell groups; which mind is negative to the positive central mind of the individual, especially when the latter is concentrated and intelligently applied.*

You may ask me the question "Well, but what about all the various metaphysical, religious, and semi religious theories advanced to account for the cures performed by the various cults and sects of the 'New Thought' and similar movements?" Answering this I would say that the various cults and sects perform cures not *because* of their dogmas, but often *in spite* of them—the real cures being performed by Mind Power, pure and simple, called into operation, and employed, in various forms, and ways, under many coverings, disguises and draperies. It is all the same grand old principle, but "with fringe on"—the style of fringe depending on the particular theories and dogmas of the sects.

There has been much written, spoken, and taught concerning mental healing, under some name or other, but the majority of the writers have been attached to some particular cult, church, or organization, which claimed that the whole truth rested upon the acceptance of some particular theory, idea, doctrine or dogma advanced and held by it, in accordance with the particular views of some certain teacher or teachers. And, accordingly, the writings have been colored by the hue of such belief and dogma. One has but to look around him in order to see that the many conflicting schools of mental or spiritual healing *are all making cures*, in spite of the claim of each that its particular school or sect, or church, has a monopoly on truth, and a corner on "true metaphysical healing." The truth is that they *all make cures*—the percentage being about the same in each instance, taking the personal qualifications of the healers into consideration. In spite of the several claims that "we have the only Truth—all others are in error, and ignorant of the real Truth," etc., etc., *all* of these "erroneous people" are getting fine results. Their differing and often contradictory theories do not seem to cut any figure in the real work, and one who closely studies the subject is soon forced to the conclusion that *there must be some underlying principle of cure which they are all using.* And so there is! And I call this "underlying principle" the effect of positive central mind upon negative body mind—you may give it any other name you choose, but you will get the results just the same.

The various theories, statements, forms, observances, dogmas and what not, have no other effect than giving a strong suggestion to people who are impressed by the same. Some people get better results when the mental healing is accompanied by some religious or semi religious talk and explanation, which appeals to the emotional parts of their nature and makes them more receptive to the healing process of the mind. (Sacred shrines, images and relics cause cures in this way.) Others get better results when some technical metaphysical theory is urged upon them, with a great wow and use of long high sounding words—they may not understand the words, but they think that there "must be something in it, for she used words that I couldn't begin to understand, and yet she knew all about them," etc. Others prefer the scientific explanation of the school of Suggestion, which avoids metaphysical or religious theories, and yet get the results. Others, still, adhere to the Mental Science idea of the Universal Mind, and the Personal Mind, and they, too, get results. Others like the Subjective Mind, and Objective Mind idea—and they get results, too. *They all get results*—but some take more kindly to certain forms, and thus get better results.

I have frequently advised people to go to healers of certain cults and schools and churches, simply because I knew that the ideas of these particular schools, cults and churches would fit the particular temperament of the person in question, and thus the best results would accrue. I am most catholic in my ideas on this subject—I believe in a person employing any phase of mental healing, from Bread Pills to Christian Science—providing that the particular agency employed will invoke the faith, confidence and belief of the patient to the utmost. Whichever form will best do this, that is the form I believe the best for the patient.

I can see very well why a person of a warm religious temperament would be better benefited by mental healing in a religious form or phase than from mere suggestion, or ordinary Mental Science—it opens up a part of the nature that is conducive to the cure. And I can see why others are impressed by technical, complicated metaphysical talk, which causes them to wonder and be impressed, and thus arouses an interest and an "expectant attention" which goes a long way toward making the cure. And I can see why others still, would rebel against either of the above mentioned forms, and would be better reached by a plain, scientific presentation of the subject. Every man to his taste—in mental healing as in everything else. In this respect I am like the Irishman who said he was glad that all men did not have the same taste, for if they did every mother's son of them would be wanting to steal his wife away from him.

But, you may ask, why is it that faith, belief, confidence, etc., play such an important part in the cures, if it be true that the real cure is effected through the mind in the cells, and cell groups—what have cells to do with faith? This is a good question—and here is the answer. While it is true that the mind in the cells is the medium or cause of the cure, still it is a fact that these cells are negative to the influence of the central mind of the person. And if that central mind be filled with the mental states of disease, fear, undesirable beliefs, etc., then the negative cells and organs must be affected. And, if on the contrary the mental states of the person be changed from fear to hope, confidence, love, faith, belief and expectancy, then it will be readily seen that the effect upon the cells will be changed for the better. And, if to these improved mental states, there is added a still more positive state—a state of conscious control and power, then will the curative effect be greatly magnified and increased.

To tell the truth, I earnestly believe that the one great potent factor in mental healing, is the *removal of fear* from the mind of the patient, by whatever means itmay be accomplished, whether by reason, argument, faith, hope, or even by superstition. Fear is the most negative of the mental states, and simply paralyzes the whole system. Fear and worry actually *poison* the cells of the body. This is a scientifically demonstrable fact. And if this pall of fear can be lifted by any means, then a big step in the direction of a cure has been effected. *And hope, confidence, and belief, will lift that pall.* That is why I believe in everything from Bread Pills to "C. S.," as I said a few minutes ago—whichever agency induces the greater degree of hope, belief, confidence, and expectancy, is the best for the particular case. But in all cases the principle of cure is the same—*mind.*

It should not be necessary for me to recite the oft repeated facts of the phenomenon of disease being created by mental states, and of cures arising from the same. Every man or woman who reads these lessons has heard this tale over and over again, many times. It is no longer a debatable question, this matter of the effect of the mind in health and disease. The books are full of it. It is as "old as the hills," and at no time in the history of the world has this form of Mind Power been accorded greater attention and interest. And therefore, I shall omit this part of the story, and proceed to business in the direction of telling you "just how" to apply the Mind Power in healing, both present and "absent."

In the first place, the principles of mental healing are precisely the same principles that are applied in all forms of Mind Power, as we have seen them in the previous lessons. It is all a matter of "*Mentative Induction,*" first, last and always. And this induction may arise from either mentative currents, or by mental suggestion. Please fix this statement in your mind, so that I will not have to repeat it.

Now, let us see what happens if mentative induction is set up in the mind of a person by means either of mentative currents, or mental suggestion, when what is called "general treatment" is given. We will suppose that the mental state of the person has been changed by induction (either from currents or by suggestion) to a strong positive state—and that is what one must aim to produce in the patient. This induced positive mental state in the central mind, is of course, strongly positive to the mind in the body and its cells. The mental image of *a normal, perfect, healthy, well body*, being held in the central mind of the patient, it follows that the physical material of the body, and cells will begin to materialize in accordance with the pattern set before the mind of the cells, by the central mind of the person. It is the old story of mental visualization, and physical materialization over again. Of course, the effect is wonderfully heightened if the patient will direct his desire and will strongly to the recuperative or reparative action, in which effort he may be materially aided by the healer.

The desired mental state in the patient may be induced either by auto suggestion (self suggestion) on his own part; or by the suggestion of the healers, (here is where the ceremonies, and "frills and fringes" of the cults, come in); or by the direct mentative currents of the healer, applied as indicated in the previous lessons. In this form of healing, the healer works *by arousing the mind of the patient, so that he really cures himself.* This "arousing" is of course affected by either suggestion, or mentative currents—the effect being the result of "induction" in either case, as you will readily understand. This form of mental healing, which I call "general treatment" includes both the form of "present healing," that is when the healer is in the personal presence of the patient, or else along the lines of what is called "absent treatments" or "distant treatments," when the healer and the patient are not in each other's presence.

Leaving the subject of "general treatment," for the moment, let us consider the broad principles underlying "local treatment." By "local treatment" I mean mental healing effected by the mind of the healer being directly and specially applied to the mind in the cells and organs themselves. You will remember what I have said about there being "mind in the cells and organs"—"local treatment" is an application based upon that fact. The mind of the healer is brought to bear in a positive, direct, special manner upon these cells and organs, and the suggestions, and mentative currents are directed immediately to these organs and cells, without the intermediate employment of the central mind of the patient, as in the case of "general treatment." Of course one may apply "local treatment" to himself, by directing his mind directly to the cells and organs, instead of indirectly by means of general mental treatment. You may wonder why I speak of directing "suggestions" to the cells—you may well ask, "can the cells *hear*?" The cells cannot hear, but the utterance of the words of the suggestion, by you, will enable you to direct your mind more directly and forcefully upon the cells and organs. You will see, as we proceed, that I advocate" speaking right up" to the cells and organs of the body, and telling them just what you want them to do. You will be surprised when you try this and see how they respond.

Now, that we understand the general principles of both of these phases of mental treatment, let us pass on to a consideration of the practice of mental healing—the actual "how" of the subject. We shall begin with "general treatment," both present and absent, and will then take up the second phase of "local treatment." In both cases we shall see the actual methods of treatment, in detail. But I must ask you to pay close attention to what I have to say about these treatments, for I am condensing a whole course of lessons in mental healing into two chapters, and you will miss something unless you watch closely.

The first step in the personal form of general treatment is to induce in your patient a mental state of calm, and relaxation. This is quite important because this mental state causes the patient to become receptive to the impressions that you wish to make upon his or her mind. The best plan is to have the patient seat himself in a comfortable position (or if he is lying down, let him assume a comfortable attitude), and then talk to him a little in order to induce a comfortable, easy frame of mind, which will react upon the physical conditions. Have him relax every muscle, and withdraw the tension from every nerve, so that he will be relaxed, and "limber" all over, from head to feet. The best way to determine whether or not the desired condition has been effected is to raise one of his hands and then allow it to drop back to his sides or lap. If he is fully relaxed, his hand will drop just as if it were not attached to his body. The mental state producing this physical condition may be best stated by the word's "Let Go!" One must *mentally "let go,"* before he will be able to "let go" physically. The patient must feel perfectly at ease, and comfortable, in order that the best results be gained.

The healer should endeavor to quiet the mind of the patient by an earnest, confident, sympathetic conversation, leading the subject toward bright, hopeful, happy topics, and especially avoiding anything likely to arouse antagonism or argument. He should throw earnestness and feeling into his tones, and speak as if his one object in life were to cure the patient, and of which cure he entertained not the slightest doubt. The healer should forget himself, and concentrate his mentality completely upon the subject of *curing the patient*. He should be very careful to *act out* the part of the confident, successful healer, because sick people are very suggestible, and take on impressions very easily, and so, if the healer manifests an apparent lack of confidence in his outward demeanor, the patient will be most likely to accept the suggestion, and the work of healing will thus be rendered doubly difficult. If you have studied the principles of mental suggestion, you will see the psychology of this fact.

It will be well to begin the treatment by a preliminary suggestive treatment, in a conversational tone. You should point out to the patient the conditions that you intend to bring about. You should endeavor to obtain the patient's co operation by means of his holding a mental image of the desired condition. That is, if it be a case of stomach trouble, he should form a mental image of a strong, healthy normal stomach, doing its work properly, and digesting the food that is given it, and manifesting a good, hearty natural appetite. If the patient will do this he will be able to do much toward aiding you. You should then tell him that his stomach is *Strong, STRONG, STRONG*, (speaking the words *with intense feeling and force*) and that normal conditions are reasserting themselves under the power of the mind. You should, in many ways and forms, keep before him constantly *a picture of the conditions you wish to bring about*, for by so doing you will change his mental image of disease into a mental image of health, and the best result is sure to follow. If you prefer the use of the hands in healing, by all means use them, as such practice gives a most powerful suggestion, as well as possessing other advantages.

You will find that you will be able to impart a wonderful degree of forceful, earnest intensity to your voice, if you will but practice "visualization" in your treatments. That is, you must endeavor to actually *see mentally*, the conditions that you wish to bring about. And when you are able to do this, you will be able to hold the attention of the patient as his mind follows your words in your description of the successive steps of the cure that you intend bringing about. He will be able to see himself as gradually improving, and growing well, not only in a general way, but also in the sense that he will be able to form a mental picture of the formerly diseased organ actually growing strong and normal. *Always keep before you the mental image of the conditions that you wish to bring about*—see them before you *as actually existing right now*—and your mind, and actions and voice will conform to that mental image, for by so doing the patient will receive the best possible suggestion, and your mentative currents will be stronger and more dynamic.

In the following chapter, we pass on to a consideration of the actual methods of applying Mind Power to the healing of disease.

CHAPTER 26

MENTAL HEALING METHODS

And now to the actual work of mental healing by mentative currents. In this work I must again repeat my injunctions given in the preceding chapter regarding the holding of the proper mental image in the mind of the healer. In the degree that the proper mental image is held, will be the degree of success in the treatment. "Visualization" is the key note of this form of mental healing, and the healer should devote himself earnestly to acquiring the art of visualizing. You must be able to see the patient as healed, and the organs, parts, and cells as functioning normally and properly. Cast aside all negative thought, and doubts, and throw yourself earnestly into the work before you. You will find that as the ability to visualize is acquired, there will come to you a feeling of strength and power, and a sense of certainty about your work.

The process of transmitting the mentative currents is not especially difficult or strenuous. In fact, this part of the work seems almost "automatic." All that you will have to do is to concentrate your full attention upon the mental image that you have visualized, and earnestly desire that the picture materializes, and do not bother at all about the currents, for the latter will begin to flow freely without any voluntary effort on your part. Occasionally you may throw a little Will Power into the work, in order to stimulate the healing process, but ordinarily the unconscious use of the Desire Force will accomplish the result. It is not necessary to use the strenuous effort that so many mental healers employ in giving treatments—this is all waste energy, and tires one out without any corresponding advantage to the patient. The clear cut mental image produced by the practice of visualization performs the work for you, as I have said, almost "automatically." The more realistic your picture is made to appear to you, the greater the force sent forth, and the greater the degree of success will you have in your healing.

Some excellenthealers have found thatthey gained additional force if they would add to their mental picture or image, the picture of the mentative currents actually leaving their minds and travelling toward the patient, and then enveloping and surrounding the latter. One very good healer has told me that she always can see, mentally, the patient being "bathed in a perfect stream of her Mind Power." I feel that this lady is right, and that by adding this feature to the mental image very good results may be obtained. The student of these lessons will find this last image easy to produce if he will remember what we have said about thought forms. I do not advise too long treatments, for I believe that the best results are obtained in a treatment extending over say not more than fifteen minutes. Yon should then leave the patient with a few earnest words of encouragement and hope, bidding him aid in your work by keeping the proper mental images of health before him, and especially avoiding all fear and worry.

The above process of giving a mental treatment may seem very simple to those who have not practiced it. But you will find that it contains the real essence of the healing process, without the "fringe" and "trimming." And more than that you will find it wonderfully efficacious—it will "do the work." You will never begin to even faintly realize the virtue of such a treatment, until you begin to practice it. You will then find yourself so filled with such a sense of power, strength and healing force, that you will seem like another person. And your patient will likewise feel an immediate benefit. I might write page after page, giving you directions about the treatment, but, after I was through, it could all be boiled down into the plain, simple directions already given you. I have given you the basis of the practical treatment—you may add the "trimmings" yourself, if you feel that you need them. This same basis you will find to underlie all of the treatments of the various sects and cults, after you have trimmed off the "fancy additions," high sounding words, and metaphysical terms. I have studied all these forms of treatment, and know just what I am talking about when I say this to you.

And now for the "absent treatments" along the lines of general treatment. There is practically no difference in the methods. The principal additional process is that of the healer endeavoring to form a mental image of the patient, as if he were right before him in person. If you have ever seen the patient you may easily reproduce his mental image. But if you have not seen him personally, you can form a mental image of "a man," or "a woman," without filling in the details of personal appearance, and the result will be similar. You will find the following method will help you in the treatment. Sit down in your chair, after drawing up another chair right before you, but about two or three yards distant. Then picture your patient as sitting in this other chair, and use your imagination to the fullest in this respect. Many practitioners of successful mental healing actually *feel* that the patient is sitting before them in this form of treatment. Then with your patient sitting before you (as a mental image) talk to him just as if he were present in person, using the same words, tones, and manner. Throw yourself earnestly into the idea of a personal treatment, and endeavor to forget that miles are between you. By so doing you will be able to start the mentative currents flowing freely in his direction, and he will be affected by them, and will obtain the best results. I have been told frequently by persons who have taken this form of healing from some of the world's best mental healers, that they could *almost see the healer* before them—they could certainly *feel* his presence very distinctly.

This "talk" to the distant patient should consist of the same calming, quieting, soothing suggestions at first, followed by the positive, stimulating, forceful suggestions given afterward. Follow the precise instructions given for use in personal treatments, and you cannot go astray. There is no difference, in reality, between personal treatments and absent treatments—if you will remember this, and act upon it, you will have the key to the matter. And, then, after the suggestive talks, you should then give the same silent mentative treatment as indicated in my instructions regarding personal treatments. You should form the same kind of mental image, and proceed just the same, in every particular. Even bid him "good bye" as you would in a personal treatment. If you have set a time for the absent treatment, your patient should place himself in a comfortable relaxed position. But this is not necessary—it is not necessary for the patient to even know the hour of treatment. All that he needs to do is to open his mind, receptively, to the treatment that you are to give him some time during the day—that is, he should express his mental "willingness," and thus take off the resistance of his will which otherwise would have to be overcome.

The healer who wishes to give absent treatments should study carefully the portions of this work relating to telementative induction, the currents, thought forms, etc. Remember, please, that all the work of mental healing is done along the lines of mentative induction, just as is the work of all forms of mentative influence. There is but one great law underlying all of these forms of manifestation, and if you understand the fundamental principle you will be able to reproduce any or all of the manifestations of it. The instruction regarding mental healing is not confined to this chapter alone—it must be gained from a study of *all* these chapters, for the reasons just stated. Strive always to acquire a clear knowledge of the underlying principles, and you need not worry about the details of operation or manifestation.

And, now, just a word about self healing, along these lines. *There is no difference between self healing, and the healing of others*. Here is a good method—simple and efficacious. All that is necessary for you to do is to imagine yourself as a patient coming to yourself for treatment. Suppose your name is "John Smith," and you wish to treat yourself along the lines of the general treatment. All you have to do is to let the central mind part of you (or the "I") proceed to *treat the body* of "John Smith." *Talk to "John Smith" just as if he were an entirely separate individual.* Tell him what he should do, and what he should know, and what you expect to do for him. Give him the same suggestions that you would give another patient. Talk up to him, and tell him just what you mean to do for him, and what he has got to do himself. Then give him the Silent Treatment just as you would another patient. Even give him the parting words, just as you would a patient. In short, treat him first, last, and all the time as you would another patient. You will be surprised to note how efficacious this plan is. This method is original with myself, so far as I know. There is a good, strong psychological and occult reason for this plan of self treatment, which is not necessary to go into here—the principal thing is that it "will do the work." Try it. The ordinary method of self treatment is to say, "I am well" and so on, giving the suggestions in the first person. I consider that my own plan gives better results, but you may try both, and decide for yourself.

And now for the "local treatment" methods of mental healing. These are very simple also—so simple that I fear some of you will undervalue them. But do not deceive yourselves, good friends, the "simplicity" represents years of hard work along experimental lines, and is really the "boiling down" of many methods far more complicated and technical. It is the "essence" of the thing, again. I wish that I could have obtained this information as easily as you are doing—but I couldn't, for I had to work it out for myself, in connection with other experimenters and investigators. The underlying theory of this local treatment in mental healing is (1) that *there is mind in every cell; cell group; organ; and part, of the body;* and (2) that *the mentative energy in such mind is negative to that in the central mind of the individual, and consequently, yields to its positivity when properly applied.* That is the whole story in a nut shell. Now see if you can grasp its importance.

The above principle of the "local treatment" is really also employed in the general treatment, because the central mind of the patient is stirred into induced activity and positivity by the suggestion, or mentative currents of the healer, or both. The central mind of the patient, so stirred up by induction, then acts upon the mind in the cells, organs, etc., unconsciously, and the cure results. Do you see just what I mean? Well, then in the local treatment, instead of going about it in this way, the healer brings his mentative energy to bear right directly upon the mind in cells, and organs themselves. So you see the process is really the same at the last, that is, it is the application of the positive central mind upon the negative mind of the cells, organs and parts.

Now, then, how may one treat the cells and organs of another person, in this way? The process is very simple, when you once learn it. All that is necessary is for you to "treat" the organ, or part, just as you did the patient, in several forms of general treatment, as stated a little while ago. You must learn to "talk to" the organ or part affected, and to give it suggestions and mental treatment just as you did your personal patient. In short, the nearer you can come to *considering, and treating the cells or organs as if they actually were "personalities" or "entities,"* the better will be your success in this form of treatment. This is no mere trick, or bit of superstition—it is based upon good psychological principles, and has its reason in well defined occult laws. *There is mind in the organ and cell, and you are reaching out to it.* The way to reach the mind in the cells; cell groups; ganglia; organs; nerves; parts, etc., of the body, is to *address yourself directly to it, just as you would to a person.* You must think of the mind in the affected parts, as a "person" who is misbehaving. You must remonstrate with, argue with, coax, order or drive the "person" residing in the organ, just as you would different individuals. Sometimes coaxing is much better than driving, and sometimes the forceful method is necessary, as we shall see. You may either talk aloud to the mind in the organ, or else (and this is the better way in treating others) you may do your talking mentally. Tell it just what you expect of it—just what you intend it shall do—just what is right for it to do, etc. *And it will obey.* I know a lady, who is an excellent healer along these lines, and who obtained the principles of this particular form of healing from myself. She tells me that she followed my plan, as above stated, with the exception that to her *the organs, nerves, and parts, always seem like disobedient children*, who must be managed one way or another. And so she proceeds just as she did when she was a successful schoolteacher, And I am inclined to think that she is right, and has made an improvement on my original idea. For these "cell minds," or "organ minds" closely resemble the minds of undeveloped children, and are often unreasonably stubborn, although if they are reached the right way, by a firm though kindly tone, in most cases they will obey orders, and mend their ways.

It is well to use the hands at the beginning of this form of treatment, in the direction of tapping or patting the part of the body directly over the organ. This seems to have the effect of awakening the attention of the organ mind, so that it becomes more receptive. It is akin to tapping the shoulder of a man on the street, to whom you wish to speak. In such cases, it is well to send the mental command: "Here! Listen to me!" The hands of the healer may also be passed over the body as the mental commands are given, and they serve to give an additional and strengthened suggestion when properly used.

A plain, simple way of giving this treatment is to awaken the attention of the mind in the organ or part, as above stated, and then proceed to mentally lecture it calling it by name, as for instance. "Here, stomach!" or "Now, you liver," etc. Don't smile at this advice—just try it on yourself and you will stop smiling. *Then go on and tell the organ mind just what you would tell it if it were an actual personality—a childish mind, for instance.* You will soon find how quick the organ mind is to awaken to your words, and to act upon your suggestions or orders. Follow the laws of suggestion in giving these treatments to the organ minds—that is, remember the suggestive phases of repetition, authoritative demand or command, etc. Don't be afraid, but start in to give the organ mind "a piece of your mind," and it will obey you.

Dr. Paul Edwards, one of the world's most famous mental healers, whom I met quite often a number of years ago when he was living in Chicago, informed me that the result of his practice has taught him that there was a great difference in the "intelligence" of the mind in the several organs. For instance, he believed that the heart was *very* "intelligent," and quite amenable to mild, gentle, coaxing suggestions and advice or orders; while on the other hand, the liver was a most mulish, stubborn, obstinate organ mind, which had to be driven along by the sharpest and most positive suggestions. I have since investigated along this line, and I am now fully convinced of the correctness of Dr. Edwards' theory in this respect. I have found the heart to be very gentle, and obedient, as he said, and I have moreover found it needed but the slightest word to attract its attention. I have found the liver to be brutish, stubborn, and obstinate, and needing the most forceful, insistent methods—something like driving a stubborn donkey along the road. I have also found the liver to be lazy and sleepy, and needing much effort to rouse it into a receptive condition. The stomach I have found quite intelligent, particularly if it has not been brutalized by "stuffing," and it will readily respond to the treatment. A peculiar thing about the stomach is that it seems to like "jollying," or "flattery"—tell it how good a stomach it is, and how well it can do its work; and how much you trust it to run things right for you; and lo! it proceeds to "make good," and justify your praise and commendations.

The nerves respond readily to this form of treatment, along gentle coaxing lines. The circulation of the blood may be increased to certain parts, or restrained, in this way. In this way the blood can be swept all over the body, creating a pleasant glow; or it may be drawn away from an aching head, or a feverish brow. The bowels respond readily to a firm, kind treatment, in which they are to be told to move regularly—it being well to name a certain time at which you expect them to establish a regular habit, *in which case be sure to keep your appointment with them and give them a chance*. The organs peculiar to women will respond quite readily to this form of treatment. Regular menstruation has often been established by treating the proper parts in this way a month ahead, and keeping it up every day until the regular period—in this case it is also well to "fix a date." Suggestions of "*firm*, now—be firm and strong" have relieved many cases of womb weaknesses. Profuse menstruation has yielded to commands of "*slow*, now; *easy, easy;* not so free a flow," etc.

There are no fixed forms of treatment along these lines. You must acquire the "knack" by practice. The proper words will suggest themselves to you. The thing to do is to *know what you want done, and* then *command the organ mind to do that thing; using the same words that you would use in talking to a real person in the place of the organ*. You will soon acquire the art, by a little practice. Those who have treated a large number of persons in this way have told me that the mind in the organs and parts seems to instinctively recognize the healer's power over them.

Just as a horse or dog will recognize men who are accustomed to managing animals of their kind, so will these organ minds instinctively recognize their master in one who has studied this art of mental healing, along these lines.

Remember always that you are mind talking to mind, not to dead matter. There is mind in every cell, nerve, organ and part of the body, and in the body as a whole; and this mind will listen to your central mind and obey it, because your central mind is positive to it—the organ is negative to *you*. Carry this idea always with you in giving these treatments, and endeavor to visualize the mind in the organs etc., as clearly as may be, for by so doing you get them in better *rapport* with you, and can handle them to better advantage.

And, also remember, that the virtue lies not in the mere sound of the words that happen to reach the organ or cells—they do not understand words as words, but they *do* understand *the meaning behind the words*—they recognize the mental state of which the word is the outward symbol. But without words it is very hard for you—to think, or clearly express the feeling—and so by all means use the words just as if the organ minds understood their actual meaning, for by so doing, you can drive in *the meaning of the word*—and induce the mental state conditions necessary to work the cure.

While this local treatment is adapted especially to personal healing, still it may be also used to great advantage in absent healing, by combining it with the regular general form of absent healing. That is, after giving the general absent treatment, proceed to place yourself *en rapport* with the organ mind in the patient, and then talk to it just as you would if the patient were actually present. Visualization will enable you to do this effectively. I have heard of some wonderful cures having been effected by the use of this form of local treatment in absent healing, in connection with the general treatment.

And in case of self healing this local treatment acts with wonderful force. One can, of course, "talk up" to his own cells and organs just as he can to those of another and with equal effect if he goes about it right. This opens up a wonderful field for self healing. The methods and practice of local treatment in self healing are precisely similar to those used in treating others. I am personally acquainted with a lady who has learned to make her body obey her perfectly. If the body looks tired or droopy or lacks freshness and beauty, she just "talks up" to it and tells it how much she thinks of it and how much she appreciates all that it is doing for her, etc., and at the same time encourages it to manifest activity and interest, etc. The result is that the next morning after the treatment she will find that all of her suggestions have been accepted and acted upon by the body, and that the latter looks fresh, active and beautiful, manifesting all the appearance of youth and perfect health. I have heard of women managing to retain their youthful appearance in a similar manner. I have known men to "coax up" their bodies, when under the strain of unusual work, with the best of results. In fact, I believe that in this form of treatment of one's own body there are possibilities as yet undreamt of by the race. Perhaps this hint may start some investigator to exploring the field to the limit—I have not found time to carry my investigations along this line quite as far as I would have liked. There is a great unexplored field here. Here is a chance for some fine work for the students of this book.

And now I seem to have reached the end of this chapter. Remember, please, that within its pages I have condensed information sufficient to have filled a good sized volume or two. Read it carefully and do not let the simplicity of my methods lead you to ignore the wonderful possibilities open to those who will practice them. I have not cared to dress up my "treatments" and methods in fancy garb for the purpose of bewildering the eye and creating an impression upon the foolish and childish minds of those who run after these things. I do not want a "following" of this sort—I want, rather, the earnest sympathetic co operation of my students who appreciate the virtue in these apparently simple methods. As I have said before, these "simple" methods and forms of treatment represent the work and experience of myself and others extending over a number of years. They are the "boiling down" of many systems, and the result of my own experiments.

They embody the simplest, plainest, and yet the most effective methods known to the world of mental healing today. Take my word for this—I base this statement upon eight active years of earnest, patient, careful investigation, experiment and study along these lines under circumstances with which few are fortunate enough to be favored. I say these things not in the spirit of boasting or "booming my own wares," but merely that you may understand just what is behind and under these "simple" forms, methods and treatments.

You will notice, I hope, that in order to practice these methods of mental healing you are not required to "join" anything—nor asked to connect yourself with any new religion or semi religion. *You may adhere to your favorite beliefs, and still make as many cures as the best of those who believe and claim that the healing is done because of some fantastic theory, dogma or belief!* There is no more sense in building up a religion around mental healing than there is in building one up around Homeopathy, Allopathy, or Osteopathy, or Hydropathy, or any other "pathy." There is but one healing power of the mind and that is free and open to all. It is the gift of the Infinite to its finite reflections. It is a natural force, working under certain laws—and *free to all*. Take it and use it toward "the healing of the nations," beginning with yourself.

CHAPTER 27

MENTAL ARCHITECTURE

"Architecture" means "the art or science of building or construction," and "Mental Architecture" means" the art or science of Mind Building." By "Mind Building" I, of course, mean "Brain Building," for as I have told you in a previous chapter, the brain is the "machinery" of the personal manifestation of mind, or the "converter" or "transformer" of the Mind Power. But as the word "mind" is generally used as synonymous with "brain," in the case of individuals, I shall speak of "Mind Building" in this lesson, although I always mean "Brain Building" when I so speak.

The differing manifestations of mind in the various persons with whom we come in contact is at once recognized as depending upon the character, quality, degree and grade of their brain material The brain is composed of a peculiar substance called "plasm," or elementary living matter. The word "plasm" is derived from the Greek word meaning "a mould or matrix," and its use in connection with the brain substance is peculiarly appropriate, for it is in the cells of the brain that "mental states" are "cast or moulded," as it were. The brain is composed of an enormous number of tiny cells which are the actual elements in the production and manifestation of thought, or mentation. These brain cells are estimated at from 500,000,000 to 2,000,000,000, according to the mental activity of the person. There is always a great number of reserve brain cells remaining unused in every brain, the estimate being made that even in the case of the wisest man, or most active thinker, there are always several millions of unused brain cells held as a reserve. And the most advanced science also informs us that the brain "grows" additional cells to meet any demand upon it. And brain building is the development and growth of brain cells in any special region of the brain; for, as you probably know, the brain contains many regions, each region being the seat of some particular function, quality, faculty or mental activity. By developing the brain cells in any special region, the quality, activity or faculty which has that region for its seat is necessarily greatly increased and rendered more effective and powerful.

The investigators along the lines of Phrenology have long since recognized the fact that brain centers or regions could be developed by proper exercises, etc., and the text books on that science give us many interesting facts regarding the same. These cases show us that not only is an individual able to develop and cultivate certain qualities of mind on the one hand, or restrain them on the other, but that also the very outward shape and size of the skull manifests a corresponding change, for the bony structure accommodates itself very gradually to the pressure of the increasing number of cells in some particular center or region of the brain. It is a fully demonstrated scientific fact that a man may "make himself over" mentally, if he will but devote the same degree of attention, patience and work to the subject that he would in the case of a desired development of some part of the physical body—some muscle, for instance. And the processes are almost identical in the case of muscle and brain center—use, exercise and practice along the lines pointed out by those who have investigated and experimented along the particular line.

Prof. Elmer Gates, of Washington, D. C., one of the most remarkable men of this age, has given to the world an account of some remarkable experiments along the line of brain growing, the experiments having been tried upon various animals. He tells us that his early experiments along this line were in the direction of training dogs to develop some one particular sense, that of seeing or hearing particularly. He would specially train a certain number of the animals according to his methods, and at the same time would keep a like number of the same animals of the same age, etc., without any extraordinary use of the particular faculty in question, and still a similar number without the opportunity of using that faculty at all. At the end of a certain time he would kill some of the animals belonging to each class, and upon examining the brains of each he made the discovery that the number of brain cells (in the regions of their brains in which the sense or faculty was manifested) showed a startling difference, depending upon the degree of use and exercise of the particular faculty. His specially trained animals showed a much greater number of brain cells than had ever been found in animals of the same breed and age. Prof. Gates continued these experiments over a number of years and obtained some remarkable results. He specially trained the faculties of some of his dogs so that they were able to distinguish between seven shades of red and a like number of green shades. I have not the time here to speak at length of the wonderful results of Prof. Gates' experiments, but he has firmly established the scientific fact that brains may be "grown" at will, if the person will apply himself to the subject with sufficient zeal and ardor. I have conducted a number of interesting experiments (not with dogs, or through vivisection, however) which have proven conclusively to my mind that the entire natures, dispositions, characters and faculties of people may be entirely changed by intelligent psychological methods along the lines of Suggestion or Auto Suggestion, accompanied with certain other methods to be mentioned in this lesson.

The great school of "New Thought" people of the various sects, cults and associations have been doing some excellent work along these lines during the past ten years or more. Their systems of "affirmations" and "denials" really developed or restrained their brain centers and desirable qualities were increased and developed and undesirable ones were restrained. But the mere use of "affirmations," "auto suggestions" or even strong, positive suggestions given by another, forms only one third of the work necessary in order to produce the best results. It is all very well to assert "I am Brave," "I am Industrious," "I am Active," etc., etc., but if the work stops there it remains only one third done. It is true that these affirmations and auto suggestions undoubtedly do stimulate and develop mental faculties and brain centers and play an important part in character building. But in order that they be used to the best advantage there must be visualization, and there should be a certain *physical acting out of the mental suggestions or affirmation*. There must be *seeing* and *doing* as well as *saying*.

You will remember what I said in my lesson on Mental Suggestion regarding the fact that "mental states take form in physical action," and its twin truth that "physical action produces mental states." It is a case of action and reaction in both instances. For instance, if you will start in to feel angry, and keep it up a little while (even though the emotion is assumed for the experiment), you will find that your brows will form into a frown and that your hands will clench and your jaws will fasten into a savage "bite." You know this to be true, of course. But then, on the other hand, if you will assume the above mentioned physical characteristics accompanying anger and will keep them up earnestly for a short time, you will find yourself *actually feeling angry*. And the same thing is true of the feelings and actions of pleasure. Think intently of some pleasant thing and you will find your face breaking into an expression of pleasure—you will smile; your eyes will twinkle and you will manifest all the outward characteristics of pleasure. And, on the other hand, if you will "throw yourself into the part," and will smile and manifest all the outward signs of pleasure, you will find yourself beginning to feel "bright, cheerful and happy" in a short time. I have seen a sign bearing the simple word "*smile!*" in big letters cause people to change their mental states in a few moments. They would take the suggestion and being amused at the sign they would begin to smile—then the smile's physical actions would react upon their minds and they would begin to "feel good" and so on.

I defy anyone to manifest the physical actions of any particular emotion or feeling, earnestly and actively, for a short time, without the corresponding mental state actually manifesting itself. Go into a business house manifesting the outward signs of good nature, confidence, self reliance, etc., and you will not only impress others by suggestion, but you will also *impress yourself*, and you will begin to actually *feel* the thing that you have been acting out. Go into the same place manifesting the outward appearance of failure, lack of confidence, fear, etc., and not only will your suggestions be taken up by the others, but you will sink deeper and deeper into the mental state you are acting out.

I have known people to acquire a masterful, confident, reliant character by a systematic and persistent "acting out" of the part—

their "second nature," so acquired, growing stronger than their original nature. The exercise of the faculty, in this way, developed the brain cells in the proper area and the people were indeed "made over." I know men who, when feeling "blue" or "discouraged" will always force a smile to their faces and in a short time they will regain their accustomed or desired cheerful state.

I have known at least one man to rouse feelings of stern determination by similar methods. This man was in a position in which there would frequently arise the necessity for the manifestation of the most determined sternness and an almost angry display of will. The man in question was by nature a good natured, easy going, kindly person, and he found it almost impossible to manifest the desired qualities upon the occasions mentioned. But one day he was roused to a state of intense determined sternness by a most annoying exhibition of careless action in the office, which although soon settled, left him with the physical reflex of the mental state just experienced. Before this physical condition had passed away there arose, unexpectedly, a case of genuine necessity for the exhibition of the stern, determined action mentioned in the first place. Meeting the man to whom this attitude must be manifested, our man found that, much to his surprise, he displayed a wonderful degree of the desired trait and gave the other man a talking to that made his hair stand on end, and brought the desired result instantly. No one was more surprised at this occurrence than our man, and after it was all over he tried to "figure it out"—and did. He came to the conclusion that when he was manifesting the physical conditions of the mental state, it required but a trifling effort to induce the state itself—in fact the state came almost "automatically." He had discovered, by accident, a well established psychological law. And he made use of it ever after. Thereafter, whenever he had to "work himself into a state," as he called it, he would walk about his office a few moments before he would see the other man, and during his walk he would "bite" hard and protrude his jaw; he would frown and clench his fists and make his eyes glare, etc., etc., and before long he would feel himself in the proper mood to see the other man and give him the necessary" laying out." The plan worked like a charm. I almost dislike to tell you the sequel, however. Our good natured, "easy" man so developed these opposite qualities by this practice that in a few years he was known as a man to be dreaded by those who had occasion to receive treatment at his hands, and his whole nature seemed to have changed, and even his best friends would then hesitate to call him "easy" or "good natured." He had made himself over—that's all. And from this story you may build up a whole process of character building if you have sufficient imagination and ingenuity—for the principle is the same in all cases. Character is plastic—and may be moulded at will, by intelligent methods. But it takes more than "holding the thought" to do it—one must learn to *act out the part desired*, until it becomes second nature.

I wonder how many of you will realize what a wonderful field is here opened out for you if you will follow the idea taught by the past few pages? How many of you will realize that I have herein given you the "Secret of Making Yourselves Over?" I wish that I could fairly "pound into you" this truth. When I think of what many of you *are*; and then of what you *might be, if* you would realize the inner truth and importance of what I have just told you—well, then, I feel like printing the tale in big, black faced type and capital letters—so that I could make you read it.

I think that the facts and principles above stated are self evident and need little or no backing up by authorities. But I think I will give you' a quotation or two to help fasten the idea in your minds. Prof. Halleck says: "*By restraining the expression of an emotion we can frequently throttle it; by inducing an expression we can often cause its allied emotion.*" I wish that every one of you would commit the above words to memory—they are golden. By expression Prof. Halleck, of course, means the *physical* manifestation or expression—the physical action which springs from the emotion.

Prof. Wm. James has this to say along the same line: "Refuse to express a passion and it dies. Count ten before venting your anger and its occasion seems ridiculous. Whistling to keep up courage is no mere figure of speech. On the other hand, sit all day in a moping posture, sigh, and reply to everything with a dismal voice, and your melancholy lingers. There is no more valuable precept in moral education than this, as all of us who have experienced know: If we wish to conquer undesirable emotional tendencies in ourselves we must assiduously, and in the first instance cold bloodedly, go through the *outward movements* of those contrary dispositions which we wish to cultivate. Smooth the brow, brighten the eye, contract the dorsal rather than the . ventral aspect of the frame, and speak in a major key, pass the genial compliment and your heart must indeed be frigid if it does not gradually thaw." Aren't those words fine? Read them over several times so as to be sure to grasp their full meaning!

If you wish to *cultivate a quality* in which you are deficient, you must think about it, dream about it, concentrate upon it—live it out in your thoughts as a "day dream" or "mental picture"—hold the visualized mental image of it always with you—and last, and equally as important, if not more so, *act out the physical manifestations of it—play the part out*. Act your part, earnestly, ardently, constantly, eagerly, steadily. On the other hand, if you wish to *repress a quality*, the best way to do it is to *cultivate the opposite quality*, and the undesirable quality will be "crowded out." If you wish to get rid of darkness in a room, you don't have to shovel it out—just open the windows and "let a little sunshine in." Prof. James has told you the same thing in the quotation given a few moments ago. It is psychological law. Kill out the negative by cultivating the positive. That's the rule! But don't forget to *act out the part!*

What is called auto suggestion, or self suggestion, is one of the most active agencies employed in Mind Building. Auto suggestion covers all the various forms of affirmations, denials, statements, etc., employed by the several "New Thought" schools, and is the underlying principle of all forms of "self impression." "Self impression" would be a better name than any of these terms, for it described the process exactly. One "impresses" his mind with certain ideas, suggestions, feelings and mental states. There is a dual aspect of mind which enables one to play two parts at the same time, *viz.*, (1) the part of teacher or master, and (2) the part of scholar or pupil. One may charge his mind with the task of waking him up at a certain time in the morning—and he wakes up. Or he may charge his mind to remember a certain thing—and he remembers it. This form of self mastery may be carried to great lengths, and one may bid his mind collect data regarding certain subjects, from amidst its heterogeneous collection of mental odds and ends of knowledge; and then bid it combine the information into a systematic form—and the mind will so act and the combined information will be at hand when needed. I find myself doing this, almost unconsciously, when I start to write a book—fact after fact and illustrations appearing at their proper time and place. The field of self impression has just had its outer edges explored—there is a great region of mentation here awaiting some of you.

And so, this auto suggestion is a case of "says I to myself, says I." And the queer thing is that if you will impress your mind sufficiently, strongly, and with sufficient repetition, you will find it taking the impression and acting upon it. Repetition is a great thing in auto suggestion. You remember the case of the man who told a certain lie so often that he got to actually believe it himself—repeated auto suggestion works along the same psychological lines. Hearing a thing impressed upon it sufficiently often, it takes it as a fact, and proceeds to act it out accordingly. Constant affirmation and statement, made to one's self, will manifest in actual conditions.

Many a person has changed his whole physical and mental condition by a careful, persistent course of auto suggestion. Of course, if one combines the mental image, or visualization process with the auto suggestion, he will obtain a doubly efficacious result. And,if, in addition to these two, he will practice *acting out the part* along physical lines, he will reap a ten fold harvest of results. These three forms combined, employed and persisted in, will work miracles in anyone. For instance, if one suffers from fear in meeting other persons—an abnormal timidity or bashfulness, commonly called "self consciousness"—the first thing for him to do, is to brace himself with constant affirmations or auto suggestions of "fearlessness"; then he should visualize himself as absolutely fearless; then he should endeavor to reproduce the physical appearance and outward demeanor (an acting out of the part) of the fearless man. And thus will he gradually develop into that which he desires. His ideal becomes real—his dream a fact—his feelings actions—his actions feelings. And this rule and example will hold good along the whole line of personal qualities or characteristics. All come under the rule—the same principle works in all cases. Get the principle and you have the secret of the whole thing.

But here I am going to suggest a little variation along the lines of auto suggestion, which I have found to act admirably in this class of cases. The ordinary auto suggestion, or affirmation works along these lines, *viz.*, one affirms or suggests to himself something like this: "I am fearless—I fear nothing—I am courageous—I am filled with confidence," etc., etc. Now this in fine—no one who knows anything about the subject will dispute the fact that a man "holding the thought" that" I am fearless," will be filled with courage, and will manifest the qualities that he is claiming for himself. It is the old tried and oft taught plan of affirmation or auto suggestion that has worked wonders for so many people. And I positively advise you to follow this plan of "holding the thought," and *making the affirmations or auto suggestions in the first person*, when you are "going into action." As a "bracer" it is unexcelled. But there is something else not so old—and here it is.

You will see in the previous chapter, entitled "Healing Methods," (in that part devoted to self healing) I tell you to imagine yourself as "John Smith," or whatever your name may be—that is, as a separate person, and then to "treat" him as such—just as you would a patient. Well, this plan also works admirably in cases of character building by auto suggestion. While the "I am," etc., plan is good as a bracer, and when going into action, still this last mentioned plan of mine operates far better when it comes down to steady "treatment" of oneself for mental failings; weaknesses and character building. Just try both plans yourself and see if I am not right—but practice my plan a little until you acquire the "knack" before finally deciding the matter. Here is how it works in practice.

Suppose you wish to cultivate fearlessness in place of the fear thought that has bothered you so much. Well, in addition to the mental image of visualization and the never to be forgotten acting out the part, you wish to try auto suggestion. The old way, you remember, was to claim to yourself, "I am fearless," etc. Now my new way of "treating" yourself is to imagine that you are "treating" some other person for the same trouble. Sit down and give a regular treatment. Imagine yourself as sitting before your personality—the central mind giving a treatment to the "John Smith" part of you—the individual "treating" the personality. The individual (that's *you*) says to the personality of "John Smith": "Here, John Smith, you must brace up and do better. You are "fearless, *fearless*, fearless! I tell you, you are *fearless!* You are courageous, and brave, and bold! You are confident and self reliant! You fear nothing! You are filled with strong, *positive* Mind Power, and you are going to manifest it—you are going to grow more and more positive every day! You are *positive* this minute—do you hear me? Positive *this very minute!* You are positive, fearless, confident and self reliant *right now*, and you will grow more and more so every day. Remember now, you are *positive, positive, positive—fearless, fearless, fearless!*" etc., etc., etc.

You will find that by this plan you will be able to fairly pour in the positive suggestions to "the John Smith part of you," and the latter will take them with the same effect as if there were two persons instead of one. And there *are* two persons, according to the occult teachings—the individual and the personality. This plan will afford a welcome variation to the monotonous "I am this and I am that" methods which have caused so many once ardent followers of the "New Thought" to throw up the whole matter in disgust. This wholesale "I am this and that" business has tired many a good soul who thereby let go just when in sight of attainment. To such and to all others I would say: "Try this new plan!" Learn to actually "treat yourself" by this method and you will be surprised at the rapid progress you will make as compared with the old plan. But don't forget to impress upon the "John Smith" part of you that he must hold the mental image or visualization; and that he *must* start right in to *act out the part*! Don't let him get away from this—insist upon it—cross examine him about it before each treatment and hammer it into him hard. For as our colored brother would say. "He sure needs 'em all" to carry him through.

Now, please experiment with this method on yourself and find out its wonderful possibilities by your own experience. Don't rest with my say so, but prove it for yourself. When once you have found out just what this method will do for you you will wonder that you had never thought of it before. You will cultivate a sense of individuality which will recognize the personality as a plastic something that can be moulded and shaped at your will by this "treatment." And, best of all, you will learn to know that the individual is *you*, and *you* are the individual and that the personality is merely something that "belongs to you." When you have reached this stage you will have called to your hand the forces of the great Mind Power and will indeed have a right to call yourself "positive" and an "active center of power" in the great Ocean of Mind Power. And all this will have been brought about by this new plan of "Says I to myself, says I." Is it not "worth while?" Then start in to "make yourself over as you will!"

CHAPTER 28

MAKING OVER ONESELF

Now comes the question "In what respect shall I make myself over?" And this is a question that I cannot answer for you, because each one of you would have to be answered differently, and I would have to understand the requirements of each particular case before I could so answer. But, after all, each and every man or woman who studies these chapters has a very good idea of his or her particular strong or weak points of character. Each one knows just about what qualities need to be strengthened and built up, and just which ones need to be restrained. Every person knows his short comings in the lines of personal qualities or character, for he or she has been forced to this knowledge by coming in contact with the world. If you are considering the question of character architecture in your own case, I would advise a strict self examination with a pencil and paper, in which you must set down the degree of development of each particular quality, without fear or favor toward yourself. When you have done this you will know just how to proceed. You will have given yourself a mental diagnosis. I herewith give you a general list of qualities, etc., as an aid in this work of self examination as a basis of mental architecture. In using it ask yourself the question: "*What degree of this quality do I possess?*" And answer the question "on honor."

Below I give you a list of the "faculties" usually given in works on phrenology, which will aid you very materially in preparing your report on yourself. Each faculty relates to some quality of character possessed by you, and regarding which you are asking yourself the question mentioned above:

Sexuality.	Ideality.
Friendship.	Mirthfulness.
Love of Life.	Sense of Size.

Physical Appetites.	Sense of Order.
Cautiousness.	Memory.
Firmness.	Language.
Faith.	Judging Human Nature.
Ingenuity.	Parental Love.
Imitation.	Stick to it iveness.
Sense of Shape.	Determination.
Sense of Color.	Secretiveness.
Sense of Locality.	Self Esteem.
Musical Taste.	Hope.
Comparison.	Sympathy.
Domestic Qualities.	Sublimity.
Love of Places.	Observation.
Fighting Qualities.	Sense of Weight.
Acquisitiveness.	Sense of Number.
Love of Praise.	Sense of Time.
Integrity.	Originality.
Veneration.	Agreeableness.

Every one of the above mentioned faculties or qualities may be increased or decreased by the practice of the methods given in this lesson. Auto suggestion, visualization and acting out the part—that triple method of character architecture will enable anyone to "make himself over" in any one or more of the above qualities. You will, of course, always remember that the methods named act in the direction of stimulating the growth of the brain cells in the particular centers, areas and regions in which the particular faculty or quality is manifested. The immediate cause of the growth of the brain cells is the *desire* of the individual manifesting itself along physical lines; coupled with that law of Nature which causes increased physical or mental growth in accordance with necessity or need. The earnest desire, heightened by visualization and auto suggestion, stimulates the brain centers manifesting the desired qualities, and by so doing causes a more rapid production of new cells and the greater development of the existing ones. Then the acting out the part, with its physical manifestations, creates a direct demand upon the brain for means of manifestation, and the brain responds by growing additional cells to meet the demand.

There is in Nature a law that tends to furnish to the organism that which is needed for its development and necessities. The horse has evolved from a three toed animal into a one toed one, in response to the demands of its environments, and the necessities of its life. Birds of prey have claws and beaks adapted to their needs and wants; beasts of prey have great teeth, claws and shape of body adapted to their wants and necessities—and so it is all through Nature. But remember this, that animals constantly change as their environments alter, for Nature always is ready to supply that which is demanded by the necessities of the organism. Evolution gives us many convincing illustrations of this fact, which I regret not being able to mention here. If a part of the body is brought into unaccustomed use, it becomes tired at first and then Nature sends to its relief increased nutrition and development so that in time it can meet the new requirements with ease. And so it is in this matter of the brain cells. Make a demand upon Nature for increased power along certain lines and she responds. And the way to make the demand for new brain cells in order to manifest certain qualities to a higher degree is to follow the methods given you herein—auto suggestion; visualization and acting out the part. I trust that you now understand not only the "how" of this subject, but also the "why" of it.

It is impossible in the space of a few chapters to give detailed instruction regarding the development of each separate faculty of the mind. That would require a good sized book by itself. But I have given you the general principles and directions and you should be able to work out the rest of the problem yourself. I shall, however, give you special directions for the development of the particular qualities most necessary to the dynamic individual mentioned in the chapters on personal influence. Before proceeding to this last mentioned phase of the work, however, I wish to say that not only may one "make himself over" by the methods given, but he may "make over" other people by the same methods applied in the forms of suggestive treatment. This is particularly true in the case of children, whose characters are extremely plastic, and who yield readily to constructive shaping and guidance. It is not necessary for me to go into this matter in detail, for in my chapters on "Mental Suggestion" and "Mental Therapeutics," as well as in the present lesson, I give the principles of such treatment and the methods of applying the same. I trust that you have paid sufficient attention to what has been taught to be able to understand and apply this form of suggestive treatment to others. What I have said about treating the "John Smith" part of you is true when you are actually treating others. The same principles apply. In addition to these you may advantageously use treatments by mentative currents, which will tend to induce in the mind of the other person the desired mental state, which in time will result in the production of the new brain cells needed to "establish" the mental character cure. In treating others for a change of character, proceed exactly as you would in treating them for a physical ailment—the principle is the same, for the trouble arises from a similar underlying cause. In both cases you are treating mind, remember.

And now to the building up of the dynamic individual. We have seen what he was like, and now we must try to "make ourselves over" to resemble him. The methods given in the present chapter, and the one immediately following it apply to this work, of course. Let us now form a mental picture of the dynamic individual and see what qualities he possesses, and then learn how to develop and cultivate those qualities.

Our dynamic individual is possessed of a strong desire. He knows how to "want" a thing the right way. No mere "wishing" or "sighing" for a thing—when he wants a thing he *wants* it. We all think that we *want* things, but the majority only want them in a half hearted way. The flame of desire burns feebly and gives little light or heat. One of the first things you will notice in coming in personal contact with the men "who do things" in the world is that they are filled with that intense, eager, longing, craving, hungry, ravenous desire that urges them on to mighty effort and achievement—which makes them *demand* things instead of begging for them.

Even among the animals that we speak of as "strong" and "masterful," you will find that this desire quality is strong, so much so that it impresses itself in their every movement and action. And on the other hand, you will find a lack of that same quality in the species of animals that are preyed upon, hunted and devoured by the others. This class of weak desired animals impress us as "weak" and "spiritless." And so it is with men. No one ever did anything or got anything unless, he was filled with a strong, hungry desire for that thing. If a man feels a hunger for attainment, just as he feels a hunger for his meals, he will make mighty efforts to satisfy that hunger. Just think of what you would do to satisfy a craving hunger! Well, these men feel the same way about other things for which they are hungry. Desire *is* a form of hunger" And the hungrier a man is for a thing the more Desire Force will he manifest and the greater efforts will he make to get that thing.

People have fallen into the habit of speaking and thinking of "desire" as an unworthy, low, animal, selfish quality—but they are seeing only a half truth while thinking that they are seeing the whole thing. They seek to escape by speaking of "high desires," "aspiration," "ambition," "zeal," "ardor," "love," and a number of similar terms—but these things are merely our old friend "desire" with a new name. Let me give you a few words used in speaking of some form of desire. Here they are: Desire, wish, want, need, exigency, mind, inclination, leaning, bent, animus, partiality, penchant, predilection, propensity, willingness, liking, love, fondness, relish, longing, hankering, solicitude, anxiety, yearning, coveting, aspiration, ambition, eagerness, zeal, ardor, appetite, appetency, hunger, thirst, keenness, longing, craving, etc., etc. Quite a formidable list!

The truth is that all of the "feelings" that incite one to action of any kind or sort, are forms of desire. Without desire one would cease absolutely from action. Preceding every action there must be desire, either conscious or unconscious. Even those people who make a virtue of renunciation of desire, and who claim to have "conquered desire absolutely," are acting in response to a more subtle form of desire. How is this, you ask? Well, simply because they are carrying out *a desire not to desire certain other things*. Desire is at the bottom of the renunciation, just as it is at the bottom of the very desires they wish to renounce. This must be so always, for desire is a fundamental natural law, and is always manifest. Not only in the *doing* of things is desire manifest, but also in the *refraining from doing* the same things. One man desires to smoke—another desires not to do so. Desire in both cases! "Lack of desire" to do a certain thing simply means a desire to pursue an opposite course of conduct and action. And so it goes—desire is manifest in every action and refraining from action—so long as one has the capacity for action. Nothing has ever been done, created, or manifested without desire. The very atoms manifest desire in their combinations. And so, all the universe has been built up through the operation of the law of desire, and the law of will—both of which are phases of the one law. Desire underlies all life—it rests in the very heart of life itself. And the greater the manifestation of vitality, the greater the force of desire.

But remember always, that there are *wise* desires and *unwise* desires. And the dynamic individual learns to distinguish between the wise and the unwise desires—between the "good" and the "bad" ones—and governs himself accordingly. He examines his desires and picking out the "good and wise" ones he discards the "bad and unwise" ones—then he proceeds to develop and build up the ones he has selected.

And how does our dynamic individual develop his desire when desire in itself is not a separate mental faculty, but, instead, manifests through and in each faculty? He proceeds to *hold up to it the mental image of the things to be desired*, and the Desire Force within him flows forth, and manifests more and more energy according to the stimulus. Desire Force is always inherent in the person just as is Will Power, but both need *an incentive to action*—a stimulus to manifestation. It is a well known law of psychology that desire flows out and manifests itself in response to an object. This object of desire is always something that affords pleasure, satisfaction or content to the individual, or else that will rid him of pain, discontent, discomfort, or dissatisfaction, either immediate or remote in both instances, and sometimes indirectly; that is, the pleasure or pain may be occasioned by the pleasure or pain, immediate or remote, of some other person in which the original person is interested.

The clearer the mental image of the object of desire, the greater will be the degree of desire manifested, all other things being equal. A child may be filled with discontent—it wants something, but does not know what it wants. Then the child thinks of "toys"—and it begins to want still harder. Then it sees a toy—and then its want becomes very intense. One may feel hungry in a degree, but when he *sees* some particular object of taste, the hunger becomes far more intense. And so it follows that if one will keep on presenting to his desire the suggestion and mental image of the object, then will the desire begin to burn more fiercely and strongly and may be cultivated to almost any degree. You know how one may awaken desire in another this way, by means of suggestion, and by presenting the mental image of the object, in conversation, etc.—how many of us know to our cost how the "sight" of an unthought of thing makes us begin to "hanker" after it and long for it? The book agent plays upon this trait of character in us—and so does the department store man on bargain days and by his window displays. You will remember what I told you in the chapters on suggestion, about the steps in "salesmanship," the important point being to "arouse desire" in the customer—and what I said about the same thing in the case of the advertiser. This idea underlies all forms of suggestive influence and is manifest in the lives of every one of us, every day of our lives. And if this be so, can you not see that by auto suggestion you may arouse the same degree of desire in yourselves that others arouse in you and you in others?

The threefold method—auto suggestion, visualization and acting out the part, will develop desire in you. In auto suggestion, along these lines, you must "treat" yourself for desire. Tell the "John Smith" part of you how much he desires this or that—how much he aspires to this or that—how strong is his ambition for this and that, etc. Then visualize the object, that is the thing desired, until you can see it plainly and clearly. See yourself in possession of it, or as having attained it. Keep this mental image always with you, for it will act powerfully in arousing your Desire Force. Then act out the idea of gaining headway and moving on to the possession or attainment. Cultivate the outward actions and demeanor of the man who has "arrived." If you are after success, then act out the part of the successful man. You need not be told *why*, after what I have said.

In conclusion, I will again remind you that the objects of this development of desire are, (1) that your will may be called into play, and (2) that your Desire Force may be set into activity and thus begin in its "drawing," "attracting" work. Read what I have said about Desire Force in the previous chapters. Now, do not dismiss this part of the subject lightly. It is most important to you. Desire and will are the two phases of Mind Power, and you must develop both of them in order to get the best results. Keep the flame of right desire ever burning brightly. Feed its lamp with the ideas of the objects of desire by auto suggestion, visualization and acting out. Remember my parting words about desire: The first thing in the direction of doing things, or getting things, is *to want the things hard enough!* A strong, ardent, keen desire will clear away the undergrowth of the path of success. It will attract you to the people and things needed for its satisfaction, and will attract to you the people, things, circumstances, environments, etc., needed for its satisfaction. *Desire is the soul of the law of attraction.*

And now let us consider the second attribute of our dynamic individual. It is *will power*. Our man is an example of *living will*. He is filled with the force of action. He is determined. He keeps his will on an object just as a machinist keeps his chisel on the hard metal, letting it bite in deeper and deeper until the desired impression and end is obtained. I have told you how the will is always set into operation by the urge of desire. When you develop and cultivate desire you are doing much to cultivate Will Power. So I need not repeat this part of the process—I have just told it to you under the head of desire. But there is another feature about the use of will which I must call to your attention. It is the feature of its determined application and manifestation. It is all very well to have a strong will, but it will avail you nothing unless you learn how to apply it.

The secret of the resolute will lies in determination and persistency. And the first thing to be acquired is the capacity for attention. Writers on psychology will tell you that a "tenacious attention is one of the strongest factors of a cultivated will." That is it—you must acquire tenacity of attention. You must acquire the art of patiently dwelling upon a thing until you accomplish your purpose. You must learn to do things thoroughly and completely. You must learn to concentrate your will upon a thing and not allow it to be distracted or to wander off until you do what you set out to do. You must cultivate stability, decision, perseverance, tenacity and stick to it iveness. And you can do all of these things by the triple method given in these chapters. Each quality is capable of cultivation and development in the same way. You can do these things "*if you want to hard enough*." First stir up your desire to accomplish the task—then will that you shall do it—then do it. Thousands of others have done these things—and so may you if you are an individual and are not a mere personal shadow. I shall now give you some advice regarding will development, to which I ask you to pay close attention.

The first obstacle to be overcome in the work of cultivating Will Power is to overcome the old habits of weak will, and to replace them by new habits of strong will. This question of habit is a most important one, for we are all more or less slaves to habit. Habit is second nature which is often much stronger than our ordinary natural impulses. In order to develop the dominant will you must cultivate some new habits. And of these things I shall now speak. The following rules for the development of new habits will prove of great benefit to you, if you will study them carefully and then put them into practice.

Rule 1. Get control of your physical channels of expression and master the physical expression connected with the mental state you are trying to develop. For instance, if you are trying to develop your will along the lines of self reliance, confidence, fearlessness, etc., the first thing for you to do is to get a perfect control of the muscles by which the physical manifestations or expressions of those feelings are shown. Get control of the muscles of your shoulders that you may throw them back manfully. Look out for the stooping attitude of lack of confidence. Then get control of the muscles by which you hold your head up, with eyes front, gazing the world fearlessly in the face. Get control of the muscles of the legs by which you will be enabled to walk firmly as the positive man should. Get control of the vocal organs, by which you may speak in the resonant, vibrant tones which compel attention and inspire respect. Get yourself well in hand physically in order to manifest these outward forms of will, and you will clear a path for the Mind Power to manifest itself—and will make the work of the will much easier. But it takes will to do these things and you must be prepared to use it. Keep your attention on these outward forms of expression until you acquire the habit and make it "second nature."

Rule 2. Learn to concentrate. By so doing you will be able to focus your will upon any object desired, and thus get the greatest effect. In using the will endeavor to make it "one pointed" as the orientals say. That is, have for the object of the will some one main object and then focus the will firmly upon that object. Cast from your mind all ideas and thoughts not in harmony with the one idea upon which you are concentrating your will. In the beginning it will be well to avoid all persons, environments, etc., calculated to distract you from the main idea. But after a bit you will be able to interpose a resistance to these distracting things and banish them from you by a mental command. While acquiring will in this way you will find that it often takes even more will to turn away from these outside objects than to follow your main object. You must learn to master these temptations even if in so doing you find it necessary to act like Ulysses who made his companions stop up their ears with wax lest they be fascinated by the song of the Sirens.

Rule 3. In acquiring a will habit use every occasion in order to *repeat the effort of the will* along the lines of the habit. Give your will much exercise. Every time you do a certain thing the easier does it become to repeat it, for the habit becomes more firmly established. Habit is a form of "impression," and the oftener you sink the die of the will into the wax of the mind, the deeper is the impression. Exercise, *exercise*, exercise—practice, *practice*, practice.

Rule 4. The greatest struggle is at the beginning of the practice or formation of a new will habit. Here one has to fight with all his might—but the first battle well won, the after fights moderate and finally become mere skirmishes. Hence it behooves one to gird on his armor firmly and grasp his sword with strength at this first fight. Let one stop smoking or drinking, for instance, and he will find that three quarters of the entire struggle is condensed in the fight of the first week if not the first day. Remember the case of Rip van Winkle with his "well, this glass don't count"—*he never could get started.* And, beware of a single slip at the start, for such slips weaken one more than he can regain in a whole day of success. After having made up your will to acquire a habit, you must not allow a single slip for this reason. A well known writer on the subject has compared these slips to a ball of cord which one is endeavoring to wind—each drop of the ball unwinds more than many windings can replace.

Rule 5. Endeavor to fix the habit as a strong mental impression by any and every means that suggest themselves to you. For when this habit becomes firmly impressed upon your mind you will find it most "natural" and easy to act along its lines, and most difficult to break away from it or to act contrary to it. You are building "second nature," remember.

Rule 6. "Look before you leap," and "Be sure you're right, then go ahead." Always take a good look at a thing before plunging in. Give it the benefit of your judgment and do not be carried away by the judgment of others. Use your reason and judgment—that's why you have them. But, after once having decided a thing is "right" for you to do, then you must learn to *"go ahead" to the finish*. Learn to *"place your hand upon the plow and look not backward."* Learn to control your Will Power and do not let it leap into action until you are sure it is right to do so. And all of this means rigid self control and mastery of one's moods as well as one's passions and emotions. Guard yourself against yourself. And also guard your desire from the influences of others, for through your desires your will is called into action. Children, savages and undeveloped individuals manifest little or no mastery over their desires but allow themselves to be affected by every little wave from within or without and then let their will fly into action in response thereto. The individual learns to "inhibit" (that is to "check, restrain, hold back, forbid, prohibit," etc.) emotional states and feelings. By so doing he will hold his Will Power under control for use when it is advisable. Pull the trigger of your Will Power *yourself* after you have taken deliberate aim and at some object worth while. Do not allow others to pull it for you nor do you, yourself, pull it in response to a whim, a dare, an unrestrained feeling. A useful rule along these lines is given by Prof. Hoffding, who says: "Even if we cannot prevent a feeling from arising, we may possibly prevent it from spreading, *by inhibiting the organic movement which accompanies it*, the indulgence in which augments it." In other words, restrain the physical action and the feeling dies. This idea of physical expression and "acting out" runs shoulder to shoulder with the idea of mental states all through the subject of psychology.

Rule 7. Keep the mind filled with mental pictures of the thing which you wish to become a habit, for by so doing you are constantly adding oil to the flame of desire—and desire is the cause of the manifestation of will. The feminine desire *asks*, and the masculine will seeks to gratify the request of his mate in any direction indicated by her. Therefore, the more she *sees* what she wants the more she *asks*—and the more she *asks* the more eager does he become to please her. The apple was *shown* Eve, then she *told Adam it was good* and asked him to take a bite, and then Adam ate and the mischief was done. But this rule works for good as well as for bad—"it's a poor rule that won't work both ways." But the principle is the same in both good and evil cases.

Rule 8. Act out the habit as often as possible, and as well as possible. Learn to go through the motions until the part becomes perfect and easily performed. I needn't tell you students the reason for this again—it should be an old story with you by this time.

Rule 9. Practice doing disagreeable things. This will strengthen the will wonderfully, for reasons that should be apparent to every student. What would be the condition of your muscles if you never had to use them? And what will be the condition of your will if you never have to exercise it by doing something unpleasant or disagreeable? Anyone, even the weakest, can do a thing along the lines of non resistance—pleasant, agreeable things, without opposition or resistance. But it takes a true man or woman—a true individual—to do things against resistance from without or from within. And when one has learned to master *himself*, that is his own moods and feelings—then he is able to master the outside world. And not until then, either! Therefore often set yourself an unpleasant or disagreeable task to perform, for by so doing you acquire mental muscle, which is but another name for will.

Prof. James, the eminent psychologist, advises his readers to systematically exercise themselves in the direction of doing some particular things *for no other reason than that they would rather not do it*. Even if the task be nothing more than rising and giving up a seat in a street car *when you want to retain it very much indeed*. Prof. James compares this exercise to the paying the premiums on insurance on one's property—one is laying up reserve resources for a day of need. He tells us that a man who trains himself in this way can be counted upon in any emergency—*he may count on himself* to manifest Will Power. As Prof. Halleck says, in speaking of such a man: "While another would be still crying over spilt milk, the possessor of such a will has already begun to milk another cow." The men who have attained great success have, in nearly every case, so trained their wills that they can undertake a difficult or disagreeable task with a minimum of effort. *They have acquired the habit*. When one learns to say "Yes! or No!" to himself, he can say "*yes!*" or "*no!*" to others with the greatest force.

Rule 10. Cultivate fixity of purpose. The man of strong will must learn to see an object ahead of him and then to "want it hard enough," and then to fix his will upon it and hold it there, while he moves to it in as straight a line as possible. But no matter how he may have to swerve from his straight line of approach, by unforeseen obstacles, nor how many times he may stumble, *he still always remembers what he is after*—and he keeps after it. The shifting, changeable, weathercock sort of men manifest but little will, and accomplish little or nothing. The successful men are those who *know what they want and never forget it.* It may take them some time to find out just what they do want, but when once they find it out they hold firmly to it to the end with an invincible determination and unswerving purpose—and these qualities always win in the long run, if for no other reason than because so few possess them and the majority of men get tired of the struggle and drop out of the race. It's the fellow with the "staying qualities" that pulls through in the end no matter how much of a start the others may have had on him in the beginning. Concentrate and cultivate "stick to it iveness."

CHAPTER 30

MIND BUILDING

I shall now briefly run over the mental faculties most necessary to be developed by the man who wishes to gain the dynamic qualities. I shall add a few words of advice regarding the development of each of the said faculties.

I. Continuity. This faculty has been so named by the phrenologists, and defined as the faculty that enables a man to "stick to it" until it is done—that gives him patience to complete his task—that gives him stability. Its lack makes a man restless; changeable; shifting; disconnected; scattered; unstable; and unreliable. To cultivate this faculty follow the three fold method, in the direction of concentrating, dwelling upon, and sticking to a matter once undertaken; doing thorough work; and fighting to make a change.

II. Vitality. This faculty is defined by phrenologists as the one that makes a person tenacious of life; and which causes him to fight off death, sickness, or weakness. This is a necessary faculty for the dynamic individual to develop, for by so doing he not only becomes stronger, but also imparts a certain quality of strength and resistance to his personality that will be felt by others. As an example, contrast the "fight for life" in an animal of the cat family, and then the lack of it in a sheep or rabbit—then think which of them is more respected and regarded in the world of animals. By all means cultivate that resolute fight for life, that is manifested by all strong creatures. Try the three fold method along the lines of holding on to life, and manifesting the "will to live."

III. Combativeness. This phrenological faculty manifests in the direction of resistance; opposition; courage; boldness;

defensiveness; defiance; spirit; self protection; determination; "let me alone"; "get out of my way"; etc. It goes with all strong characters. It is true that its perversion renders one a nuisance and a quarrelsome and brawling person, and such state is to be avoided. But its absence makes of one "a human door mat," and the world proceeds to wipe its feet on him. The dynamic individual must have this faculty well developed, and also well controlled. It must be the case of the "soft voice and the big stick," of which we have heard so much of late. The world loves the brave man, and hates a coward. And this means mental bravery, and mental cowardice, principally, in these days of mental struggle. By all means learn to stand up like a man, and, looking the world firmly and calmly in the face, say in the words of the old verse: "Come one; come all! this rock shall fly from its firm base, as soon as I." Don't be a brawler, but don't be a weakling. Avoid the rabbit and sheep mental attitude. Develop this faculty by the three fold method, along the lines of debate; argument; mental conflict; mental resistance; asserting your individuality; insisting upon your rights; self confidence; self assertion; and "I Can and I Will."

IV. Destructiveness. This name is not well chosen, in my opinion, by the phrenologists, but I shall not attempt to change it here. It is used by them to indicate the faculty that manifests in: Determination to overcome obstacles; beating down resistance; brushing away barriers; making headway; pushing to the front; clearing away underbrush; pushing through the crowd; holding your own; etc. Its perversion renders one a hated man, and one who is not sufficiently regardful of the rights of others, and whom it becomes the duty of society to restrain. But, still it is a quality that is needed by the dynamic individual, lest he allow himself to be walked over with impunity; outraged; and treated with contempt by the world; or which will cause him to be pushed aside and imposed upon. Its absence also causes one to be overcome with impotence when obstacles confront him, or resistance shows itself. Its absence causes one to be a whining "I can't" person; and also causes one to be too much subject to precedents, pretended authority, etc., and kills off his originality. To develop this faculty, use the threefold method along the lines of breaking new mental ground; striking out into new paths; breaking down barriers; overcoming restraint; holding your own; pushing to the front, even if you have to elbow the crowd, etc.

V. Acquisitiveness. This term is used by phrenologists to indicate that faculty which manifests in: Getting; acquiring; possessing; drawing to oneself; obtaining and securing desired things, etc. It may be perverted into miserliness; penuriousness; meanness; hoggishness, etc., but nevertheless its proper use and development is necessary. Unless one has a desire to have and hold, he will not be apt to make any progress in the world. One must want to get things, before he will act energetically. And so far as money is concerned, while I freely admit the evils of an extreme greed and desire in this respect, yet I am just as fully convinced that a man must possess a certain amount of this "money wanting" quality in order to make him an active center of force.

For when one wants money, he really wants the things that money buys. Money stands for nearly all that is necessary for a man's well being and sustenance. Money in itself is nothing—and a man is a fool who loves or seeks it *for itself*. But it is also a "symbol" of almost everything else, and without it he can get practically nothing else. So, just as I think it justifiable and proper for a plant to desire and seek, and draw to itself the sustenance of the soil, air, water, and sunlight, so do I think it proper, desirable and praiseworthy for a man to desire, and insist upon drawing to himself the proper sustenance of life—and money means just that, to the sane man, and nothing more. The people who decry this "desire for money," are principally those who either (1) have failed to accumulate money themselves, by reason of lacking the necessary qualities (the really *unfortunate* ones do not join in the condemnation of the *desire*); or (2) those who have inherited money of which they did not know the labor, excitement, or satisfaction of making for themselves, and who, therefore, grow righteously disgusted at the money which they did not have to use their heads or hands to acquire. These people are like those who take no exercise, and get indigestion at the sight of a good dinner; while those who have worked well come to the dinner with a good appetite, and cannot understand the "sick feeling" of the others. It is a law of Nature that makes both of these classes of people "sick" at the sight of that for which they have not worked; or (3) that class of "parasites" who live by hard work of others, doing nothing themselves, and deeming themselves far above those "muckers," or "money grubbers," who work, and toil and labor to support these "parasites."

People are *all after money*—every blessed mother's son and daughter of them—in one way or another. What is the use of denying it. Some day we may have better economic conditions—I pray to God that we may—but until that time all of us must chase the nimble dollar to the best of our ability. For unless a man does this thing, then shall he not eat; nor be clothed; nor have shelter; nor books; nor music; nor anything else that makes life worth living for one who thinks and feels. Therefore I feel justified in saying to you: *Develop a normal degree of acquisitiveness*, if you wish to amount to anything in the world's work. Develop it by the threefold method, along the lines of realization of what it means, and what it will do for you, in this stage of the world's economic evolution. But—Don't Be a Hog! To be sure, "while you're getting, get all you can," *but give the other fellow a chance.* "Live and Let Live!"

VI. Secretiveness. This is the name given by the phrenologists to that faculty that manifests as: policy; tact; concealment; self repression; self restraint; etc. Its perversion leads to deceit; double dealing; duplicity; lying; false living, etc. But a certain amount of it is necessary, lest one fall into the error of wearing his heart on his sleeve; transparent simplicity; loose mouthedness; "blabbing"; lacking ordinary prudence; indiscretion, etc. Develop this faculty by the threefold method along the lines of tact; diplomacy;

reticence; cautiousness; politeness; etc., the main object being to acquire the faculty of keeping your own secrets; keeping your affairs to yourself; avoiding that "leakiness" that has ruined so many men—and women. Regarding this—"and women," I would say that my business experience has taught me that in spite of the alleged "secret telling" of women, it is true that the women stenographers in an office are far less liable to disclose their employers' secrets than are the men employes. And then again, while a woman may have a tendency to "pass on a secret," still she knows how to keep certain secrets that concern herself, or the man she loves—or the child she loves—in a manner, and in ways that cause a man's hair to rise in bewilderment.

VII. Cautiousness. This faculty manifests in carefulness; prudence; watchfulness; foresight; judgment, etc. Perverted it leads to timidity, irresolution, etc. But a certain amount of it is necessary. One should learn to use judgment and reason—to "be sure he is right, before going ahead." If deficient in this quality, develop it by the threefold method along the lines of care, prudence, watchfulness, thought, use of judgment, etc., and by "looking before you leap." If you have too much of it, restrain by similar methods, along the lines of boldness, daring; "don't worry"; take a risk on it, etc., and a general spirit of not crossing a bridge until you come to it.

VIII. Approbativeness. This faculty manifests in a desire for approval; praise; flattery; fame; show and ceremony connected with one's personality, etc. It is seen frequently in a perverted sense. Very few of us need to develop this quality—we have enough, or more than enough of it already. If you wish to restrain this faculty, you may use the threefold method along the lines of indifference to public approval or opinion; "what does it matter anyway"? "they say; what do they say? let them say"; "do not worry about it—your friends will not care, and your enemies will persist anyway, so what's the use"? "what care I for the opinions of the crowd, anyway?—they are 95 per cent fools at the best"; etc., etc., etc. Learn to live your own life, and stand upon your own feet. Other people would like to even "breathe" for you if you would let them—but say "scat" to them, and shake them off when they bother you. You've got to live your own life, and why bother with the people who are always telling you "you mustn't do it this way—do it as I say," when their own lives are glaring examples of the folly of "*their way*."

Pick out a right object—follow a right course—and let the crowd mind its own business, if it will—and *if it won't, forget it.* You will find it ready enough to shower favors upon you when you finally succeed. And do not be deceived by its praise or flattery—the same people who are singing your praises to day, will damn you to morrow if occasion offers. They are throwing roses at you now—to morrow they may throw rocks with equal grace and delight. Don't be a slave to the crowd or its opinions—make yourself master of it, if you would rule it. It is managed through its selfish fears and interest, rather than through its love. It has a mean trick of turning on the thing it loves, "and tearing it to pieces, just as a female spider devours her mate. But when it fears—*well, then, it lets you alone.* Not high spiritual teaching, perhaps—but a bit of worldly wisdom. Shake off the crowd from your heels—you mind your own business, and tell it to do the same. And look it in the eye while you are telling it, too. It will understand you, if you don't truckle to it. But never cringe to it—else it will rend you to pieces.

IX. Self Esteem. This is the faculty of self respect; self reliance; self love, etc. Perverted it means tyranny; superciliousness; imperiousness; hauteur, and other forms of egotism carried to extremes. This quality is necessary to be developed, normally. One must learn to respect himself; value himself; rely upon himself; love himself; hold his head high; look the world in the face; believe in himself; and take his own place in the world, without false modesty, or shrinking. Develop it by the three fold method, along the lines of realizing just what you are—a centre of energy, power, and strength in the Universal

Ocean of Mind Power. Think of yourself in the word of Black Hawk, the Indian chieftain, who said to Jackson: "I am a Man!" Be a "man among men," and insist upon the fact. Learn to say "I Am." Feel that back of and under you is the great Ocean of Universal Mind Power, and realize that you are of and in this wonderful thing.

Believe in yourself; love yourself; look out for yourself. I tell you friends, *I* believe in you, everyone of you, for I know what you are and what you have *in* you—and I want you to believe in yourselves. I want you to say "I" without being afraid. Don't be afraid to "Assert the I." Don't be afraid to say "I." Say "I; I; I; I; I; I; I," until you begin to realize what a wonderful thing that "I" of you is, after all. Recognize the "Ego" as a centre of power, and stop all this foolishness about being a "worm of the dust." Don't be "meek and humble" like Uriah Heep. On the contrary, stand up, with head thrown back, looking the world straight in the eyes, without fear, and say firmly and positively: "I believe in Myself." You have heard it said that "God helps those who help themselves"—and He *does*, unquestionably. But this is also true—God *believes* in those who believe in themselves. And so does the world, because God has made it so! So start in now, and say, early and often, "I believe in Myself!"

X. Firmness. This term does not have to be defined—you all know what it means. It is the faculty of stability; fixity; decision; perseverance; tenacity; manifestation of the determined will. Too much of it may make you mulish, and stubborn—but very few of you have too much of it, along the right lines. You need to develop it by the threefold method along the lines of "putting your hand to the plow, and looking not backward"; sticking to your original plans, despite the talk of others; resisting tendencies to "sidetrack" you. This is the faculty that keeps the will to the task, like the chisel to the metal, until the work is done. Be firm as a rock against which beat the storms, but which yields not an inch, nor is it hurt a particle. Have a mind of your own, and hold to what you believe is right. *See your object, and march straight to it, firm in your determination and purpose.* By all means develop the faculty of firmness.

XI. Hope. This is the faculty of expectation, and anticipation. It gives us one of the three features of success—"Earnest Expectation." You must believe in your success and must "earnestly expect" it. Cultivate hope and "earnest expectation" by all means. Be not a mere dreamer or visionary, through excessive hope—but cultivate desire; then develop earnest expectation; then will to act. Each of these features is necessary to the great three. Develop it by the threefold method, along the lines of "looking on the bright side," visualization; "looking aloft"; not worrying; and belief in the efficacy of earnest demand accompanied by earnest work. Visualization is the greatest incentive to hope and earnest expectation. When you can see the thing done "in your mind's eye," you have started to build in earnest—the rest is a mere matter of detail and work.

XII. Mirthfulness. This is the faculty of humor. By all means cultivate the sense of humor. It will save you from more follies and ridiculous positions than anything else. And cultivate the cheerful spirit for it will make life easier for you, and will lubricate the machinery of work and endeavor. It will also make friends for you, and will tend to remove the obstacles which the world throws in the way of people who are sour, disagreeable and "grouchy." Smile and the world smiles with you; frown and you get a frown. Develop this faculty, by all means, by the threefold method, along the lines of humor, joy, cheerfulness.

And, so, now I have called your attention to the faculties most prominent in the dynamic individual. I have not spoken of his religious or moral faculties, because these lessons are dealing with another part of his make up. But do not imagine that the qualities named here have no connection with the religious or moral life. There is nothing that I have recommended here that will not apply as well to the minister as the business man—to the priest as well as the salesman. The same mental qualities that make a bad man "great" and "strong" will make a good man "great" and" strong." Morals are one thing and degrees of strength another. Good men may be strong or weak; bad men may also be strong or weak. And in the degree of "strength" will be the degree of influence, for good or evil, that a man will manifest. With this in mind, I think that it would be a great thing for the world, if some one were to distribute this book among the "good" men of the world. The evil men have a knowledge of the subject, already.

In closing this chapter, let me remind you that these mental states, cultivated and developed as I have shown you, will manifest themselves in your outward manner and demeanor, as mental suggestions to those with whom you come in contact. The symbol will spring from the inner reality. And they will also manifest in the shape of currents of Desire Force and Will Power, which will sweep far and wide, as well as near and close, influencing and affecting those within their field of induction. From these mental states will flow a strong stream of power which will tend to "draw" to you that which you demand and desire; and which will also tend to "force and compel" the things that you so will. You are a great centre of power, which radiates from you continually. Realize this, and endeavor to charge that force with the best qualities and properties, that while you are asserting your own individual rights, you will still be doing something toward the great work of strengthening the race, to the end that it may produce more real individuals ready and capable of playing their part in the great drama of life on the stage of the universe.

This talk is along new lines and is radical in the treatment given the subject. It is as "meat for strong men, and not milk for babes." There is no "bromide" or "pink tea effects" in it. It is vital, radical, and positive. Its message is "Strength." All truth that is worth while, renders its possessor stronger—if any teachings cannot stand this test, discard them. Nature's Law is toward producing strong individuals—fall in with it, and Nature will come to your aid, for then you will be one of its chosen ones. Fall in with the law of evolution—do not run contrary to it. In the one case, you are nourished, supported, strengthened and encouraged—in the other, you are relentlessly crowded out by the operations of the law.

If you get one half the benefit from the study of this book that I obtained from the writing of it, you will be well repaid for your task. It is as a "live wire," charged with the elemental force, energy and truth about certain occult natural laws. It contains a message for you, which I trust you will heed—for you need it. If you are an individual, this teaching is just what you want. And the same is true if you are *not* one, but *want* to be one. But, if you are a weakling, and prefer to remain so, instead of rising and claiming your birthright of strength—your heritage of power; then by all means remain as you are, and go on your own way. Leave these teachings for the others of your brethren, who will not sell their birthright of power for the mess of pottage of negative content, and sheep like passivity, but who are boldly claiming their own, and demanding their rightful portion—these strong brothers of yours, the individuals who are the coming inheritors of the earth.

I have tried to infuse my words with the strong, vital energy, which I feel surging through me as I write out this message of strength to you. I trust that these words will act as a current of verbal "electrons," each carrying its full charge of dynamic power. And I trust that each word will act to so fill you with the Mind Power that gave them birth, and will thus awaken in you a similar mental state, desire and will, to be strong, forceful, and dynamic—determined to assert your individuality in being and doing that which the universal creative desire and will is hoping that you will be and do. I send to you this message charged with the very dynamic vibrations of my brain, as it transforms and converts the Mind Power into thoughts and words. I send it to you—yes, *you*, who are now reading the words—with all the energy, force and power at my command, to the end that it may pierce your armor of indifference, fear, and doubt, and "I Can't." And that reaching into your heart of desire, it may fill you with the very spirit of individuality, conscious egohood, perception of reality, and realization of the "I." So that from hence on your battle cry will be changed, and you will plunge into the thick of the fight, filled with the Berserker rage, like the Icelandic hero of old, and shouting your positive cry of freedom, "I Can; I Will; I Dare; I Do!" you will mow your way clear through the ranks of the horde of ignorance, and negativity, and reach the heights beyond. This is my message to you—the individual!

BIBLIOGRAPHY

Atkinson, William Walker. *The Secret of Mental Magic*. Chicago, IL: William Walker Atkinson, 1907.

Atkinson, William Walker. *Mental Fascination: Reveals the fantastic powers of the mind. Contents: What is Mental Fascination; Among Animals; Impressionability; Experimental Fascination; The Dangers of Psychism; Oriental Fascination; Future Impression; Establishing a Mentative Centre; Personal Atmosphere; Direct Personal Fascination; Eye Impression; Fascination of the Eye, plus more.* Chicago, IL: The Fiduciary Press, 1907.

Atkinson, William Walker. *Mind Power or The Law of Dynamic Mentation.*

Chicago, IL: The Progress Company, 1908.

Atkinson, William Walker. *Mind Power or The Law of Dynamic Mentation.*

Chicago, IL: The Progress Company, 1910.

Atkinson, William Walker. *Mind Power: The Secret of Mental Magic.* Chicago, IL: William Walker Atkinson, 1912.

Atkinson, William Walker. *Mind Power: The Secret of Mental Magic.* Chicago, IL: Advanced Thought Publishing, 1912.

NOTES